JONA

Other Titles in the Biblical Classics Library:

JONAH

An Exposition

R.T. KENDALL

PATERNOSTER PRESS

CARLISLE, UNITED KINGDOM

© R.T. Kendall 1978

First published in the U.K. 1978
by Hodder & Stoughton Ltd., London
Second edition 1985

This edition published 1995
by Paternoster Press, P.O. Box 300, Carlisle CA3 0QS, U.K.

01 00 99 98 97 96 95   7 6 5 4 3 2 1

British Library Cataloguing in Publication Data

Kendall, R.T.
  Jonah:Exposition. – New ed – (Biblical
Classics Library)
I. Title II. Series
224.9206

ISBN 0-85364-653-8

Printed in the U.K. by Cox and Wyman Ltd., Reading

TO LOUISE

AND

ROBERT TILLMAN II

AND

MELISSA LOUISE

Through whom I know
a husband's delight and
a father's joy

Contents

Preface

No one was more surprised than I to hear that my sermons on Jonah would become a book. I had no idea that these would be desirable for printing save possibly in the *Westminster Record* (in which in fact they have appeared). That they should comprise a book never once entered my mind.

First of all, I began preaching them in February 1977 as the Visiting Minister of Westminster Chapel. I originally projected eight sermons from the whole book of Jonah during the time I was to be Visiting Minister. My family and I fully planned to return to the United States at the end of six months. Two unexpected things happened during this time: my sermons expanded to twenty-three and I eventually accepted the Call to become the Minister of Westminster Chapel. (One sermon preached on the day I accepted the Call, does not appear in this book.)

Secondly, these sermons were preached with the members of Westminster Chapel in mind. I was preaching to them and for them only, thinking entirely in terms of what I felt were their needs at the time. They had been without a consecutive ministry for about three years; they were in a discouraged state and their numbers were comparatively small. My goal was to build them up as best I could in order that another minister could follow me and help make the Chapel the powerful influence it once was. These sermons therefore contain comments along the way that could be quite irrelevant for another congregation or situation.

Thirdly, the sermons themselves were not written out in advance of delivery but preached largely extemporaneously from a few notes. They were taken down verbatim from a tape recorder. They therefore do not read particularly well. They have been an editor's nightmare. Very little could be done with them without re-writing the sermons entirely. This was decided against however and they are presented to the reader with minimal editing.

Homileticians and Bible scholars may find my approach disappointing. Some theologians may not be happy with what will be easily detected as a definite theological position early on. I merely preached from my heart with the needs of the people in mind.

Many have continued to ask why I really chose the book of Jonah as the basis of sermons at Westminster Chapel. While I answer this question at the beginning of the first sermon, I must admit that the strongest reason that lay behind the sermons is simply that I utterly identify with Jonah – all the way from his abortive journey to Tarshish to his carnal display at Nineveh. I have thought that I understood Jonah if nobody else ever did. Because I am Jonah.

I wish to thank Mr Edward England of Hodder and Stoughton for his advice and encouragement. I am grateful to Miss Pamela Harris who had the laborious task of typing my sermons from the tape recorder and for Mr Richard Alderson who first proof-read the manuscripts. I want also to thank the copy-editor at Hodder and Stoughton who bravely worked through the material in an attempt to make it more readable but who finally decided to let it meet the reader 'warts and all'.

R. T. Kendall

London

April 1978

1 Introduction

Jonah 1 : 1–3

WHY SHOULD I choose the book of Jonah to inaugurate this ministry? The book of Jonah is one of the most relevant books for the present time. First of all, it is analogous to the modern church. It presents a story that ominously parallels the situation at the present time. I am referring to the church, speaking generally. The church today is in retreat. It is not really in the battle. The church has an inferiority complex and, like Jonah, who ran toward Tarshish from the presence of the Lord, has determined to run from God and go in another direction. The church has done this; the church has been given a message to preach but is not preaching it. The church has been in rebellion to the revealed will of God and has missed her calling. The church has looked to Tarshish and not Nineveh. The church is like Jonah who paid the fare to sail on the ship going in the opposite direction from what God demanded. The church has spent its energy, its time and its money on the wrong things. The church at the present time is like Jonah, asleep in the sides of the ship while the world is tossed in unprecedented bewilderment. The world is afraid – the church is asleep. The world asks questions – the church has no answers.

What is missing in the church today is the note of authority. The word of authority is not here; the church has lost it and the world outside has rejected the church. The church has ceased to command the respect of the world; the church has lost its authority because it is not preaching the message that God gave her to deliver to that world. Thus what is missing today is a word of authority; a word from beyond; a word not from a man, not what man can produce but that word that comes from beyond, from God to man. This

11

generation has witnessed, by and large, an anthropocentric gospel, a man-centred gospel, and the world does not respect the church. The reason is, the church is like Jonah running from God.

I will go a step further. The trouble with the world today is to be traced to the sad state of the church. You remember what Jesus said, speaking to the church, 'Ye are the salt of the earth. But if the salt has lost its savour it is thenceforth good for nothing but to be cast out and to be trodden under foot of men' (Matt. 5:13). These are the words of Jesus, our Lord, to the church. We are the salt of the earth but when we've lost our savour we are good for nothing. Jonah became good for nothing and had to be thrown overboard. It is time for all of us to accuse ourselves, to see that it is our own fault that the world does not respect us. We are like Jonah – good for nothing and we deserve the world's rejection.

A few years ago one prominent minister in the United States startled his denomination when he made the statement that if the Holy Spirit were completely withdrawn from the church the work of the church would go right on as though nothing had happened.

Now it may be easy for us here this morning to accuse those outside our walls. It used to be that the Anglicans would accuse the Catholics and that those in the Free Church tradition would accuse the Anglicans and we may want to accuse other Evangelicals. But as long as we justify ourselves and blame everybody else, I promise you, this work may go on just like it has without the unction of the Holy Spirit. For I suspect that we are no different here. If the Holy Spirit were completely withdrawn from us the work would go right on as though nothing had happened.

There is an old Negro Spiritual sung in the South of the United States. Like many Spirituals it is not grammatically sound but it has a profound theological message:

It's not my brother, nor my sister but it's me, O Lord,
    Standing in the need of prayer.
Not the preacher, nor the deacon but it's me, O Lord,
    Standing in the need of prayer.

You may be able to accuse anybody else but may God hasten the hour when you see this folly and begin to accuse yourself, not your wife, not your husband, not your mother, not your father, not your children, not the one sitting next to you, not that one you are inviting to church. You must accuse yourself.

The fact is, we are bankrupt. We are, in fact, little if any different from the world outside. The world laughs at us. The world does not respect us. Are we to be on the defensive? And prove why we are good? I think not. The hope of the world is that God in mercy will prepare a great fish, as it were, to swallow us up and make us see our folly and repent.

There is a second reason that I have chosen the book of Jonah. I identify with Jonah. I confess before you openly. You are looking at a man who knows what it is to be a Jonah. I know what it is to have the Lord come to me 'the second time saying: Get up now, go to Nineveh that great city and call out against it' (Jonah 2:1). I know what it is to be a Jonah. You see, Jonah is a type of the Christian life. There is not one of us, I hope, who has not known the chastening of the Lord. I say, I hope there is not one of us because if you do not know what it is to be chastised of God you have just told me you are not a Christian. For Hebrews 12:6 says 'For whom the Lord loves he chastens and scourges every son whom he receives.' Yes, if God chastens you, He deals with you like a son.

Let's be honest, we are all Jonahs. We know what it is to be thrown overboard; to be swallowed up until finally we surrender and admit that God's way is right. You see, Jonah is illustrative of how God keeps His own. What a great doctrinal truth underlies this whole book. I possibly shall be saying more about this than anything else – that God has a way of preserving His own. In reformed theology we call it 'the perseverance of the saints'. Southern Baptists call it 'eternal security' and there is the cliché over there 'once saved, always saved'. Fair enough, I defend it. Jonah is a proof of that. God has a way of getting His way.

There is a song that we sometimes sing in the States and I suggest that this be our motto, that God does not compel us against our will but makes us willing to go. Now, I may be talking to someone here who is truly converted to the Lord Jesus Christ but you are not living like it. You may well be a Christian but one would hardly suspect it by the way you live. And maybe you know what it is to be swallowed up and to be brought to the bottom of the sea and maybe God is still doing that with somebody. Let me tell you; if you are a Christian, God is going to win out. Do yourself a favour and quit fighting; come around. The word of the Lord has come to you – you have run the other way. Let God make that 180° turn in your life. He will do it. For God does that to His own.

There is a third reason that I have chosen the book of Jonah. This book, this story, shows in many ways how God converts a sinner to Himself. I cannot think of a more evangelistic book than the book of Jonah. It shows how God saves men. How many of us went the opposite way when we first heard the word of the Lord. How many of us heard the Gospel and rejected it, heard it and rejected it, heard it and rejected it, until finally, like Saul of Tarsus, we found out that it was hard to 'kick against the pricks' (Acts 9:5). How many of us have even experienced the severity of God's wrath in our rejection of Him. I have known some to hear the Gospel, reject it and go on and on in their rejection for weeks and months and sometimes years, and eventually find out that God is going to have His way. You see, you may win the battle but God will win the war. And when God gets His hook in your jaw you may fight like a giant blue marlin; you may take off in the sea and run in the other direction; but God has a way of reeling you in, and this may be painful for you. You will learn that 'salvation is of the Lord' (Jonah 2:9). You may win the battle – God will win the war.

Now let us examine this text. We are told that God in His faithfulness came to Jonah. 'The word of the Lord came to Jonah' (Jonah 1:1). God's faithfulness to you is in letting you hear the Gospel. The kindest thing that anybody ever did for you was to invite you to hear the Gospel. And the most valuable thing that you will ever hear are the words of the Lord that there is good news – Christ died for sinners.

14

The most valuable thing that ever comes to any man is the word of the Lord. Has it come to you? Has the word of the Lord come to you? Listen, that is the most valuable thing in this world. People today are looking elsewhere for values, laying up for themselves treasures on earth. But there is something more valuable than money. It is the word of the Lord. The greatest deprivation ever to be brought to any man is that he does not get to hear the word of the Lord. Maybe you are discouraged; maybe you are despondent and perhaps the outlook is gloomy; I grant that it is. But has the word of the Lord come to you? That is the most valuable thing ever to come to any man. The worst thing that can ever come to a country is not the famine of financial reverses. Recently here in England we knew what it was to have a famine of rain and many people are still suffering losses as a result of that, but the worst thing of all is a famine of the word of God and I suspect this is at the bottom of all our troubles. I ask you, have you been one of those to whom the word of the Lord has come? If so, you are a blessed person, indeed. Oh, what value has been imparted to you that you could be singled out to hear that word. Has it come?

But do you know something? When God speaks to men He speaks in a *personal* way to them; He speaks familiarly with them. One old Puritan in the seventeenth century on his death bed uttered these words to those who had come to say good-bye. He said: 'One thing that I have learnt is that God deals familiarly with men.'

We are told that the word of the Lord came unto Jonah and it identified him, 'the son of Amittai'. Maybe you are living in a world that does not care about you. Do you know what it is to walk from this place, go to the Underground, but nobody knows your name? You can go home and nobody all the way will know your name. You can go to work and on the way nobody knows your name. A large city like London can be the loneliest place in the world. You feel nameless. Nobody knows you, much less do they care. Listen! God calls you *by your name*. He knows who your parents are, He knows your background. He knows every care you have.

When Isaiah gave the prophecy to Israel the words were:
'Fear not, O Israel, I have redeemed thee, I have called thee
by thy name' (Isa. 43:1). You see, when God singles you
out, He calls you by your name. It's like that story of the
Rich Man and Lazarus (Luke 16:19ff). We don't know the
name of the rich man but we know the name of the man
who went to heaven. And you will remember when Jesus
was resurrected from the dead and the angels had a word to
those disciples that came to the empty tomb, the angels
said: 'Look, go your way, tell His disciples and Peter' –
singling him out by name – 'that He goeth before you
into Galilee' (Mark 16:7). 'God deals familiarly with
men.'

It is Christianity that gives you personhood, that gives
you authenticity, that gives you purpose. Do you wonder
why you are alive, why you have been thrown into the
world? As the existentialists put it: 'Thrown into your existence.' The existentialist says there is no purpose in it. It is
absurd, there is no meaning – you are here today, gone
tomorrow. When you die, you die like a dog; like a fly. But
it is Christianity which gives you personhood, meaning for
life, reason for existence; for it is the great Creator of the
universe, who made the stars, the planets, the sun, who gives
you life, who gives you breath, who knows your name and
who calls you by your name and is calling you now.

Your Creator invites you to take Him as your partner.
Do you not have a partner? Maybe you have a partner and
don't trust your partner. Or, it may be, you have a friend
who has turned his back on you. God wants to be your
partner: your partner in business; your partner in school;
or your partner in the home. Is your marriage in trouble?
God wants to enter your home and bring you back together.
Most marriages can be saved. Oh yes, God is interested in
those things. You can go to a psychiatrist, or a psychologist
(and I do not underestimate their help), but what will give
you personhood is when you realise that your Creator would
come to you and bring you in and deal intimately with you
and be your partner in your frustration with your financial
problem, with your sickness, with your disease, with your
trouble. That is the kind of God who calls. And so, the word

of the Lord goes forth familiarly. 'The word of the Lord came to Jonah.'

We are told that the word of the Lord in this case (to Jonah) was to go to Nineveh. We learn from this something of God's ways with nations. Now the first question to be asked is, Why Nineveh? Nineveh was a pagan city. Nineveh would not be on Jonah's schedule. It wasn't on his chart; converting Nineveh wasn't anything he had planned to do. Why Nineveh? Nineveh was a city with a population we are told of 120,000 souls. Why would God ask Jonah to go to Nineveh?

God may ask *you* to do something and it does not make sense to you. God may have a plan for you and you are trying to figure out the end from the beginning. Why would God say to Jonah: 'Go to Nineveh'? We don't always know why God picks certain places to do things. You don't know why you were born where you were born and not in another country, under different parentage, on a different date in history. And God may be directing you in a certain way you don't understand. It may be the thing that God is asking you to do. You say, 'I can't do it. It's too big for me, it's too great. That step would be a giant step and I am not big enough to do it, I am afraid. I can't take that step. I cannot go that direction. Besides, I can't understand why God would say: "Do that".' You see, God knows all places and you never know what God is going to do next. Who would have thought that God had any plan for a place like Nineveh?

We don't even know whom God is going to convert next. The next person to be saved on God's calendar may surprise you. Who would have thought at one time in the early Church that the next person to be saved was Saul of Tarsus? For every Christian was running from that man and I would suspect that when different Christians were praying for certain people they weren't even thinking of praying for Saul. Sometimes we look at a particular individual and we say: 'That person will never be saved,' or, 'what a gigantic task it would be for God to save that man, that woman. This particular individual is beyond help.'

Listen, if God can *save you* He can save *anybody*. Can

you think of anybody more difficult that yourself? And you don't know whom God is going to save next, and it could be that the person that you are wanting to see converted seems so far from God. Many times we give up because the task is so great; we say: 'It is too much.' But God can do it and when God tells us to do something we'd be better off to begin to obey at the beginning.

But we are told that Jonah had other thoughts. Despite the fact Jonah was given the word of the Lord; despite the fact that God came to Jonah in such an intimate way, calling him by name, knowing his background, singling him out – such a favour God did Jonah – we are told that Jonah wanted to do other things. Jonah rebelled; Jonah disobeyed; Jonah rose up to flee from the presence of the Lord. Jonah had other thoughts.

When Jonah rose up to flee from the presence of the Lord that *might* have been the end. When Jonah paid the fare to go to Tarshish that *could* have been the end. We might *not* have known that there was any more to the story and I would remind you that when you have disobeyed, when you have rebelled, when God has said one thing and you have done another, I want to remind you that that *could* have been the end of *you*. God *could* have finished you off right there. God was not obligated at all to keep on dealing with you. God could have just struck you out. But that was not the end of the story of Jonah. God stayed with him: 'But the Lord sent out a great wind into the sea', and we are going to examine what happened.

You have found that God was not finished with you. You have gone your way but you have been miserable and you have been making it miserable for everybody else and you have been accusing others and blaming others. Let us learn to accuse ourselves and thank God, in His mercy, that He sends out the great wind and that He prepares the fish and He brings us back.

2 Jonah's Folly

Jonah 1:1-4

THE BOOK OF Jonah gives us a sharp profile of the character and the attributes of God. Now, when we think of the attributes of God, we should know that theologians refer to God's omniscience; He is all-wise. He knows everything. Did you know that God cannot learn? But don't feel sorry for Him; it is because He already knows. And you see, God does not make mistakes; God does not err; God is perfect in every way. He not only knows all from the stand-point of having all knowledge, but He is all-wise. So that, what God purposes is right and even what God permits is right. God does not err – God does not misfire. God does not have to say: 'I made a mistake', for God is right from the beginning, and Paul tells us that God has dealt with us in all prudence (Eph. 1:8). So that you can be sure, you can be positive, you may have assurance that God's guidance over your life is perfect.

Well then, God is all-wise but there is an attribute called the omnipresence of God and we learn this as well from the book of Jonah, that God is everywhere. There is no place where God is not. We shall see that this was part of Jonah's folly in imagining that he could run from the presence of the Lord. If there is anybody here who begins to think he can do this, may God help you to see that this is foolish thinking. You cannot really run from the presence of God in this sense. You can go from here to Australia and find that God is there, for God is everywhere.

And then there is that third big word, God's omnipotence. That is, He is all-powerful. That means, God can do anything, and the book of Jonah shows us this, how that God is even in control of nature. It was God who sent out a great

19

wind into the sea – God is all-powerful.

Now, I ask you: Would you want God to be any other way? There are those who don't like the fact that God knows everything but I ask you: When you are in trouble, when you are desperate, how would you feel then if you were calling upon a God who didn't know His own mind, much less the mind of others? I tell you, there is nothing more comforting in a time of distress and turmoil than to rediscover that God knows all, that He is everywhere and can do anything.

But I also mentioned the character of God. We will go a little more deeply into this question, Who is God? For the book of Jonah is full of this. You see, God is essentially to be understood as a God of glory. Now, the glory of God is to be understood in two ways. The first way is one that we cannot really comprehend, as in this great hymn.

> Immortal, invisible, God only wise,
> In light inaccessible hid from our eyes.

The glory of God is that which no man can see and live (Exod. 33:20). So we are told that we can only see the glory of God by reflection, as in a mirror, and in that mirror we see the face of Jesus Christ (II Cor. 3:18–4:6). For in Christ dwells all the fullness of the Godhead bodily (Col. 2:9). 'He that hath seen me hath seen the Father' (John 14:9). The glory of God, then, must be understood in this sense so that *directly* it is that which no man can see.

The second sense, though, in which we use the term 'glory of God' is to be seen as *the dignity of His will*. God, you see, has a will of His own, and I suspect this is the most painful lesson that we have to learn. God has a will of His own. The church is in its present state because it has not recognised this. We have wanted to go one way while God has a will of *His* own and we don't like it. The glory of God is the dignity of His will and the greatest thing that can ever happen to a man is to see and love the glory of God.

The highest state of grace to which you will ever attain is loving the glory of God. When William C. Burns was leaving Scotland for China one put it to him sarcastically:

'I suppose you are going to China to convert the Chinese?'
He replied: 'No, I am going to China to glorify God.' May
God hasten the hour when we all have devotion like that;
when we see that God has a will of His own and that the
ways of the Lord are right.

Well then, the book of Jonah shows us that God's prerogative to do what He wills may not be on our schedule.
What God wants to be done may not be that which we anti-
cipated.

Now, I raised the question: Why Nineveh? But I want to
put another question: Why Jonah? Why would God ask
Jonah to go? Now, we really don't know much about this
man Jonah. He is only referred to one other time in the Old
Testament. You will find that in 2 Kings 14:25 Jonah had
once been used of the Lord. Perhaps not in a spectacular
way but Jonah nonetheless had seen God use him. But
then, why would God come to Jonah at a particular time
and say: 'Go to Nineveh'?

We sometimes want to ask, Why is God asking *me* to do
this? Do you remember the time when you were under great
conviction of sin; or before you came into the assurance of
your salvation? Conviction – do you know what it is? It is a
miserable feeling and it was at that time that you were
wrestling with God. You were like that giant blue marlin I
was talking about, racing into the sea going the opposite way
– though God's hook was in your jaw beginning to reel you
back. You had that feeling of knowing God had tapped you
on the shoulder. You began to say: 'Why me, why this
miserable feeling?' Could I be addressing someone who is
beginning to experience this now? Perhaps you have always
thought you were a Christian but you are coming to the
realisation that you are not a Christian. Or perhaps you
have always been aware you are not a Christian but now
something is making you reassess things and you don't like
it. You are having to reassess the way you thought about
things and you are unhappy in this and you think: Why
has this happened to me? Why me? Why Jonah? Or since
you have been a Christian perhaps God has put His hand on
your shoulder and asked you to do something for Him.
Perhaps the task is something that makes you say to your-

21

self: 'I am not capable of doing this.' You can look at someone else and say: 'Lord, why don't you ask *that* person to do that? Why me?'

The book of Jonah shows us that God's prerogative is to do what He wants to do. God has a work for you to do and perhaps when it first comes to you that this is His will your question is: Why me? You'll be a wise person if you begin *now* to obey. Don't get into a lot of trouble, arguing with God, rebelling against Him, because, I remind you, I warn you, God has a way of getting His way.

You see, God has a claim over every man: You are bought with a price, your life is not your own (1 Cor. 6:19–20). Oh, I know what it is to be situated in a very comfortable situation and then have God interrupt that state. Do you know what I am talking about? To be comfortable; to be happy and then God interferes and you rebel. We don't like the thought that we are not our own, but I remind you that you are not. You are bought with a price and God has a claim over your life. I don't care who you are. So, you are not to argue. But we don't like it when God manifests that claim over our lives. We don't like it. The fact is, we are not our own.

God then not only has a claim over every life, but now back to the question: Why Nineveh? Well, God has a claim over every *nation*. Perhaps one of the most unexplored areas in theology is the matter of the relationship between God and nations. God's purpose in the world is much broader than merely dealing with individuals. We are told in Isaiah 40:15 that the nations to Him are but a drop in the bucket. And God is dealing with nations, not merely individuals – nations.

There is that very interesting verse in Matthew 25 where we are told our Lord has come to set up His throne in His glory and the words are: 'before Him shall be gathered all nations' (Matt. 25:32). God has a claim over every nation. Now, it is quite right for you to believe that God is interested in all the details of your life; your marriage, or whom you will marry, who you should keep company with. Boys and girls, it is perfectly all right for you to ask God to help you with your school work. God is interested in your job, your health, your finances, even your grocery list. But, don't forget that God is simultaneously interested in others as well, including nations. When is the last time you prayed for Peru, or Bolivia? You see, God is interested in France, Germany, Argentina, China, Poland, Mexico, Australia — even the United States and the United Kingdom! It shouldn't surprise you that God would want to raise up particular nations most of us had not taken note of.

I once knew some Dutch people very well. And they told me that for a long time they sincerely believed that God spoke Dutch. Since I have been in this country I have found out that some think God speaks English, with an English accent! Jonah thought that God spoke Hebrew and Nineveh was hardly on Jonah's prayer list. But God's prerogative to do what He wills with whom He wills the way He wills is something that we need to learn. And after all, God can do it differently from the way He has done it in the past. Peter was told by Jesus on one occasion how he was going to die. You know what Peter's question was immediately: What about John here? (John 21:21). And it could be that God will want to do something in the world with a nation that you had not thought of, or with an individual you would not suspect. And God may actually want to do something through *you*, and you ask: Why me? Why not this other person? Why not that one? You see, God may deal with you in a totally unexpected way and you may not find a precedent for the way God is dealing with you; but that is what I mean by God's glory — loving His glory; the dignity of His will. When He says to do something, happy are you if you begin to do it.

Well then, what about God's discovery of Nineveh's sin? Perhaps the most marvellous insight of all from this passage is the very fact that God *discovered* Nineveh's sin. An important line to be noted in the Old Testament is the way the word *discover* is used with regard to sin. When God discovers (i.e. uncovers) one's sin in the Old Testament it is a sign of His mercy. God, you say, already knows everybody's sin; He doesn't need to discover it. But God uses the word *discover* to accommodate us. Of course, He already knows the sins of the world; He knows everything.

We have already established that. But one of the amazing things to be observed in the Old Testament is how God may discover sin; how He will discover evil and wickedness. He takes note of it and it is a sign of His mercy. We are told that Jonah was to go to Nineveh and cry against it 'for their wickedness is come up before me'. Nineveh should be thankful for that.

The greatest curse that can ever be brought to a nation is for God *not* to discover its sin. The greatest curse of all is when He ignores sin. Look what happened as described in Romans chapter one. We are told that they refused to retain God in their knowledge and God just 'gave them up'. It didn't say that God pushed them, it didn't say God clubbed them. There were no bright flaming letters in the sky to say what God was about to do. God just 'gave them over to a reprobate mind'; that is, a mind void of judgement, a mind that cannot grasp the truth. The worst thing that can ever happen to you is for God to pass over your sin in that way. Maybe you feel you are pretty clever because you have sinned grievously and you have not been caught. Don't feel good about that for God has by passing over your sin indicated wrath for you, not mercy. There are those who hide behind the doctrine of justification by faith. This is the folly of some antinomians. They say, 'God doesn't see our sins'. And so they live as they please. You see, in this sense, for God *not* to discover your sins is a sign of His wrath. And do you know what we must begin doing? We must begin praying that God *will* see our sins. It is one thing to know that 'as far as the east is from the west that is how far our transgressions are removed from us' (Psa. 103:12); but when there is unrepented sin and God overlooks it, that should worry you, not give you cause for rejoicing. For, I say, the greatest curse is for God to pass over your sins in that way. There is that interesting verse – I have been fascinated by it for years – in Psalm 147 verse 17 when the Psalmist raised the question: 'Who can stand before His cold?' – when God just ignores you. So, when we see a nation that is accelerating in its wickedness and its sinfulness and God, seemingly, is doing nothing about it, it's a time not of rejoicing but it should be the basis of our mourning.

You see the evil that is in the world, the wickedness, and you wonder, 'why doesn't God take note of it?' This is what is meant by this Old Testament phrase 'discovering sin'.

Let me tell you this: as an individual, you had better be like David who said: Search me and try me, and see if there be any wicked way in me (Psa. 139:23–24). For if God deals with you directly and discovers your sin and grants you repentance, thank Him for it. And so it is with the church – the church that is in retreat – we must pray that God will discover our sin and have mercy on us. And as a nation, whether in the United Kingdom or the United States, where the Marxist threat is so real and where wickedness and unconcern are accelerating every day, we ought to fall on our faces and ask God to discover us! It is a great mercy when this happens; and so it was to Nineveh. 'Go to Nineveh, for their wickedness is come up before me.'

But the main thing that I want us to see now is what I have referred to as Jonah's folly. How thankful Jonah ought to have been that God came to him. How thankful you ought to be that the word of the Lord came to you. But we find these words – perhaps the saddest two words in the whole book – verse 3: 'But Jonah'. He ought to have been thankful; 'but Jonah rose up to flee'. It reminds me of the event when Israel would not listen to the words of Samuel and they wanted to have a king. They would not listen and God said: All right, you can have a king (I Sam. 8:19–22). But Jonah's *doubt* must be seen as the key to this whole dilemma. For the root of Jonah's folly was his *unbelief*. That is the root of sin always. This is why Jesus said, referring to the Holy Spirit, 'when he is come, he will reprove the world of sin ... of sin, because they believe not' (John 16:8–9). It goes back to Genesis. God had commanded Adam and Eve not to eat of a particular tree. Then came the serpent who, at the very beginning, laid the groundwork by implanting doubt in Eve's mind with the words: 'Hath God said thou shalt not eat of every tree of the garden?' (Gen. 3:1), implying doubt. Satan still operates this way. He did it with our Lord in the Temptations. Satan's words were, 'If thou be the Son of God' (Matt. 4:3), implying He might not be. So, the first thing Satan does is to get us to doubt God's word. And this is the root of the problem of the modern church. The church is in retreat because it has doubted God's word. And so it was, Jonah doubted that this would really be God saying: 'Go to Nineveh', and Jonah went the other direction. The root of our problem is unbelief in God's word.

And so it was, Jonah doubted God's word, for had he been fully persuaded he would have obeyed. Full persuasion always results in obedience. This is why it is very important to see that repentance cannot be real until there is a persuasion first. Assurance must come before repentance: assurance of what is right, assurance of what is true. The greatest contribution of Calvin in the sixteenth century was his doctrine of the Holy Spirit. For he said it is by the *internal witness of the Spirit* that we are persuaded God's word is true. This is the problem with the modern church; apparently we no longer believe this by the internal witness. What has happened is that men today say: 'I will believe the Bible if you can prove that it is true externally'. That is to say, by using radical criticism – Form Criticism it is called. And we can prove, they say, that the Bible is true on certain hypotheses. The interesting thing is, they seldom get around ever to seeing that it is true. The same danger is in archaeology. There are those who say: I will believe the Bible is true when archaeology verifies it. These are *external* witnesses. It is not the call of the church to wait around for science, or for archaeologists, to verify Scripture. It is the Spirit who gives the *persuasion;* and may God hasten the hour when that persuasion sweeps the church so that once again we see that God's word is infallible. It *is* true! His word is in heaven and it will not be broken.

Jonah doubted and the church is doubting. Moreover, the church today, seemingly, is waiting in the halls to see what science is going to say next. The church no longer influences the world; the world influences the church. Because science says such and such today the church, seemingly, follows along and says: 'Now we have got to fit what we thought was true in with what science says', not realising that science is always changing. And how foolish it is always to be following science, accepting uncritically what science is saying. I mentioned radical criticism. Out of Germany, this century, came a phrase called 'demythologising'. The idea is that we can no longer believe the miracles of Scripture; no longer believe the historic faith as we once did. Modern man sees this as mythology, so we must demythologise it and bring it down to the level of modern man. Now it is interesting that British scholarship, by and large, has rejected that term, but not always the idea. I went to Oxford to hear an address by a famous theologian. He was speaking on the subject: 'History and the preacher'. I went because I thought I would learn something from him. He began by saying that there are certain things we no longer believe because of what science has shown us. He said that we cannot believe the early chapters of Genesis, and no longer can we believe that man was once perfect and has since fallen, as the book of Genesis tells us.

And this is what has happened: the church doubts what should be an assumption, that the Holy Spirit gives us the *persuasion* that God's word is true. Who knows, maybe fifty years from now, science will come along and say: The Bible is true after all. Is the church going to agree with them then? Must we wait? Must we wait a hundred years? What does it matter? God's word is true, it authenticates itself and it is the Spirit that gives us the persuasion. And the reason we are not in obedience today is we don't have the persuasion that God's word is true. And this was Jonah's folly: doubting God's word.

There was another folly of Jonah. It is what I would call the folly of over-familiarity with holy things. Jonah once experienced God's using him. Jonah knew what it was to be used of the Lord; he had seen God work and we have every reason to believe that Jonah was well acquainted with God's ways.

This can happen to the maturest Christian, especially when he discovers certain theological truths. I think that the worst thing that can happen to a person sometimes, for example, is to discover the doctrine of the sovereignty of God. Now, it is a great thing to learn this; but it is often a disastrous thing. I love to see people discover the glorious doctrine of justification by faith but I tremble sometimes

27

when I see them discover the doctrine of Christian liberty. And many, when they see that God is sovereign, lose their zeal; or when they see justification by faith, they take lightly God's command to live holily in the world. And I suspect that Jonah had a bit of this in him. He wasn't very afraid. He knew the truth, he didn't know the verse but no doubt knew that all things work together for good to them that love God (Rom. 8:28). And I have known Christians like that. They say: 'Well, I might as well do this because I know that Romans 8:28 is true'. It is. But you may wait twenty years before you have the joy of it. And so it was that Jonah knew some of the deep things of God and he suspected, having seen God use him before, that he would get by with disobedience.

Jesus said that we must be like children (Matt. 18:3). Children take things at face value, and we as mature Christians must accept the simple promises of God's Word; such things as 'Preach the Gospel to every creature' (Mark. 16:15) and 'holiness without which no man shall see the Lord' (Heb. 12:14). It doesn't surprise me one bit that God is using Pentecostals today and passing up most of us. It doesn't surprise me. God honours those who believe in the simplicity of His word. Perhaps the reason God is withholding some of the deep things of His word from the church is because of what it has done to some. So, I suggest to you, Jonah was a victim of the folly of over-familiarity with holy things.

Jonah was also a victim of the folly of ingratitude. Jonah should have been thankful that God gave the commandment to go to Nineveh. He should have been thankful that God saw the sins of Nineveh and was going to discover them, and there were a hundred and twenty thousand souls there to be preached to. But Jonah was unthankful. The doctrine of sanctification is sometimes called the doctrine of gratitude. (I would have thought it is an assumption that we don't think we are saved by being sanctified – that would be a theological error. It is rather true that we are sanctified because we *are* saved.) But some of us tend to under-estimate how much God *wants* our gratitude. What do you think all the Psalms are about concerning praising the Lord, giving praise to Him; showing thankfulness to Him? We show our gratitude by the way we live, by our obedience to Him. But there is the folly of ingratitude; the folly of running from God and thinking that we can get by with it.

The last thing I will mention now is that Jonah felt confirmation in his disobedience. This always happens. I use the term guardedly but use it in a way that I think will arrest your attention. It is what I would call the 'providence of sin'. Jonah determined to go to Tarshish and lo and behold he *found a ship going* to Tarshish! He, no doubt, convinced himself that he was right. It is like Eve in the garden. After she succumbed to the doubt she looked at the fruit and she saw that it was good for food (Gen. 3:6). I suspect that by the time Eve partook of the fruit she was convinced she was doing the right thing. And so, Jonah, now making a 180 degree turn from God's commandment, going the other direction, found a ship and it gave him comfort.

You see, when you are living in disobedience to God's commandment you will find many providences, as it were, to confirm you in that disobedience. I have talked to businessmen who say: 'I must be doing something right, look how God has blessed my business'. But God blesses atheists as well! I have had people come to me and say: 'My sin just happened this way; it was so convenient. I was at this particular place the right time; it seemed the thing to do!' Ah yes, sin can be very providential. The way of disobedience has a way of having confirmations, and the problem with the modern church is that she finds confirmation for the things she wants to believe and convinces herself in her folly. I wonder how many of us are here today, living in rebellion to God's will but because of certain confirmations, things that have 'just happened' so conveniently, we have become further persuaded we are right.

These are sad words: 'But Jonah rose up'. I close however with happy words, and thank God for these: '*But the Lord* sent out a great wind into the sea'. 'But Jonah ... But the Lord'. How kind He is, despite our rebellion, despite our determination to go the opposite direction. He stays with us! Thank God we cannot run from Him. 'If I make my bed in hell, behold thou art there' (Psa. 139:8). He is omni-present. God has a way of following us. 'Surely goodness and mercy shall *follow* me all the days of my life' (Psa. 23:6). God is on *your* trail. You may have been confirming yourself in your wayward ways. But that wind you are experiencing, that makes everybody else miserable: *that* is God warning you. Thank Him for it.

'But Jonah . . . But the Lord'.

3 Jonah the Sleeper

COMMON GRACE ???

Jonah 1:1-6

THERE IS TO be seen in the story of Jonah an important teaching we have not yet examined. It is a teaching, I fear, that has been rapidly perishing from the church, but one with which I want us to be well acquainted. It is the teaching of 'common grace'. This may be defined simply as God's goodness to all men. Now, common grace may be contrasted with saving grace. Saving grace is that which applies to believers. Saving grace applies to God's elect. Saving grace applies to those who have been born of the Spirit. But common grace is a realm that transcends this. This is to be seen in our Lord's words that God makes His sun rise on the evil and on the good and sends rain on the just and on the unjust (Matt. 5:45). James put it this way: 'Every good gift and every perfect gift comes down from above, from the Father of lights with whom is no variableness, neither shadow of turning' (James 1:17).

There are many realms of life that illustrate common grace. When we get into politics, or the arts, or the sciences, we are dealing with common grace. Now, there are some who feel that there is a sharp dichotomy to be seen, a radical disjunction between the sacred and the secular. I use this language because I think you will be familiar with what I am getting at, although I am not sure it is a fair dichotomy. In any case, we should understand that God has deposited with His Son a Kingdom that has a two-fold realm. It is not merely the church but also the whole world and so we must see that we are serving a God who is the Governer of all men, of all nations. We that are in the church should be thankful indeed for the fact that there is common grace in the world. When you get sick and need a doctor, you may be

31

thankful for that doctor, that God has raised him up. And it is the same when you consider the arts, the sciences and politics. Yesterday I drove past Sir Winston Churchill's statue in front of Westminster Abbey. What a man! What an honour it would have been to have met him – a man of the century. God raised him up at a critical time in England's history. Common grace did that. Christian people, does it surprise you that God would raise up men in affairs that we tend to call the secular? But that which can make you enjoy a Tchaikovsky concert or a concerto by Rachmaninov or enjoy a man like Artur Rubinstein playing the piano is a gift of God. Look at science. Look at a man like Albert Einstein, who some say was the most brilliant man that ever lived. This is an example of common grace.

But it is not only these spectacular men who have been blest with common grace. God has given gifts to *all* men. There is something that you can do better than anybody else. If you are not a Christian today, I want you to hear this: there is something you can do better than anybody else, and God gave you that. God has given us doctors, nurses, hospitals, medicine; God has given us policemen; He has given us Scotland Yard; He has given us government, law, order, decency – these are the virtues of common grace. You see, God through common grace supplies these things. This is what Calvin called 'special grace within nature'.

Moreover, such a person visited with this kind of grace may or may not have the gift of *saving* grace, and more often than not he does not have saving grace. Yet it is a gift of God. You should be thankful for such common grace if you need to have surgery or you need to have an operation on your brain for a tumour. You are not going to look in the realm of saving grace for a man to perform that operation and I suspect you are not going to be too concerned whether the man is even a Christian. If you were to hear there are two doctors, one who has performed a thousand operations successfully but is an atheist, and the other who has just started but is a Christian, whom would you pick? The chances are you would be thankful for the man that God used in the past. We should be aware of this – God's work in nature. And so, as I say, we have what is sometimes called the sacred and the secular. I am not happy with this language but I put it before you so that you will know what I am talking about.

So, there is common grace on the one hand – the world, nations, government, business, the fact that you have natural abilities, reason, the fact that you can think – *God* gave you that. But on the other hand there is saving grace – the church, the sacraments, conversion – these are provided in this special realm where we are told our Lord Jesus is the Head, even the Head of the Church. But do not forget that God has deposited with His Son this kingdom that is comprised of both church and state; the people of God, the people of the world; the elect, the world, but all under God's sovereign rule. Christ is the Head of the Church, He is also the Ruler of nations.

I have said all of that to say this: Jonah's retreat brought him more noticeably into this realm of common grace. Jonah thought that he was leaving the presence of the Lord, but merely went from one realm of God's kingdom into another. We are told that he rose up to flee to Tarshish from the presence of the Lord. He went down to Joppa, found a ship going to Tarshish and paid the fare, but the Lord sent out a great wind into the sea. Here is God's work in nature. God is at work everywhere. And so the wind came into the sea; a mighty tempest so that the ship was nearly broken. Jonah eventually found out what the Psalmist meant when he said: 'Whither shall I go from thy Spirit? Whither shall I flee from thy presence? If I ascend up into heaven thou art there; if I make my bed in hell, behold, thou art there. If I take the wings of the morning and dwell in the uttermost parts of the sea, even there shall thy hand lead me and thy right hand shall hold me' (Psa. 139:7–10). So it was, Jonah could not really run from the presence of the Lord. Instead of rubbing shoulders with priests and prophets, he was mixing with mariners, sailors, and was soon to be approached by the ship-master. Jonah, instead of preaching and teaching and ministering, was found paying a fare on a ship going to Tarshish. Yes, Jonah, instead of preaching faith and repentance and obedience, became a tourist on a Mediterranean cruise, and settled down for a nice nap!

You cannot run from God. You might think you can flee from the church to the world, as if God will not see you. There is an old spiritual that goes like this:

> He sees all you do, He hears all you say,
> My Lord's a-writin' all the time.

Are you here this morning and you have been running from God? Could I be talking to somebody like that? Well, maybe not in the explicit way like Jonah. Perhaps you are not aware of what you are doing. Are there sins you have been nurturing that nobody knows about but you? The word of the Lord has come to you and has said one thing and you have been doing another. You are running; you are in retreat and you think nobody knows about it. Let me remind you that if you are running from God you are doing something that cannot be done.

Very well, then, Jonah's retreat brought him more noticeably into this realm of common grace. But God manifested special love and mercy by sending the wind. This wind we may call the chastening of the Lord. God's chastening may be defined as His simultaneous wrath and mercy. Now, Habakkuk the prophet prayed: 'O Lord, revive thy work in the midst of the years, in wrath remember mercy' (Hab. 3:2). But chastening is somewhat different from that. It is simultaneously wrath *and* mercy. How can this be? Well, isn't that the way you deal with your children? You may be angry with them and yet love them at the same time. I could never understand that as a small boy when my father would take off his belt and look at me and say: 'Son, I'm doing this because I love you'. It made no sense to me. I saw no love in his eyes; he looked angry. But I know now that is what it was. I am thankful for every spanking I ever got from him. And that is what God's chastening is. It is simultaneous wrath and mercy, but while that wrath is being poured out we are not aware that it is His mercy. It is only when we look back that we can appreciate what God has done and we can be thankful for every time He had to chasten us.

So this is what is going on; the wind now begins to blow, a tempest is stirring – God is angry. But this is God's way of going to great pains to show you how much He loves you. You see, this is a sign of His special grace. The fact that God sends the wind may be in the realm of common grace because everybody is affected by the wind. God can do that simply to get at you. The fact that God would go to great pains to stir you up is a sign that He loves you. 'For whom the Lord loves he chastens and scourges every son whom he receives' (Heb. 12:6). The word 'scourge' means 'to whip with thongs'. And so it is; it is not pleasant. Luther used to say that you must know God as an enemy before you can know Him as a friend. It is simultaneous wrath and mercy. But, maybe, you say to yourself: 'Why is it God does this to me when I see others who don't have to undergo this?' Have you wondered why it is that others can commit sins and get away with it and you cannot? Have you wondered why it is that the person who lives across the street or next door to you can wade knee-deep in sin, in evil, in wickedness and get away with it? They are able to buy things you cannot buy, go places you cannot go. They can do things like that and you know what they are doing. They do not care about God; they just go their way and it seems the worse they behave the more they are blest. The Psalmist experienced the same thing and this is why he wrote the thirty-seventh Psalm: 'Fret not thyself because of the evil doer who prospers in his way' (Psa 37:1, 7). But that the great Creator of heaven and earth would pass by the masses and single you out by sending a strong wind – be thankful for that. You see, this is why it is no sign of mercy for you to get away with unrepented sin. It could be that you are persisting in a sin that nobody knows about and you've got away with it. It is no sign of God's mercy. You may have justified yourself. You may have said: 'This is because I am special. God understands me. Nobody else could do this but I'm a particular case.' Do you know that is one of the favourite tricks of the devil, to make you think your situation is different; that you have a particular trial, or a particular temptation that is unique so that nobody has gone through this before, but you? Therefore although no-one else should do it, you would not advise anybody else to do it because you are different and God understands that. Be careful, be very careful, for if you are permitted to go on and on in unrepented sin, it is no sign of God's mercy. It is more than likely a sign that God is passing you by, 'giving you over' (Rom. 1:28). Are you at this moment on the brink of doing something dangerous and you know it is wrong? Break it off! Break it off! May God grant you repentance now. God does not chastise for sin repented of. It is no sign of His mercy if you are getting away with those things.

And so it was, Jonah made a one-hundred-and-eighty-degree turn from the plain commandment of God's word. Now the chastening process begins. We are going to see that it is a hard process in this case. May God grant that it need not be that way with you. I hope it will not. I hope that through the preaching of the word you will make your one-hundred-and-eighty-degree turn from the direction you are going and come back to God's word. It can happen. Don't wait for the wind to get worse. Don't wait for the fish to bring you to the bottom of the sea. May God help you to see it now and manoeuvre you in such a way that you conform to His will. Spare yourself further agony by doing that. And so it is, the wind is a sign of God's mercy. Let me ask you: 'Are you experiencing the wind?' That wind can take many forms. Is there a rocky marriage? Is your marriage on the brink of disaster? Did you know that most marriages can be saved? Do you know *your* marriage can be saved? The wind may be God's way of reminding you that He is at the bottom of all this to get you to wake up and come to your senses. Are you in financial trouble? Could it be you have been stingy with your giving – giving to the church? Do you know God has a way of getting it? You can give willingly or He can take it another way. It may not get to the church but you will lose it. Is God trying to show you something? Are you one of those who make it miserable for everybody else, and you blame them? It is always the other, you say, yet wherever you go you make everybody miserable. Are you like that? That is the way Jonah was. See the winds blowing, see the boat rocking.

Don't wait to be thrown overboard. Come forward now; come back to God! Come to your senses! It can be done; it can be done now. See these winds as mercies from God — simultaneous wrath and mercy.

But now I want to return to the point that I have been making, that the story of Jonah is an analogy of the modern church. Like Jonah, the church has retreated into the realm of common grace. The church was not meant to subsist on common grace. You see, when we come to the place in the church where we depend on our natural abilities, or we think that the church is going to grow because the church is comprised of Einsteins or poets, brain surgeons or first-class musicians, then we are subsisting on common grace. The church was meant, instead, to subsist on special grace, as Zechariah the prophet put it: 'Not by might nor by power but by my Spirit, saith the Lord' (Zech. 4:6). 'Without me ye can do nothing,' said our Lord Jesus (John 15:5). So it is, the church today seems to be existing not on that special grace for which the church is made but on the very abilities that the world has. This is why I said to you that if the Holy Spirit were completely withdrawn from the church today, the church would go right on as though nothing had happened. This is why men outside see the church as being no different from the world. While it is true that Jonah could not really run from the presence of God, because God is omnipresent, I want to say this to you: there is nonetheless something precious that Jonah lost. This expression 'the presence of the Lord' is used in more than one sense. Though I have been using this phrase up to now simply to show God's omnipresence, that He is omnipresent — that there is no place where God is not, so that by running from the kingdom of grace into the kingdom of common grace God is still there; Jonah did lose something. And I want you to know that when you run from God you lose something. It is that special presence of the Lord. With Israel, it was called the pillar of cloud by day and fire by night (Exod. 13:21). It was described in the book of Acts when it was said of the church: 'Great grace was upon them all.' We are told in Acts 4:33: 'And with great power gave the apostles witness of the resurrection of the Lord Jesus, and great

grace was upon them all.' John called it 'the unction – the
anointing'. He said in 1 John 2:20: 'Ye have an unction
from the holy one and ye know all things', and in 1 John
2:27: 'But the anointing which ye have received of him
abideth in you and ye need not that any man teach you but
the same anointing teacheth you all things.' This is what the
church has lost – unction; the anointing of the Spirit. That
presence that makes unsaved people miserable. Does it not
alarm you that the unregenerate can walk through our
doors, sit through our services, hear our sermons and go
back into the world untouched and unmoved? And so it is,
we may have successfully fled from the presence of the Lord
but we've lost that special presence.

At the beginning of this century, in America, there was a
man by the name of Phineas Brezee. He was the founder of
a movement which became the Church of the Nazarene.
That church, for a time, was the fastest-growing movement
in the United States. The reason was that there was an
anointing there, an unction, and wherever the church was,
unsaved people (if they got near the place) were often converted. Unsaved people were actually afraid to walk
through the doors less they should get saved. And Phineas
Brezee, in his final days, gave the church a message. His
words were: 'Keep the glory down.' What he meant was
this – he meant by the glory that special presence I'm talking about. He knew that that particular movement had no
genius within itself; that it could not perpetuate itself beyond
that special presence. So it is today. We must see that we
don't have this unction. Are we kidding ourselves? Are we
playing games with ourselves? You say: 'Well, we are
keeping the faith; we are the orthodox ones. Look what has
happened to other churches. Look at us; we are still holding
to the faith.' Are we so foolish? The fact is, the world
laughs at us and we should hang our heads in shame.

So it was, Jonah lost that special presence and we ourselves are like Jonah. While the wind was rocking the ship,
Jonah was fast asleep. The mariners were afraid and cried
every man to his god, but Jonah was asleep. Now here is
an interesting point. Within this realm of common grace we
find the mariners calling upon God. It should have been

Jonah calling upon God, but Jonah was asleep. Here we have things turned around, where there was more fear of God in the realm of common grace than there was with this man who was running. Does it surprise you that this could be? Many times the world outside calls upon God and you may not know about it. General Douglas MacArthur used to say that there are no atheists in fox-holes. Many times those in the world can get alarmed when the church is asleep. Isn't it strange that there are people in the world concerned about things and the church is not? The world is asking questions. The church, like Jonah in the side of the ship, is asleep. At the present time, I suspect, the world outside is more alert than the church. We are lagging behind. The world is asking questions and while we have the Communist threat at our doors we have no answers. With the youth rebellion, with our young people on drugs and continuing openly in sex and all manner of evil and wickedness, the church is asleep. We just say: 'Isn't it awful what the young people are doing today?' We don't realise that the young people have been asking questions and we are not giving the answers. And I suspect the time is coming when even the young people now are beginning not to ask questions. I stood with Francis Schaeffer in his garden in Switzerland and I said to him: 'What are the young people asking now?' And he said: 'That is what disturbs me. In the 'sixties they bombarded us with questions but now they just don't seem to have them – it is a different breed.'

The fact is, the cause of the condition of the world must be traced to the church. We are the salt of the earth. 'How,' we may ask, 'could Jonah sleep through this storm?' It doesn't make sense; it is irrational. How could Jonah be fast asleep while this storm was going on? You see, Jonah confirmed himself in his rebellion. The church lost its persuasion of the word of God and has continued to confirm itself. Jonah was determined to go to Tarshish. And we are told that, lo and behold, the ship was going to Tarshish! It looked providential, that he was doing the right thing. I made this point earlier. Let me take it a step further. The church today, in rebellion against the word of God, looks for confirmations, and it finds them. 'And so,' scientists say, 'look at the evidence that we have for evolution, or this belief or that.' The church today has largely accepted the prevailing assumptions of science; and also the notion of Form Criticism that has come out of Germany, where it is hardly purported that the Bible is the Word of God – infallibly true. Rather, we are told that by studying the forms of the words we can get behind the real statements of Jesus and find out what was just put there merely by the church. And so the church goes further and further in this direction because it sees these evidences. The fact is that we had long before departed from the Word and with our confirmations we justified ourselves in what we wanted to believe. Oh, how we need to wake up and see that the church is to subsist by simply believing God's Word, which will not fail.

There are certain characteristics of sleep. Many of us would deny that we are asleep. Did you know that you do not know you were asleep until you wake up? Have you ever relaxed on the couch and said: 'I am just going to rest, I am not going to sleep, I am just going to rest'? Then you look at your watch and you have slept for an hour. 'Was I asleep?' You didn't know that you were asleep until you woke up. And this is the condition of the church – not aware of its condition; not aware that it is asleep. Another characteristic of sleep is that you dream of things you would never do if you were awake. Now I know that this has Freudian implications, that we are unguarded in our sleep; we don't have inhibitions and we dream things and we wake up and we think: I had the craziest dream, I would never do that. But, you see, the church is asleep today and the church is doing things that it would not do when it is awake. We don't like the sound of an alarm. We want to sleep on, it's so comfortable. And no-one likes the alarm of the prophet. This is why Israel killed its prophets. The fact is, while we are asleep we do things that we would not do when we are awake.

Let me put it to you this way. Maybe when you look at someone else involved in a particular sin, or crime, you say: 'I would never do that.' Are you so sure? Are you sure you would never do that? What pride and folly is that! Let me tell you this: when you depart from the simplicity that is in Christ, when you depart from the simplicity of the Word, you have set yourself up to do things you didn't think would be possible! But you are capable of the most heinous crime apart from God's grace. And I want you to know that within you is the capability of repeating any crime, any sin that has ever been described in the history of the world. If you depart from God's Word you are inviting the flesh to take over and do things that you didn't think were possible. And so it is, many of us today condone things that we wouldn't have condoned ten years ago. We do things we once wouldn't have done; we justify ourselves. We say things we once wouldn't have said and we have reasons. Could it be we are in that state of sleep while the storm is raging?

I suppose one of the most embarrassing things that can happen to a backslidden Christian is to have somebody come up to him and say: 'I want you to pray for me.' And the church today is in this kind of condition. The world wonders what is happening. We should be there to help. What an opportunity we have! We should have the answers. But we don't have them. You will remember how the Apostle Peter put it: 'Sanctify the Lord God in your hearts and be ready always to give an answer to every man that asketh you a reason of the hope that is in you with meekness and fear' (1 Peter 3:15).

It finally turned out that the mariners had to wake up Jonah. I wonder if it is going to be that the world will be the source of our awakening? The mariners woke up Jonah. The ship-master came to *him* (Jonah 1:6). Is that what it is going to take? Will the world wake *us* up? God knows something must do it. The storm is raging; we are asleep.

But I close with this happy note – thank God for the storm! God didn't have to send the storm. God could have finished off Jonah. God could have finished you off. He could have cut us all off. Thank God for the storm. It is a sign that God is doing great things to get to us. We wouldn't listen to His word. We began to doubt. In this secular age, in this scientific age, we have become afraid to believe in the simplicity of the Scriptures and so now we are asleep. God is at work; He has not finished with us. He *is* going to

41

wake us up; for God loves His own. The gates of hell shall not prevail against the church. The church will not perish. And the same is true of you as an individual Christian; you will not perish. Thank God for the wind. He has not finished with us. He is still after us.

But may I remind you that the greatest pains of all that God went to was when He sent His Son into the world? We are told that the Lord Jesus was smitten of God and afflicted. It pleased the Lord to bruise Him. All we like sheep have gone astray. The Lord laid upon Jesus the iniquity of us all (Isa. 53 : 4–6). That was the greatest price of all. God is not through with us because the glory of His Son is at stake and that is our hope today. May God help us to see that we can look to that place called Calvary and find that though we have done these foolish things; though we have nurtured our secret sins; though we have doubted; though we have done everything that would justify God in dropping us, He is *not* going to drop us. He has not finished with us, because His Son died on the cross. He shall see of the travail of His soul and be satisfied (Isa. 53 : 11). Jesus who died shall be satisfied. And there is forgiveness for us all.

4 Jonah Found Out

Jonah 1 : 7–10

THERE IS TO be seen in the story of Jonah, especially in this section, a pattern for another great awakening in the world, another reformation. All of us are aware of the great Reformation of the sixteenth century. We are aware of the Great Awakening of the eighteenth century. God has raised up men who have figured prominently in such awakenings. But we must keep in mind that God may work differently from the way He has worked in the past, that God is not in an historical strait-jacket. For example, the Great Awakening of the eighteenth century was vastly different in style from the great Reformation of the sixteenth century. Jonathan Edwards once stated it like this: 'The task of every generation is to discover in which direction the Sovereign Redeemer is moving, then move in that direction.' So God may work differently from the way He has worked in the past. I still say, nonetheless, that these verses in the first chapter of Jonah provide us with a pattern for a true awakening and I refer to a two-fold awakening: awakening of the church simultaneously with an awakening of the world.

Now we have seen that the Jonah story is analogous to the sad state of the modern church, a church that is in retreat. We have seen that the root of Jonah's folly is in his doubting God's word, thinking he could run from God and then in confirming himself in his own disobedience as though he were actually on the right course. We have seen that the church may be described as being asleep, like Jonah who went into the sides of the ship. This state of being asleep is owing to the church's having lived on the strength of God's common grace and not deriving its power from that special unction on which the church is meant to thrive.

43

Another way of putting it is this. The church has lost her identity. She has confused saving grace with common grace. She has confused the Holy Spirit with God's omniscience. The church has confused the anointing of the Spirit with the gifts that God has given to all men – that 'special grace in nature', as Calvin called it. And so it is, the church today in retreat has begun to think that the fact that our natural gifts come from God and we use them is a sign that God is with us. Whether it be our advancement in the arts and sciences, or anyone's particular I.Q. or other natural abilities – I could go on and on – the church has leaned on these gifts of God's common grace, supposing that this is the way the church is intended to thrive. The fact is, the church has lost its real identity in the world so that the world outside is essentially no different from the church within. So it should not surprise us when the world is unmoved by what is to be seen inside the church. We must not justify ourselves for this state; rather, we should face things as they are. We today are a church that has lost its identity in the world, like Jonah, who concealed his identity when he ran from the presence of the Lord and took a ship going the opposite direction from Nineveh. Jonah, I say, concealed his identity, and this is part of the folly of the modern church.

Now there is to be seen in these verses the analogy, not only between Jonah and the church but, as I put it, the analogy between the world and the realm of common grace. And we are to see here that the world in this realm of common grace is confused; that there is not sufficient strength from common grace to give real direction in the world. For we are told by our Lord Jesus that it is the church which is to be the 'light of the world', and if the church does not give light in the world then the world will persist in confusion. For that which flows from common grace, however wonderful it is and however thankful we must be for it, that strength is not sufficient to give real direction; for it is the church which is the 'salt of the earth'. When the church loses her identity, the world will persist in confusion. And so it was, the mariners on the boat were afraid and were so desperate that they began to cast lots. This shows the confusion of the mariners and, I say, it shows the confusion that is in the world today. The suggestion that the church has lost her identity in this world is corroborated by the fact that we are looking at a world full of confusion. I say, then, observe how confused the mariners were. They said: 'Let's cast lots.' The best they could do, you see, would be to try chance. They were wholly given to chance. Now they were so desperate they were willing to try any-thing – chance. The world today continues in this kind of confusion.

Nobody has the answer. The world persists in confusion and what is needed, it is often said, is for someone to come up with a new idea to help us through our distress, our economic distress, our moral degradation. Will somebody come forward and give us some new idea? The church to-day, having lost her identity, is simply adding to the confu-sion by merging with the world; and the world persists in the same confusion: wanting an answer and finding no answer. And the problem is that *there is a dearth on the horizon today of leaders who can say what is right*. There is moreover a dearth of men on the horizon with *a sense of destiny*, a sense of conviction. It seems all we are wanting to do is try 'something else'. We, like the mariners, are just trying anything – given over to chance. This shows our confusion. And it is a sad state when in this realm of com-mon grace there is such a dearth of leadership. It is to be traced to the church, the sad state of the church, whereby the world is lacking in truly great men. I challenge you to find a truly great man on the horizon today, speaking with authority, with conviction, having a sense of destiny.

Someone put it well when he described Sir Winston Churchill as having a sense of destiny. I watched the BBC some weeks ago and saw a particular world-figure being in-terviewed whose name you would recognise immediately. The interviewer put the question to him: 'Since Churchill had a sense of destiny, may I ask you, Sir, have *you* ever had a sense of destiny?' And this world-figure answered: 'No'. This is the problem; such confusion invites any idea that may work. No one knows what to do. The mariners, afraid, said: 'Let us cast lots.' This confusion, you see, was trace-able to Jonah. The trouble that they were experiencing the whole time was due to Jonah, who was living in disobedience to God's command. And I say that the misery of the world today is to be traced to the fact that the church has lost her identity. Jesus said it perfectly: 'Ye are the salt of the earth but if the salt has lost its savour wherewith shall it be salted? It is thenceforth good for nothing but to be cast out and trodden under foot of men' (Matt. 5:13). This is what has happened: we have lost our identity in the world and the world is in trouble; the world is confused and leaders do not know which way to turn. It is traceable to the state of the modern church.

This can even be seen in a small community, when a disobedient Christian can be troublesome to those around him. Sometimes, you see, a real Christian can make everybody else miserable. We would be tempted to say: 'That person couldn't be a Christian and act like that.' Sometimes a Christian can be worse in appearance and behaviour than is common in the world. You remember how Paul put it in I Corinthians 5:1-5. There was that man in the church who was carrying on an incestuous relationship, and Paul said that this is the sort of thing even the heathen don't do. Let us be careful not to judge people just because they are behaving in an odd way. They don't act like model Christians sometimes; they do things that are horrible and terrible and make everybody else miserable. You can hurt your own testimony as a Christian by not living like a good Christian and make everybody around you miserable. You may be blaming them when the trouble is with yourself.

It is much like the story of some naughty youngsters who played a prank on a man with a moustache. They put limburger cheese in his moustache once when he was taking a nap. (Now I don't suppose you know over here what limburger cheese is. I have not seen its equal, I am happy to say! But you don't have limburger over here. I don't know how to describe its smell except to say that it is hardly like Chanel No.5!) In any case, these youngsters playing a prank on this man who had fallen asleep – the man with a moustache – took some limburger cheese and put it in his moustache. When he woke up, he said: 'This bed stinks.' He got up, sat on the edge of the bed, took a deep breath and said:

46

'This room stinks.' He walked into the next room, took a deep breath and said: '*This* room stinks.' He went into another room, took a deep breath and said: 'The whole *house* stinks.' Then he walked outside, took a deep breath and said: 'The *world* stinks!'

All the time it was himself. It could be that you, my friend, are making everybody else miserable. You are blaming them: 'I am mistreated, people don't understand me, they don't like me, they persecute me, they are out to get me.' You are blaming them and you say if only they would start acting right, then you could have some peace. That is just the way a backslidden Christian causes things to be. You make everybody else miserable. And so it was with Jonah on the boat. There was trouble; the sea was causing the boat to rock and they said: 'What could this be? What is causing it?' They looked for an answer. The answer was to be found right there; the problem was the man on the boat. The confusion was traceable to Jonah. But there is more. This confusion was not only traceable to Jonah but to an angry God. It was God, after all, who sent the wind. God was at the bottom of the whole confusion. Now, someone is going to say that the Bible says that God is not the author of confusion. Yes, that verse (I Cor. 14:33) refers to the church's responsibility to do things decently and in order. The confusion that is in the world today is traceable to the church but ultimately to an angry God who is angry with His own people.

The world is confused and behind it all is an angry God. Someone has put it well: 'The first work of the Holy Spirit is to confuse.' Christian people, if you bring your friends to church and they go away and say: 'Well, I'm just confused', don't be too quick to get out the antiseptic and a bandage; maybe the Spirit is at work. When Nicodemus came to Jesus with a question, Jesus made a statement that confused him: 'Ye must be born again' (John 3:3). Let us not be too anxious to pacify our friends who, under the power of the Spirit, may act strangely.

The misery that is in the world today, then, is traceable to a disobedient church under an angry God; and so God is at the bottom of it all. But there is more. God overruled the

47

mariners' confusion and they saw the real cause of the trouble. They cast lots. The lot fell upon Jonah.

The thing to be seen first of all at this point is that it was out of their hands. They would try anything; they were given over to chance. The lot fell on Jonah, but that was nothing they did. God overruled and God did that. They saw that it was Jonah. The real solution to the problem was outside themselves. The irony of what happens when the church merges with the world is this: when the church confuses saving grace with common grace a real friendship between the world and the church does not follow. And so, the mariners cast lots. The lot fell upon Jonah and so they brought Jonah forward to interview him. Here is the thing: Jonah's getting on the ship to Tarshish did not result in his becoming friends with the mariners. And so it is that the church's identity being lost in the present world does not result in a genuine relationship with the world. Now it is interesting to me that many in the church have said: 'We need to relate to the world; we need to rub elbows with the world.' 'The trouble is', say these people, 'the world doesn't understand us.'

Let me tell you; the solution to making the message of the church 'relevant' (as they put it) to the world is not to be found by our concealing our identity. Jonah concealed his, and there he was right on the ship with the rest of them. The world is waiting to see something different, while we have been told what we need to do is to mix with the world. It has not solved the problem. The interesting thing is this – when the mariners came to Jonah we find that they didn't even *know* him! The mariners didn't know Jonah! They had to put questions to him the way you would put them to a total stranger. You see, the solution is not that we mix with the world as if the world were going to get to know us now. This is 'casting pearls before swine'.

The church, with the same kind of folly, often says: 'Well, we have just got to show the world that we are no different; we are just ordinary people.' The identity is lost but a friendship hasn't followed. The mariners come to Jonah and put questions to him that show there was no relationship there at all. This is the way you talk to a total stranger. 'What is thine occupation? Whence comest thou? What is thy country? And of what people art thou?' That, I say, is the way we talk to a stranger. Listen, the world will never become 'friendly' with the church by the church's trying to be like the world. James put it well: 'Know ye not that the friendship of the world is enmity with God? Whosoever, therefore, will be a friend of the world is the enemy of God' (James 4:4).

We should see the utter folly of trying to get on such good terms with the world that the world will accept us. This contemporary word, this cliché that has been used in recent years, is that we must be 'relevant'. The idea is that we must adjust our message so that the man in the street will now accept it. We have been doing it for years, bringing the message down, step by step; yet 'modern man' is unimpressed. And so it is, even in our merging our identity with the world we are strangers! We are like Jonah and the mariners. The world and the church were not meant to be 'friends', as it were.

But we can thank God for this. We can thank God that a genuine friendship does *not* exist. For in this story Jonah was *forced* to identify himself. It turns out that his real identity was entirely unlike that of the pagan mariners. Jonah had concealed his identity. He didn't want anybody to know about his background. He was ashamed, like many in the church today, ashamed of his heritage. So many in the church today are apologising that there were once people called the Puritans; or apologising that there was once a Jonathan Edwards who could preach a sermon like 'Sinners in the hands of an angry God'; apologising that there was a time when the church believed in an everlasting hell. 'But come in and try us now', they say; 'we don't believe those things any more. We are different.' Such talk shows we are ashamed of our past, our heritage, our background. Jonah concealed his identity but now, put on the spot, *Jonah was found out*. 'I am an Hebrew. I fear the Lord, who made the sea and the dry land.'

There was no greater stigma in those days than being a Hebrew. And the church has been working overtime in this generation trying to lose the stigma of the Gospel, of the past. When she recovers her identity – and may God hasten the day – the world will see how radically different the church is from the world. 'I am an Hebrew. I fear *Yahweh* – the Lord.' That is the Hebrew word used here, whereas earlier in this chapter we find the expression that every man prayed to 'his god'. Now that is the word – *Elohim*. It is used in Genesis 1:1. 'In the beginning God' – *Elohim* – 'created the heaven and the earth.' *Elohim* is a transcendent God, a God of Power, a God 'up there'. But the Hebrews had a special relationship with that God. And a Hebrew would never use the expression: 'You pray to your god and I will pray to mine'. There was that special word, peculiar only to the Hebrews – *Yahweh*. So it is, Jonah had to admit that at the bottom of this whole problem was the fact that he had a peculiar relationship with *Yahweh*. Jonah was forced to admit a special relationship between himself and the God of creation.

One of the church's greatest follies at the present time is her claiming the merit of other religions in the world. This is what many are doing now. In many places, church leaders and theologians are looking into other religions and saying that we all worship the same God, called merely by different names. One name is Buddhist, another is Hindu. There was a book written by a theologian, Rudolph Otto, entitled *The Idea of the Holy*. His thesis was that there is a common denominator in religion as a whole that repels and attracts. And so, many theologians have taken this idea – hook, line, and sinker – carrying through with it. In our effort to overthrow our past and get rid of the stigma we have been looking into other religions, saying, 'Well, we are all worshipping the same God.' But, you see, Jonah had to admit that while they had been praying to their 'god', he said: 'I fear *Yahweh*'. Our true identity as a church will force us to confess that 'there is no other name given among men whereby we must be saved' (Acts 4:12). Christianity claims for itself the one and only true way. Jesus said: 'I am the way, the truth and the life, no man cometh unto the Father but by me' (John 14:6). In our state of being asleep, and having wandered from the way, we have been taking other religions seriously. But when our identity is brought to light so that we truly see ourselves and the world sees our true identity, then everyone again will see that what makes the church the church is when unapologetically she stands for the God of the Bible and the fact that Jesus of Nazareth, who was born of a virgin, died on a cross and rose from the dead, is *the* way! And if men believe on Him they will be saved; if they do not they will be damned.

That is our identity. That is where the stigma is and we have been trying to disown our heritage. We have been trying to conceal our real identity, and the result is that the church and the world merge together, trying to be friends. But it can't be done.

Moreover, what resulted from Jonah's having been found out was the awakening of the mariners. Whereas in verse 5 we see the mariners were 'afraid', they were afraid merely because the boat was rocking; they were afraid because of the light of common grace. They were afraid of what they saw in nature. But verse 10 says that after Jonah revealed to them who he really was, 'then were the men *exceedingly* afraid'. They weren't afraid now merely of wind, of a rocking boat; they saw something authentic in Jonah. They saw something there that was different; they were awakened to the fact that there is a true God in the world! He is there; He is not silent; He is alive and He is a God of purpose who controls the wind, who is God of creation, who is a God of all power! This is why they were afraid. They saw that behind all this was a God of wrath, a God who was angry. When the world finds out that the church derives its force from that God who is there, that God who is angry, the world will be awake.

Today there is no fear of God in the land. Have you met anybody lately afraid of God? Men are not afraid of God. And the most comfortable place in the world is the church. Why, the most wicked man in the whole world can come to the church and be peaceful and not be afraid. The fear that the mariners had in their confusion was transcended by the realisation why they *ought* to be afraid. It is one thing to be afraid because of confusion. Yes, your neighbour is living in fear, your friend across the street has anxiety, depression; fears of being aliented; neuroses, psychoses.

Fears, yes, but this kind of fear, when they found out who Jonah *really* was, precipitated the fear of authenticity. That is what the world does not see in us. They don't see anything authentic. We are not afraid of God; why should they be? We sin; we get away with it. The world watches. Why should the world be afraid? We are not. We have been so successful in concealing our real identity.

But this was a genuine awakening. 'Then were the men *exceedingly* afraid.' The men knew, they *knew*, he fled from the presence of the Lord. You see, the world is not convinced of Christianity because we are not convinced. But when the mariners saw who Jonah really was, then *they* were convinced, they *knew*. And so, when the church recovers her identity the world will know who we are and the awakening will come.

But I think I can hear somebody saying: 'Yes, but that is all out of our hands; after all, God stirred the wind. They cast lots, God overruled and so all we can do is just wait.' It is like that Moderator in that Baptist association meeting, who took his gavel to William Carey, who had a burden for the lost in India. 'Sit down, young man, sit down. When God is pleased to save the heathen he will do it without your aid or mine,' said that pious-sounding Moderator to young William Carey. Most of us are like that Moderator. We've had a glimpse of one or two truths of God and that is about all we could see in the Bible. 'God is sovereign; God sent the wind; God overruled the casting of the lots; it was out of their hands. God will have to do it now.' But we are forgetting something. We are told that the men were *exceedingly* afraid; they knew that Jonah was running from the presence of the Lord *because he had told them* (Jonah 1:10). When his identity was revealed, then he began to *preach* to them. He 'told' them. Thus our identity is tied to the fact that it is *preaching* the Gospel that will save; and preaching is something that we can all do. We can do it tomorrow morning as easily as I can do it right here. We are going to have to start talking, sharing, telling. It is not enough just to say: '*God* must do it'. Of course He must. And He *has* been doing it even in this generation while we who are so orthodox say: '*God* must do it'. There are those around going to places where we are too proud to go, reaching people that we don't want to reach, and God *has* been saving His elect from every kindred, tribe and nation while most of us do *nothing*.

So this fear that came upon these men was because Jonah 'told' them. If we want to witness the world outside being 'exceedingly' afraid, then we are going to have to start telling them things. We are going to have to admit to others who *we* are. Let us not be ashamed of our past. It is a glorious past. Let's not be ashamed of our heritage. It's a glorious heritage. Therefore, let's not conceal our identity. Let's not reject the stigma. We would like to reach the intellectuals, the scientists, the university lecturers, the students. We may, but in so doing, if we think we must adjust the Gospel to a non-stigmatic level, we are fools! When the pure Gospel is preached to men as they are, it will save some and condemn others. But it will accomplish God's purpose. The time has come for us to cease to be afraid to preach this Book. Oh, there's a stigma here. You may be sure of that. Tell me, are you a backslider? Have you been concealing your identity? You don't want people to know who you are? Just as surely as I am standing here looking at you, if you are a child of God you are going to be *found out*. Jonah was found out. You will be too.

But there is a great relief in being found out. I suspect that Jonah was glad it was all over: 'I'm an Hebrew. I fear the Lord'. There is a certain security in being chastened of the Lord. The best thing you can do for your children is to show you love them by punishing them. They feel secure. I suspect Jonah was delighted that God cared enough to find him out in this way.

'I am an Hebrew.'

Who are you?

5 Jonah Overboard

I HAVE STATED that the modern church has lost her true identity in the world, so that it appears the world outside is essentially no different from the church within. I diagnosed the problem as being that of our confusing saving grace with common grace. The church has confused the two; she is existing on common grace when in fact it is God's will that the church be sustained and nourished by that *special* anointing of the Holy One. I said also that when the church recovers her true identity an awakening outside will follow. An awakening will come because the church first of all will have had her own awakening from confessing who she really is in the world; and also because the world will be moved when it sees this honest confession of the church: the world will again see authenticity and the world will be awakened. This is borne out by Jonah's words: 'I am an Hebrew; and I fear the Lord, the God of heaven, which hath made the sea and the dry land. *Then* the men were *exceedingly afraid*, and said unto him: Why hast thou done this? For the men knew that he fled from the presence of the Lord, because he had told them' (Jonah 1 : 9–10). The mariners saw that God is there and is alive. He is a God of purpose, a God of glory, a God of wrath, a God of love. The world will be awakened again when the world sees such authenticity in the church.

We need to see, however, that this awakening took place despite Jonah. We need to see that this awakening was not because Jonah consciously apologised for God. Now there are those who have the idea that if we merely preach that God is a God of wrath, God is love, God is alive, that He has a purpose in the world and so forth, such mere preaching will somehow precipitate the kind of awakening that we all want to see. But Jonah was not preaching this truth voluntarily or consciously. And so, the fact that there was an awakening was despite Jonah. It was not because he was doing something in himself to bring it about. He was forced to make his confession; he was found out. But in this unplanned disclosure the mariners saw that God *was* really there. We need to see that there will be a genuine awakening because of a transcending power which overrules the church. And so it is, we are not going to see such an awakening simply because we preach who God is, as it were, and expect that that alone is going to do it.

There must be more. This story shows the inseparable connection between the transcendent power of God and the message of the church. To put it another way, had Jonah made this confession without the storm at sea such a confession would have been utterly meaningless. Had there been no storm at sea Jonah's confession would not have meant anything. For example, had he got on the ship and announced to everybody: 'I am an Hebrew, I fear the Lord, the God of creation', I am sure the mariners would have said: 'Take your place on the ship. We are not interested in that.' Now we need to see that the message Jonah preached, albeit involuntarily, was timed in such a way that, had he made the confession earlier, it would have been meaningless.

The problem we seem to have nowadays in our efforts to precipitate an awakening is that we are controlled by what has happened in the past and we try to repeat the same thing and expect it to work again. I quote Jonathan Edwards again: 'The task of every generation is to discover in which direction the Sovereign Redeemer is moving, then to move in that direction.' God has a particular message for a particular moment in time and it is our duty as a church to perceive what it is, not just imagine that we can do something that has been done before and that God's glory will inevitably be manifested again if we preach a particular message.

As a young minister I once took the text of Jonathan Edwards' sermon 'Sinners in the hands of an angry God' to the pulpit and read it. I had read about the effect that that message had had on one July day in the eighteenth century when, before the sun set, 500 men were converted. And so I took that sermon to the pulpit and read it with all the fervour that I could. Some yawned. Some slept! It later gave me a bit of consolation when I found out (and this is not so well known) that Edwards himself preached the same sermon another time with no effect at all. We must see God's timing. It is utter folly to think that we can resurrect certain sermons or methods of the past and suppose they are going to produce results again. I always think of Christopher Hill's astute observation that one of the great pities of the Puritans in the latter part of the seventeenth century was that they were still chewing over the arid doctrines that had turned the world upside down a century before but were ceasing to make a similar impact.

I wonder how many of us are guilty of the same thing. We are on the boat to Tarshish and we are announcing who we are and what we have come to preach; but the world is not listening. We are supplying answers to questions that are not being asked. So we need to see that the significance of what took place on the Mediterranean sea lay not just in Jonah's statement but in the fact that it was given at a particular moment. There was the wind; there was the casting of the lots. All these things coalesced and there is no earthly way we can *make* these things coalesce and bring them about. The timing has to be exactly right.

We must see also however that Jonah had to be obedient to the word of the Lord and that he said so. There is indeed this responsibility of preaching the truth; we must hold to our profession of faith, our confession of faith. But let us not do it under the pretence that this in itself is going to achieve something. If it is true that it is not enough for us to imagine that if we get our theology and ecclesiology straight the church will automatically awaken the world, it is also true that we must see that it is not enough for us to suppose that God will manifest Himself in great power and glory *apart* from our obedience to the Word. This is one of the great errors of the Pietists and, more recently, of certain supporters of the Charismatic Movement, that is, wanting to see some kind of power when they don't have a clue what the Gospel is. So these things must cohere – the transcendent power of God coming upon us simultaneously with the message, obedience to the Word.

One other point: Jonah got no glory because of this awakening. It's a humbling thought. Most of us cannot rejoice in a great awakening if we think it will take place elsewhere. Now it is quite right for us to pray for a great awakening right here in Westminster, when as families we pray for our immediate needs. But I would want to know whether you, in fact, could rejoice if God *should* come in a great awakening and it not take place here? What if it were to happen in some other church in Westminster? I could name other churches, outside Westminster, which you would know by name. Could you rejoice if an awakening took place there? When God comes in power, no flesh shall glory in His presence.

What took place on the boat was despite Jonah. There is a sense in which Jonah had nothing to do with it. They certainly saw nothing particularly good and virtuous in him. In fact, what moved them was when they saw he *was* a disobedient man. But they saw behind this, that there was a real God out there; a God who was in control! God broke through the situation. And, I remind you, Jonah got no glory out of that. We need to reassess our prayers. We should pray for an awakening, for revival, for blessing. But we must ask ourselves whether in fact we are wanting God's glory or our own. 'I am the Lord: that is my name: My glory will I not give to another' (Isa. 42:8). It does not matter who we are, what God has done in the past – even here in this place. God may not be pleased to do so here. And maybe one reason is because *we* want the glory; we want to see the glory of *our* past restored. Oh, how nice it would be! But when God comes, He will come in such a way that *no* flesh shall glory in His presence (I Cor. 1:29).

Now let us look at this story in more detail. We read in verse 11 that the mariners said to Jonah: 'What shall we do that the sea may be calm?' The interesting thing here is that there is to be seen in this story the respect the mariners had for Jonah. Now he did not deserve this respect. He was a disobedient man. But they respected him. Oh how they revered

him; they stood in awe of him; they were afraid of him! And
so it is, when there is a real awakening in the world we shall
see a resurrection of the respect for the church that ought
always to have been there. But we do not see this today.
There is no genuine fear of God in the world at large. There
is no respect for the church, for holy things. There is no respect for the ministry. This is partly due to ministers who
capitulate to the desire of the masses to bring the ministry
down to the level of the common man – as if the minister is
just 'one of the boys' – so that this familiarity prevails. And
yet men do not respect the ministry.

This is a day moreover when men generally have no respect for theology. Now maybe you think that this is an un-
important point. But did you know that there was a time
when theology was the queen of the sciences? Theology was
once at the top of the ladder of the arts and sciences. The
motto of Oxford University is *Dominus Illuminatio Mea*,
from Psalm 27:1: 'The Lord is my light'. That great University was founded when theology was at the pinnacle of
learning. In those days (and it went on through the sixteenth
and seventeenth centuries) a divine – as they called a theologian then, or even a pastor – was the most revered and respected man on the face of the earth. It is hardly that way
today. The love and respect for theology has almost completely disappeared from the academic world. And many of
those who are the best known theologians of the present
generation, strangely enough, were brought up by evangelical
parents. Many prominent theologians today had parents who
were strong evangelicals. But too many of these have overthrown their heritage. Thus a new breed comes on the scene
to propagate a diluted, sick theology. At this rate, by the
arrival of the next generation there will hardly be any interest in *theology* at all because the theology that is being
taught today is really anthropology: not theology but ethics,
sociology, philosophy, psychology, and so forth. Now my
point is that when a real awakening takes place these things
are rectified. But what is happening today is that theology
for its own sake is being shunned. When a genuine awakening takes place the world outside will be affected by it. Even
things like the *ordo salutis* will become of importance

again to the man in the street. When the fear of God is brought back, men will be made to ask this kind of question.

The awakening on this ship, then, was despite Jonah, despite his disobedience, yet they did not want to harm him; they respected him now. They respected the God behind the storm. But Jonah said, 'There is only one solution. Take me, cast me forth into the sea and the sea will be calm. For I know why this has happened.' We read in verse 13: 'Nevertheless the men rowed hard to bring it to the land.' They might have seen Jonah as a disobedient man and consequently have had no respect for him. But the opposite was true; they knew instinctively that they should not touch God's anointed. We are living in a generation when men don't care about those things. There are ministers up and down this land and around the world that have been harmed, put down, hurt, and even devastated because men do not respect the ministry. Jonah knew there was but one solution. The storm was not getting any better.

We might ask, Why didn't the sea calm down with the confession: 'I am an Hebrew, I fear the Lord'? Couldn't that have ended it? It might have, but God had greater plans for Jonah. Jonah had more to learn and God had other plans as well for these men on the boat – their conversion. God knew there was more to be done to bring this about so that men should really respect Yahweh, the God of heaven and earth. It required that Jonah be taught a further lesson and be made an example to these men so that they should not forget what had happened. So Jonah said: 'The storm is not going to get better. I am sorry to say this to you, but it is because of me all this is happening. It will get no better until you throw me overboard.' The men said, 'We cannot do that.' So they rowed hard. They did their best, but things got worse. Finally they took him at his word.

We may ask the question. How could Jonah have made this request: 'Throw me overboard'? This is irrational thinking. Was Jonah irrational? Was he bent on self-destruction? Was he suicidal? How could Jonah talk like this? 'Throw me overboard.'

The answer is very simple. Jonah recovered a fundamental principle that Christians sometimes forget. Jonah
saw that *his life was not his own.* Jonah rediscovered this.
He knew he was not his own. How many of us forget those
words of our Lord Jesus Christ: 'I say unto you, whosoever will save his life shall lose it; but whosoever shall lose
his life for my sake and for the gospel's, the same shall
save it' (Mk. 8:35). The Apostle Paul had to remind the
Corinthians: 'You are bought with a price; you are not
your own' (I Cor. 6:19f). Many of us have to learn this the
hard way, after we have been Christians for a while. There
is that sin principle in us that rears its ugly head in our
hearts and we decide we must have our own way. God has
a way of getting His way, and reminding us again that
we are not our own.

Have you been guilty of taking your life into your own
hands? Trying to determine your own destiny by manipulating things? Have you been working for a promotion
by pulling strings here and there? Are you trying to solve a
problem by doing the work of the Holy Spirit yourself?
Are you seeking vindication before the eyes of men by pro-
testing your own morality and goodness and integrity? *You
are not your own;* you are bought with a price. You are
owned by God.

If there should be anybody here this morning who is not
a Christian and you have been thinking about becoming a
Christian, I am compelled to put a major obstacle in your
way. I warn you. You cannot receive Jesus Christ as Saviour
without also receiving Him as Lord. You cannot have the
benefits of His shed blood apart from having Him own
you; and when He owns you He doesn't give back! He
keeps you. He owns you. He can do what He wants with
you and He will. So if you have been thinking about becoming a Christian, think twice.

Christian people, you are bought with a price; you are
not your own. 'Well,' we may ask, 'how do we get this very
principle back?' You may be saying, 'All right, I *have* been
taking my life into my own hands. What do I do? Do I
begin now to imitate Mark 8:35? "He that saves his life
shall lose it and he that loses his life shall save it." Yes, I

have been living as I have pleased and I see I shouldn't do this.' But to recover the principle like that, by looking at it directly as though it were some kind of code of morality, will be folly. This is a very fundamental principle. You cannot just say, 'I am going to lose my life. Yes, I see, I should lose my life; I am going to do that.' For when Jonah said, 'Throw me overboard', he wasn't merely trying to imitate some moral code. Do you know why Jonah said this? He said it because there was a conviction that had been restored. He was overwhelmed at the thought that God loved him so much as to track him down at that moment. Jonah got a glimpse of the glory of the Lord. When you see the glory of the Lord, the easiest thing you have ever done is to give your life away.

Here's another way of putting it: do not try to imitate the Sermon on the Mount for its own sake. Atheists do that, for they admire such words as: 'Love your enemies. Do good to them that persecute you.' Natural men speak of putting others first. You can *try* that, but you will never truly grasp this principle until *first* you see that God accepts us *as we are*. Repentance, moreover, is only actualised when we see first that we *have* been owned by God.

And so it was, Jonah could ask to be thrown overboard because he was overwhelmed by a sense of God's grace, His glory, His power, His love! When Jonah saw that he was found out before those men he was relieved that it was over and he was glad to rediscover that God cared about him that much. Just to see a glimpse of God's glory precipitated a detachment from his own life and well-being, and Jonah could freely say, 'Throw me overboard.' It always happens this way. Jonah was willing to do anything, and I promise you that if you get a glimpse of the glory of God, it will happen to *you*. The reason that you are trying to run your own life, manipulate, vindicate yourself, and assert your own will is because you haven't seen the glory of God lately. Isaiah saw the Lord high and lifted up and he cried out, 'Woe is me', and went on to say, 'Here am I; send me' (Isa. 6:1–8). People wonder how it is that a missionary can go to a foreign field and love not his own life. But when we have a glimpse of the glory of God it doesn't matter; we are not our own.

Jonah saw this. When he saw that God *was* there, he didn't care what happened to him. It was the way David felt when he was found out and had a choice of three punishments. David said, 'Let me fall into the hand of the Lord for His mercies are great' (I Chron. 21:13). That is what a glimpse of the glory of God will do every time: you will gladly lose your life. Just to see His glory will bring about that feeling of self-expendability. You don't have to be number one, you don't have to assert yourself, you don't have to be first; you love His glory. When I lived in Oxford I walked along Broad Street almost every day, I seldom went by a certain spot on that street, marked with a cross on the pavement, without remembering a story. In 1555, old Hugh Latimer, seventy years old, was tied to the stake back to back with young Nicholas Ridley. People still wonder how they could die for Christ. What was it in these men that they were willing to be burned at the stake? I would walk by that spot on the road on Broad Street, right next to Balliol College, known in those days as Balliol Ditch, and recall the story. For here were men that had a taste of the glory of God. John Foxe records the moving story in his *Acts and Monuments*. When the flames were encircling their bodies, old Hugh Latimer called to Ridley and said: 'Fear not, Master Ridley, and play the man; we shall this day light such a candle in England as I trust shall never be put out.' The same year John Bradford of Manchester was burnt at the stake over here in Smithfield, and he exclaimed to the one being burnt with him, 'Cheer up, brother, we will have a merry supper with the Lord tonight.'

Jonah wasn't irrational when he said, 'Throw me overboard.' He had a glimpse of the glory of God. He didn't care what they did to him. And once you see God's glory you won't care either. You will want God to do anything He wants. Jonah wasn't afraid. 'Throw me overboard. I've seen the glory of the Lord. I don't care what happens to me.'

There's a man in America who wrote these sweet lines:

Let me lose my self and find it, Lord, in Thee;
Let all self be slain, my friends see only Thee;
    Though it cost me grief and pain,
    I will find my life again;
Let me lose my self and find it, Lord, in Thee.

Have you been manipulating your life? Trying to get ahead? Asserting yourself? Protecting your own life? Have you been worried about how you are going to make it – financially, emotionally, physically? Does it look like the end of the road for you? One glimpse of the glory of God will show you how foolish it was for you to worry about that. You are not your own. Those cares that you have are His cares. May I remind you that God has taken on your case? 'Well', you say, 'I have got great problems. The Lord perhaps didn't know what He was getting when He got me.' He knows. Your situation isn't unique. This is the Devil's great suggestion: Nobody has been through it like you before. Yes, they have. We all have. We are all just like you. You see, you are bought with the price of Christ's own blood, and God's glory is at stake, the glory of His Son. You are owned by Him and He's going to take care of you. There is nothing that can happen to you without His permission. The very hairs of your head are numbered. Maybe you *have* been disobedient. Are you a Jonah? Sure you are. Be willing then to be thrown overboard. Let God do anything, anything, anything with you.

6 The Mariners' Conversion

Jonah 1:11–16

WE HAVE SEEN up to now that despite Jonah's disobedience a genuine awakening was precipitated owing to the mariners' seeing *authenticity* in Jonah's passive witness. This was due not to Jonah's active witness to the true God but to the fact Jonah was forced to admit his real identity. The mariners saw that, behind Jonah's witness, however much he was forced to this involuntarily, authenticity was to be seen. Now this, I say, is what the world always wants to see – what is real. The world wants to see something real in the church. The church claims that it reflects a God of power, a God of grace, a God who is *there*; and the world outside says, 'Show me that this is true'. Very well; this *is* what happened: the mariners saw that there was something authentic behind this testimony.

What the world wants to see in fact is what could be called 'experimental knowledge'. There are two kinds of religious knowledge. There is the knowledge of *faith;* and there is *experimental* knowledge. The knowledge of faith could be called the 'direct' act by which we *immediately* see God's word: we grasp Christ's death *directly*, God's mercy immediately. This is faith: the persuasion that God is there, that His word is true. This is brought about by the *internal witness of the Holy Spirit*. And so we speak of a direct knowledge – an immediate apprehension of God's will, of His mercy, His grace. This I say is the knowledge of faith.

But there is also what may be called experimental knowledge. Any scientist who may be here this morning would know what I mean by that. One puts forth a hypothesis; one tests the hypothesis by experiment; one then draws a conclusion. Now the world out there is watching us and the world wants to be shown what is undoubted. Let's be fair: the world has some right to ask this. For the church claims to be the light of the world, the salt of the earth. The world says, 'Show us; prove your claims.' This is where experimental knowledge comes in: testing a hypothesis by experiment.

What is the hypothesis? The hypothesis is, that behind the church – behind the Christian – is God who is *there*: a God of power. What is the test? It is when the church and the Christian demonstrate that there *is* such a God. And then the conclusion is immediately drawn whether or not what the church claims to be true is true. This is experimental knowledge.

Now there is an important if not crucial thing to be grasped here: that *experimental* knowledge is for the *world* and not primarily for us who comprise the church. *We* should not need experimental knowledge. We should not have to wait and see certain 'effects' to convince us. This is because the knowledge of faith is *direct*. Experimental knowledge is the effects *flowing* from faith. Experimental knowledge is for others to see. We shouldn't have to be convinced by those effects. We have already believed the Word! It is direct. It is immediate. Such is the knowledge of faith. We do not get our persuasion by the experiment, the 'effects'. We do not have a 'delayed' persuasion, as it were, so that we test the hypothesis that God is there by experiment. Our persuasion, then, does not come by experimental knowledge; it comes by seeing directly, immediately, that God is there. But alas the church today sees little even of experimental knowledge, much less this direct persuasion. In any case, experimental knowledge is primarily for the world to see in us. The world wants to see authenticity and authority. The mariners saw this behind Jonah's witness and such experimental knowledge precipitated this awakening. Thus when Jonah said, 'I am an Hebrew, I fear the Lord, the God of heaven, which made the sea and the dry land', the men were 'exceedingly afraid'. This then was the awakening to which I have referred.

But now there is a further critical distinction to be noted. It is the difference between a general awakening in a community and the actual conversion of individuals, which we call regeneration. Verse 10 shows the awakening – 'the men were exceedingly afraid'. This was an awakening in that realm we have come to see as common grace. This however is to be seen as something different from an individual conversion. I would call it a change of atmosphere in the community as a result of seeing the true God. Thus things are not the same as they were. For we read in verse 5 that the mariners were afraid because of the storm, and each began to pray to 'his god'. They were just praying to their own god: idol worship, you could almost call it. But now we see a different situation – a change of atmosphere, when the true God – *Yahweh* – was the object of their fear. A great awakening however can change the atmosphere in a community and still not necessarily be synonymous with regeneration of all in that community.

Now what do I mean by change of atmosphere? Well, when there is real awakening it will have an effect upon the whole life of a community – from government down to the man in the street. And so, government will recognise the true God; crime will largely be checked; open sin will lose its boldness. The Great Awakening in the eighteenth century, both in this country and in America, are illustrations of this. Many historians have come to see that the Great Awakening in this country through Wesley and Whitefield saved England from despair.

We can look at the Great Awakening in New England and can see a profound impact. Did you know that in the second quarter of the eighteenth century there were only about fifty thousand actually converted? Now that is a large number but it was just a small percentage of the whole population. Indeed, that is a great number. It was something that revolutionised the church, both quantitatively and qualitatively. But let no one think that because of the Great Awakening everybody in America was converted. That was not the case. About fifty thousand were converted from about 1730 to 1750.

But there is something further to be seen in that Great Awakening. The awakening had such an impact upon the American continent as a whole that, when the Revolution came into being (and a new nation was born), there was such a general fear of God that, from the beginning, America saw herself as a 'nation under God'. To this very day every coin, every bit of monetary currency, has imprinted thereon 'In God we trust'. Now I am saying it can largely be traced back to this Great Awakening. Of course there are roots that go behind that but it was this kind of atmosphere that changed the whole community. And so it is, there is a distinction to be noted between an awakening which changes the atmosphere and conversion of individuals.

However, I want us to see that in the case of Jonah and the mariners there was more than just a change in the atmosphere. We are now going to see one of the most neglected parts of the book of Jonah. I wonder if you have seen that these mariners on the ship not only experienced a general kind of awakening that I have just described (where they saw the true God and they feared Him – and this is something that we should pray to see in our own generation so that from government down to the man in the street there is a fear of God) but in this case there was more. We are going to see that these mariners experienced real conversion among themselves.

One of the greatest proofs of this is that this conversion was brought about despite themselves. You see, that is one of the proofs of genuine conversion: when it happens despite yourself. Your conversion, I ask you, was it something that was natural or was it something supernatural – coming down from above? You see, if your conversion was something that was natural – something that would have happened inevitably, because you are just of the temperament that could be religious, I must question whether you had a real conversion. For conversion, regeneration, is something *above* nature; it is not something that man can bring about. It is above nature; it comes from above and that is what the expression being 'born again' means. It means 'born from above'. This is why I said earlier that if God can save *you*, He can save *anybody*. It took no more grace to convert the greatest sinner that ever lived than to convert you. Because potentially you *are* the greatest sinner that ever lived. And when you see yourself as one who has been changed, con-

verted, you see this could not have been done naturally.
Now this ought to encourage you when you pray for others,
when you see other people that seem so far from the Kingdom of God, and you wonder what it is going to take to
save them. Remind yourself that if God could save you,
He can save anybody. And so, one of the greatest proofs of
this conversion is that it was despite these men.

It was much in the same sense that Jonah had been a
passive witness. Let us not forget this. Jonah could get no
glory at all for what he did. You will recall that Jonah was
in the process of dying. He said, 'Throw me overboard.' Paul
said to the Colossians, 'For ye are dead and your life is hid
with Christ in God' (Col. 3:3). You see, that is where we are:
we are dead. We don't live to ourselves; we are alive unto
God but we are dead to the world, to self, to sin. We are
living totally to the glory of God, said Paul. But the
fact is, there is that flesh in us that wants to live to self;
and this happened to Jonah and Jonah had to rediscover
God all over again. He needed to be renewed and when
he did discover God's grace in his life in this amazing
way he was brought to that feeling of self-expendability.
Now that is where we are all supposed to be – dead. But
Jonah was alive, he was running, running to Tarshish.
But God brought him back until he 'died'. Jonah said,
'Throw me overboard'; Jonah was a passive witness.

But that is what convinced the mariners of authenticity. It wasn't anything Jonah did. This is what brought
about the mariners' conversion. God can use both an
obedient person and a disobedient person in His own purpose. We are going to see how that in God's permissive will
we may still be used of God though we are disobedient.
And this should give us great comfort today. For as a
church, not being what we ought to be, to think that God
could still use us is a marvellous thought. I tell you candidly
I take great comfort in this. For the fact that the church is
not what she ought to be at the present moment does not
mean that God cannot use us. For God can use a crooked
stick to draw a straight line and that is precisely what happened in the case of Jonah. Jonah was a disobedient man.
Now let no one think for a moment that I am condoning

Jonah's disobedience. For it is far better if the church is not a passive witness but an active witness; that actively the church is on fire, doing exactly what she is supposed to do so that men will see God's glory.

Consider the way it was with Moses. Through Moses men saw the glory of God, but there is one thing to be noted about that story. When God used Moses in this particular way it came to pass that when he came down from Mount Sinai with the two tables of testimony, he 'wist not that the skin of his face shone while he talked with him' (Exod. 34:29). You see that Moses wasn't aware of any personal glory even when he was actively obedient. Moses was not aware of this impact he was making because he was so full of the glory of God. I want you to notice something: when men are converted to Christ, it will be because they see Christ directly. Now if He comes to them through us, whether we are being passive witnesses or active witnesses, it must be the glory of *Christ* that they see. The fact is, many of us want to see men converted for our *own* glory. Isn't that the truth? Don't we really want to see revival in a sense so that we can get some glory out of it? And I suspect that we are going to have to take seriously, more seriously than I suspect we took my comments last time, that before we see something happen we must crave to see an outpouring of grace in such a way that we are willing for it *not* to be where we are! In fact, we must give up on it being here and pray for God to show Himself *anywhere, any place*. We may secretly hope for it and we want to see it happen here. But a love for the glory of God means that you want to see an awakening take place anywhere. And so, men must see the glory of God. In the case of the mariners it wasn't because of Jonah's active obedience, obviously not! They saw something far beyond him and it must always be this way, even when we *are* being actively obedient – that men don't see merely us. Now obviously in the case of Jonah it *had* to be God they saw! It wasn't Jonah, was it! There was no way that Jonah himself did anything. He was the object of God's chastening. But they saw *God*. It is precisely in this way that even when we are actively obedient to the Word we must not for a minute think that it is anything *we* do. It is God through us. And when God works through us this way we will not draw attention to ourselves, as Moses was not aware of the impact he was making. This was a result of active obedience but, in any case, when men are converted it will be because they see the God behind us. These mariners were genuinely converted and the first reason I suggest is because it was something beyond themselves.

Now I want us to see something else. Look how the men fought against what was happening. We read in verse 12 that Jonah said to the men: 'Now look, there is only one solution. I know you don't want to do it. There is only one way that this storm is going to calm down and that is to throw me overboard.' But we read in verse 13: 'Nevertheless the men rowed hard to bring it to the land. But they could not for the sea wrought and was tempestuous against them.' This was something beyond them. They were still going against Jonah's advice.

There are some principles to be learned from this verse, where these men rowed hard to bring the boat to land but they could not. The first principle is to see the futility of fighting against God. You should know that if God is pleased to act He is going to win. Are you fighting against God? I feel sorry for you. You are going to be a miserable person. You are going to be doing everything you can trying to outwit, out-manoeuvre God. You are going to keep trying. These men rowed hard. Jonah told them that there was only one thing to do, but they rowed hard. It is futile to fight against God. And remember this, when God is pleased to work He is going to accomplish His purpose. For example, when God was pleased to come to the rescue of the Children of Israel, when they were against the sea; they looked back and saw Pharaoh's army. They were in that moment of crisis. But Moses said, 'Stand still and see the salvation of the Lord' (Exod. 14:13). When God comes down, all hell shall be defeated! When God works, He wins! We must pray that God will work in this way in our day. This is what the Psalmist meant when he cried out, 'It is time for thee to work' (Psa. 119:126). For if God comes down, men will be slain. You see, it is not only futile to fight God, but further fighting will lead to more despair.

When I get to heaven I want to ask the Apostle Paul exactly what was going on in his mind when he was making that trip to Damascus. He was struck down and the words were, 'It is hard for thee to kick against the pricks' (Acts 9:5).

Is there anybody here fighting against God? God has said one thing and you are doing another? And it is getting worse? You are rowing hard, you are going against everything? Give up! Give up! It will get worse! It will lead to more despair, more anxiety, more trouble. Give up.

We learn something else from this story. *God has a purpose in any continuing storm.* None of us likes stormy weather. And none of us enjoys rocking on the waves. We are afraid of being dashed against the rocks. Do you know what it is to be in turmoil? In indecision? Not knowing which way to turn? Do you wonder, 'Why does God let this last?' Are you in a particular situation that is utterly inexplicable and you can't understand it? You are involved in a matter that is beyond you and you wonder why God doesn't come to your rescue. 'Surely God can handle this matter?' you keep saying. You are perplexed. You are worried. 'Why doesn't God work it out now, right now?' But we are to learn from this story that *God has a purpose in the continuing storm.* It may be rough, it may be dark, it may be gloomy. You may not know which way to turn. The solution may indeed be beyond yourself. But God has a purpose in the continuing storm.

Now, in this context it was a two-fold purpose. First, God had more to teach Jonah. We might have thought that Jonah's confession would have been enough. He admitted who he was. We might have thought that when Jonah came to grips with things that the storm could have calmed right then. After all, he had confessed and surely they could go on? But in this case Jonah had more to learn and that is why the story continued. And I have a suspicion at this moment that if *you* are in a storm – in some trouble – and it won't end – that God is wanting to teach *you* something. He is preparing a fish for you: a great university in which to learn some deep things of God. He has a purpose in the continuing storm.

But the second reason for this continuing storm is that

God wanted to convert the mariners. We usually forget the possibility of unexpected conversions. It is amazing how God works. Who will be converted next may come as a complete surprise to you!

> God moves in a mysterious way
> His wonders to perform;
> He plants His footsteps in the sea,
> And rides upon the storm.

That is the second reason for the continuing storm. First, God was saying to Jonah, 'You come this way. Let the mariners go that way. I want to teach *you* a lesson and I have got something for *them*.'

And so, finally, the mariners saw there was nothing else to do. They fought hard, they continued to row but it got worse. In despair they took Jonah and threw him over. And here came the experimental knowledge again. The sea was calm! Experimental knowledge was not for Jonah. He had to learn the lesson directly; the knowledge of faith was for him. But the world wants to see something happen, something that is real; and those men knew what was happening! They could never forget it. They knew how hard they had tried. Then they threw him over and the sea was calm! And so we find then that they feared the Lord.

But there's more. Let's look at the details of what was taking place. We can see why this was a genuine conversion. They not only feared the true God but they called upon the *name* of God. You will recall that in verse 10 they were 'exceedingly afraid', but in verse 14 they cried unto the Lord – *Yahweh*. In verse 5 the mariners were simply calling to their 'god'.

Christian people, do not ever underestimate the fact that if men ever come to conversion it will be because they are confronted with the true God. One folly of the church in the present generation is our bringing God down to a level where men will say, 'Oh, I can now go along with *that* God.' And we somehow have been afraid to make men face the true God. And so one of the tragedies of the present generation is how the Christian church has been capitulating to world religions, saying, 'Well, there is the Buddhist, there is the Shintoist, etc., we are all trying to get to the same place.' But I remind you that that is where the mariners were at one time. Each of them was crying to his 'god' but not now! They had seen something take place. They had no choice but to call upon the true God – a God who was powerful, a God who was angry, a God who was there, a God who deals familiarly with men. 'Whosoever shall call upon the *name* of the Lord shall be saved' (Rom. 10:13). Christ Jesus is Lord! 'There is no other name given among men whereby we must be saved' (Acts 4:12). Never apologise for the God of the Bible, the God of Scripture. Let them laugh, let them scoff. But if men are ever converted they will face the true God. And so, we have this extraordinary incident when these heathen men were forced to call upon the *name* of the true God.

But there is more. We find that these men, these heathen, became beggars before God. That is the way men will always be when they come face to face with the true God. They will become beggars. Oh the cheap, silly evangelism that we witness in our generation in which the Christian church in places has represented a God who is supposedly up there, but who doesn't know His own mind, much less the mind of others, and is just begging people to note Him. This God is begging people to recognise Him, begging people to make a decision for Him. No wonder this generation has no respect for God! They have the idea that if they go to church, they are doing God a favour. If they do something good, they do God a favour. But I want you to know something. When you see the glory of the true God, you will find out that He does *you* favours, you don't do Him favours. Are you unsaved today? Have you got the idea that you are doing God a favour when you come to church? Listen! Whenever you see the true God, you will be like that leper who came to the Lord Christ, looked at Him and said, 'Lord, *if thou wilt* thou canst make me clean' (Matt. 8:2).

And so we read that they cried unto the Lord and said, 'We beseech thee, we beseech thee, let us not perish for this man's life and lay not upon us innocent blood.' They were on the begging end. And I want you to know that's the posture you are going to have to be in if you ever come to the true God. Don't you think that you can snap your fingers at Him and expect Him to jump. Maybe you are the type that has had your own way in everything you do. Maybe you have got a manipulative personality so that you can get your way: you know how to move people. But not God you don't!

There is more. These men dignified God's will. The glory of the Lord is the dignity of His will. And one of the greatest proofs of conversion is when men come to dignify God's will. Men by nature hate God. One of my favourite sermons of Jonathan Edwards is entitled 'Man God's natural enemy'. Men by nature hate God. They hate Him because He permits evil in the world, they hate Him because of this or that. They want to get even with Him. And so, here was a storm. These men were rowing hard. But now they came to dignify the will of God. 'We beseech thee, we beseech thee, have mercy upon us, O Lord; *thou hast done as it pleased thee.*' 'Thou hast done as it pleased thee'. Can you pray like that? That's proof that these men had been changed. They came to agree with a God of sovereignty and glory. 'Thou hast done as it pleased thee.'

I remember being in a prayer meeting once when an elderly man about ninety years of age prayed this prayer: 'O God, I thank you that everything is just like it is'. Can you pray like that? That's dignifying the will of God. I also recall one old saint who once said: 'You know, I have been serving the Lord so long now that *I can hardly tell the difference between a blessing and a trial.*'

There is still more. The mariners saw the need of atonement – outside themselves. We are told that the men feared the Lord exceedingly and offered a sacrifice unto *Yahweh*. They were heathenish and maybe they had once been offering sacrifices. But no longer to their 'god': it was to 'the Lord' – *Yahweh* – Jehovah God. And so it is, you will never be saved until you see you need *atonement* and that it must come from outside yourself. You need a substitute: One who did what you cannot. And this is what Jesus Christ did on the cross. He did what you cannot do: He atoned for sin.

The final thing I mention is that the mariners then 'made vows'. And notice the order. They made their vows *after* making the sacrifice – after atonement. You see, sanctification is our *gratitude*. It is a way of saying 'thank you'. The mariners didn't make vows in order to precipitate God's mercy. They beheld His mercy, they offered sacrifices and *then* they made vows. Don't think there is something you can do first to attract God's mercy – to make Him like you a little better. This is where we Christians so often get muddled. We sometimes imagine there are things that we can do to make God like us a little more, or to give us a better feeling. But remember, first you see Christ. And *then* you say 'thank you' by obedience – by repentance, by sanctification. Don't try to bargain in any way. And so it was that the mariners were converted and ever pre-figured the *ordo salutis* (order of salvation) laid down in the New Testament.

But I close with this. I have been saying that it was a disobedient Jonah that led the mariners to the true God. Does that justify Jonah's disobedience? It would seem that if Jonah had not been disobedient and if he had not run from Nineveh to Tarshish those mariners would never have been saved. It would seem that way. It would seem then that Jonah's very disobedience was right – justified in itself – because had he not been disobedient the mariners would never have been converted. I say, it would seem that way.

But God's ways are 'past finding out' (Rom. 11:33). Romans 8:28 says that 'All things work together for good'. That does not mean however that all things *are* good. It means that all things *work together* for good. And there is that inside all of us that wants to think deductively. 'If *this* is true, then that means *this* is true. The mariners were converted therefore Jonah was right in being disobedient.' And so it is, maybe you can look back on your life and say, 'I know a situation in which I did something that was terribly wrong but it worked out so well that I believe I am glad I did it.' Wait, wait a minute! Don't ever think in those terms! You are giving yourself the credit. It's much like when a husband and a wife get into an argument. When a husband and a wife get into an argument she may say to him, 'See there, I told you I was right. See how it worked out!' We love to say, 'I told you so'. There is that in all of us; we love to say: 'I told you so'. But the wonderful thing about the grace of God is that it has a way of making things *appear* that it was right from the start. You see, when God makes things work together for good He does it in such a way that it *looks* as though that *was* the way it was supposed to be. But you are not to say that. You are not to say that. His ways are 'past finding out'. Don't try to play God and try to understand His secrets. 'All things *work together* for good.'

The fact that a matter is right or made right *now* doesn't mean that it *was* right *then*. Can you handle that one? God makes it right *now*. But that does not mean it was right *then*. And so, the fact that it is right now does not make it right in its original context, as in the case of Jonah's disobedience. It does not mean that it was right then.

But, if it *is* right now then everything *is* all right.

7 Jonah's Fish

Jonah 1:17

WE COME NOW to the best-known part of the book of Jonah. You have heard of 'Jonah and the whale'. We will be dealing with Jonah and the great fish, whatever kind it was, for a while now. We find Jonah in the belly of the fish. Jonah doesn't call it a whale; it's a 'great fish'. In Matthew, chapter 12 verse 40, the authorised version translates the Greek word *ketous* as 'whale', but the word really means 'sea monster'. It may have been a whale; it may not have been. It doesn't matter.

I pass over the cavil of those who question whether there is a fish large enough to swallow a Jonah and the fish still live. I pass over the cavil of those who raise the question whether a man could actually live three days in the belly of a fish. That there is a fish or sea monster in the sea equal to this feat is irrelevant. I have always been amazed that a great commentator like Adam Clark should go to such lengths to show that this miracle may well have happened because there is a certain kind of fish in the Mediterranean sea large enough to hold a man inside. I don't understand why Evangelicals sometimes feel the need to prove the possibility of a miracle. There have actually been those in the present generation who try to show that there could really be a Virgin Birth. Christian people, do you need to be told that that is possible simply because it has been shown in the real world that this could happen? I have actually read where they have shown that a man could falsely appear to be dead. This is to show allegedly that Jesus could have been dead and then revived. I don't understand why it is that Evangelicals want to prove these things.

It doesn't matter whether there is a fish now in existence

large enough to hold a man for three days. We only need to know that there was one. God does not have to have a precedent to perform any act nor does He have to do anything twice. Evangelicals who venture into the arena of proving the possibility of miracles become sitting ducks for the secular empiricist, who can make such an Evangelical look ridiculous when he finds contrary evidence. And I have been surprised at the fuss being made over the recent BBC series on Archaeology and the Bible. Why should this upset you? What do you expect from a secular mind? What would worry me is if you got encouragement from such if he came down on the side you wanted him to come down on. It may be true that it doesn't help the cause but it would be sad if it helped it because it was able to prove one or two things. And there are those who say, 'But we should try to prove these things'. But, when something cannot be proved, what then? Do you stay with Scripture? That even makes you look worse! That shows that you do not have an open mind. You are merely wanting to prove a certain thing.

We miss the whole point of the Christian doctrine of revelation when we try to work out our doctrine in the light of what science can tell us or verify. And so it is, I worry if there is somebody to be helped that much because of certain archaeological verifications that show certain things really happened in the Bible. You see, that is not the correct epistemological method by which we know things. Thus if we rejoice in what we like and lament what we don't like from such a series on television, then it shows that our whole premise is false.

The thing that has passed behind the cloud in the present generation – I suspect it happened long before the present generation – is what I think was the greatest contribution of the great Reformation: the doctrine of *the internal witness of the Holy Spirit*. How do you know that the Bible is the Word of God? Are you going to stand back and wait for science to say it is? Are you going to wait for the archaeologist to continue to dig and show that there really was a Jericho, or that Moses really lived? Is that what you need? The great Reformation principle was that it is *by the Holy*

Spirit we are persuaded that the Bible is the Word of God. And so, any time we need *external* evidence to help our persuasion along we tell on ourselves! It is rather by a direct, clear witness of the Spirit that we know the Bible is God's Word. And so, don't let things like external testimonies upset you. We are not waiting for their verification; we already have it.

It is like in the parable of the Rich Man and Lazarus (Luke 16:19–31). There was the man who went to Abraham's bosom, Lazarus. The rich man went to hell, and after he saw that he could not come back he said, 'I do have one request. I have five brothers; my five brothers do not believe that there is a place like this. They are secularists and they don't believe in the supernatural, much less do they believe in this place, hell. I don't want them to come here. Send Lazarus that *he* may tell them about this place.' The word came back, 'But those five brothers have Moses and the prophets' – that means the Bible, the Word of God. And then the rich man in hell wanted to argue: 'But you don't understand; my five brothers are not going to believe in hell by virtue of the Word saying it; they need a miracle over and above the Word. If they saw Lazarus come back from the dead then they would be persuaded.' Then the word came, 'If they hear not Moses and the prophets, neither will they be persuaded, though one rose from the dead.'

Where do we take our stand? It is on this Book, God's infallible word! This is what we hold to. This is what we contend for – without apology. Because there is that in us – the Spirit – that persuades us, though all hell shake! This is God's Word.

I also worry about those who say, 'Well, I know I *must* be a Christian because I was tempted to do this and I didn't do it.' I want to ask, 'Suppose you did? Does that mean you are not?' This is the danger of basing your whole assurance on what you do or do not do. And you see how it is, that Christ being the ground of our assurance coheres with this principle of the internal witness of the Holy Spirit. It is a direct ground. And so it is, Christ as the ground of assurance and the principle of the internal witness of the

Spirit go together! Thus we must also remember, insofar as miracles are concerned, God does not need a precedent nor does He have to do anything a second time.

But, there is one more point. It is quite right indeed to prove the principle of the guidance of the Holy Spirit, especially in the matter of first impressions. Now, you will notice in Jonah 1:13 (and I dealt with this in some detail) that the men rowed hard to bring the ship to land. I made the point that they were not going to succeed because God was going to win. But let's not be too hard on these men. They did the right thing; they should have done that. For it is quite right to test the impressions that you get. You say, 'But how do I know if it is God speaking?' Well then, do just like those men. They rowed hard. Because if God is behind a matter, He will show it to you.

How *do* we know when God is speaking? Well, of course, you know about the *theological* test. In I John we find these words: 'Beloved, believe not every spirit, but try the spirits whether they are of God: because many false prophets are gone out into the world. Hereby know ye the Spirit of God: Every spirit that confesseth that Jesus Christ is come in the flesh is of God: And every spirit that confesseth not that Jesus Christ is come in the flesh is not of God: and this is that spirit of antichrist, whereof ye have heard that it should come; and even now already is it in the world' (I John 4:1-3). John says this is the theological test by which you know the difference between the spirit of truth and the spirit of error.

Then there is another test we know about in Scripture. It is the test of *whether a man is a false prophet*. In the Gospel of Matthew our Lord put it this way: 'Beware of false prophets, which come to you in sheep's clothing, but inwardly they are ravening wolves. Ye shall know them by their fruits. Do men gather grapes of thorns, or figs of thistles? Even so every good tree bringeth forth good fruit; but a corrupt tree bringeth forth evil fruit. A good tree cannot bring forth evil fruit, neither can a corrupt tree bring forth good fruit. Every tree that bringeth not forth good fruit is hewn down, and cast into the fire. Wherefore by their fruits ye shall know them' (Matt. 7:15-20). And so it is, a prophet is to be tested: 'by their fruits ye shall know them'.

Then the third test is concerning *impressions*. One wishes to know when it is God actually speaking. I think that many Christians go astray at this point. They want to feel that they are obeying impressions from the Lord. I was once pastor of a church in which there was a very devout Christian lady who some years before had given birth to a son with a cleft palate. She was so broken-hearted that she had a baby with a cleft palate. She turned to the Lord. She got the impression that God was going to heal the baby; she was convinced God was going to do it. When the physicians came and said, 'We can operate on that baby and your baby will be in good condition,' she said, 'No; God will do it'. And they insisted that they should do it but they could not get her permission. She felt that if she let them operate she would be going against the leadership of the Spirit.

This is why we should not be hard on those men who continued to row. For *when God is in something He brings your options down to one*. These men reached the point where they had one option. Both Jonah and the mariners were agreed; there was only one solution and that was to throw Jonah overboard. When God is in something He will bring this to pass so that there is only one thing to do. There was nothing else left to do. It is quite right to test your impressions. The best test of all is the question of open doors and closed doors. You may feel led to do something. But does it work out? Does it pass the providential test? Do you have to manipulate it? Do you have to pull strings? Do you have to do this, do that, to work it out? Or does it just 'happen'? Let God hand things to you on a silver platter. God does it by the providential test. And so it was, these mariners did not want to do what they had to but they became willing to do it because there was no choice. It is like that song:

> He doesn't compel us against our will
> But makes us willing to go.

And God made these mariners willing.

Very well then, the next thing to be grasped here is that Jonah *expected* to die. Jonah was not looking for a great fish to swallow him up! I don't think that when they finally were convinced they should throw Jonah overboard that Jonah went to the rail, looked over and said, 'Don't throw me here; there is nothing but flounders and halibut here; get me over there where the *big* fish are'. I don't think it happened like that. I don't think there were any BBC cameras there to film the next series on Archaeology and the Bible!

Jonah thought he was finished. He was going to die. But we have already seen that he was *willing* to die because he had recovered that principle that *he was not his own.* You see, God has a way of bringing us back to the fundamental point of our conversion. When we were first converted it was because we lost our lives. 'He that loseth his life shall find it; he that seeketh to save his life shall lose it.' But Jonah began to *save* his life. God said, 'Go to Nineveh'. Jonah went instead to Tarshish. Jonah began to get possessive over his own life. And so it was, God had to show him a lesson. God can do that! May He do it with us! May He do it to us who have been professing Christians for years – to bring us back to the fundamental point that we recognise what we were when we were first converted! We must *continually* be in a state of *willingness to lose our lives.*

Now let us look at this verse, Mark 8:35: 'For whosoever will save his life shall lose it; but whosoever shall lose his life for my sake and the gospel's, the same shall save it.' There are two cautions about this verse. The first is, you cannot manipulate it into actualisation. You must see that this promise 'he that loseth his life shall find it' is not a promise primarily given to entice men to try it. It is rather a statement of fact. There are so many verses in Scripture like this and we sometimes confuse this matter. Mark 8:35 is not dangled before your eyes to tempt you to try it. Take, for example, evangelists today who say, 'Try Jesus and you will be happy'; so people 'try' Jesus to get happiness. It is not that they truly *see* the glory of Jesus; they want happiness and they sometimes will do anything to get it. And so, when it comes to this verse, the same principle follows. You must lose your life; yet this cannot be actualised merely by manipulating it. The second caution is, as long as you are concentrating on the second part – *finding* your life – it won't happen. It just won't happen! As long as you are thinking of *saving* it by losing it you haven't lost it yet! You cannot lose your life as long as you are figuring on saving it. 'Well,' somebody says, 'but they go together, don't they? Wouldn't they be two sides of the coin?' Indeed so, but when you *lose* your life that means you kiss it goodbye! It is *forgetting* saving it.

The same is true with the *ordo salutis*. Take the issue of faith and repentance. Faith (assurance) must always go *before* repentance. And someone always says, 'But isn't there repentance?' Some are so afraid of leaving out repentance! But I tell you, repentance will be a *feigned* repentance if there is not *first* the *persuasion* that God *accepts* us. The trouble is, we keep trying to get the *second* half! We must know the order. Thus he that loseth his life *will* save it; but, as long as you figure on saving it *while* you're losing it, you've obviously got your eye on saving it not losing it. You are not really losing it yet. Losing your life means to recognise it's finished! Hands off!

When we get too possessive of something we are in danger of losing it. But when we are truly, truly willing – and I don't want to use the word 'willing' here in the sense that one initiates it; but when we really *have* lost our life, that is when we save it.

In the book of Genesis we find the most perfect illustration of this principle. We find here also one of the most moving and touching stories to be found in all Holy Writ. You know the story. God told Abraham to sacrifice his son. Abraham obeyed. We read the story in Gen. 22:6–14. 'And Abraham took the wood of the burnt offering, and laid it upon Issac his son; and he took the fire in his hand, and a knife; and they went both of them together.' Can you imagine what was in Abraham's mind? And then, if that weren't enough: 'Isaac spake unto his father, and said, My father: and he said, Here am I, my son. And Isaac said, Behold the fire and the wood: but where is the lamb for a burnt offering?' How could Abraham answer? He answered: 'My son, God will provide himself a lamb for a burnt offering: so they went both of them together. And they came to the place which God had told him of; and Abraham built an altar there, and laid the wood in order, and bound Isaac his son, and laid him on the altar upon the wood. And Abraham stretched forth his hand, and took the knife to slay his son.' But the angel wouldn't let his hand come back down! The angel's words were: 'Abraham, Abraham, lay not thine hand upon the lad, neither do thou any thing unto him: for now I know that thou fearest God.' Abraham had been given no clue of what would happen. This is what is meant by losing your life.

But I warn you, as long as you get too possessive of something you are in danger of losing it, such as running your own life, being too possessive about your job, or your future. God has a way of reminding you that He is God – and who you are. You may get too possessive with your family – with your husband, your wife, or your children; God has a way of making you reassess your priorities. Jonah saw himself as dead. God has a right to take what is His at any time.

So it was, Jonah expected to die. But God prepared a fish.

But before we can proceed to the fish we go back again. Why did not Jonah's actual confession calm the storm? It could have. Let's be clear about that. Once Jonah came clean with the man – once Jonah recovered his identity: 'I am an Hebrew, I fear the Lord', that might have calmed the storm. And I want to say that in most cases it does; in most cases the confession is sufficient. And if you have been like Jonah, making everybody miserable by disobedience – if you have been like that, so nervous and tense because *you* are the one that is in the wrong and everybody around you is miserable, then recognise who you are. Confess. Get right with God. You will remember the verse in Proverbs 16:7: 'When a man's ways please the Lord, he maketh even his enemies to be at peace with him'. And so, in most cases the confession is sufficient and let us always remember 1 John 1:9: 'If we confess our sins, God is faithful and just to forgive us our sins and to cleanse us from all unrighteousness.'

At this point I want us to become acquainted with a most profound principle. *The fact that the story, or chastening, continues does not mean we are not forgiven.* Many misunderstand this because God continues to chasten. Many feel that God has not accepted them because He still chastens. But don't forget that chastening is simultaneous wrath *and* mercy. That in itself is a proof of God's love (Heb. 12:6). And so it was, Jonah's confession might have calmed the storm. But it didn't. Why? We must be clear that the reason the storm continued was not because God didn't love Jonah. A deeper principle underlies this whole story. The continuing storm does not mean that God is trying to get even with you.

Many Christians live under a kind of Old Testament covenant. They say to themselves, when something goes wrong, 'God's mad at me. He is getting even. I sinned the other day and I knew this was coming. God has got even.' I have dealt with people when counselling in the vestry who say, 'I know why this happened to me. Fourteen years ago I did something that I should not have done. And for the last fourteen years I have been dreading that God was going to do something to me. Now it has happened.' Rubbish! Rest your case in that glorious Psalm 103, verse 10: 'He hath not dealt with us after our sins; nor rewarded us according to our iniquities.' Listen! If God did deal with us according to our sins we would be chastened all the time! We could never lift our heads up. *Chastening is not God's 'getting even'. God 'got even' at the cross!* God was satisfied with His Son on the cross. The Lord 'laid on Him the iniquity of us all' (Isa. 53:6). God's justice was satisfied there. His chastening you is not what satisfies His justice. God got even at the Cross.

Well then, 'Why', you may ask, 'does God continue to chasten?' The answer is very simple. Why did God prepare the fish? Why the continuing storm? Why more chastening? *God's chastening is not meted out in proportion to our sins but in proportion to the lesson we have to learn.* The greater the work ahead, the greater the trial now. Jonah had some lessons to learn.

Could I be speaking to someone like that this morning?

You may have wondered, even though you have confessed your sins to God, why does the storm continue? Why the chastening? You have just told me that God is dealing with you in a special way. God *could* have finished off Jonah, surely He could have. Have you noticed how many times God might have finished off Jonah? He could have done it as soon as Jonah ran from the presence of the Lord (verse 3). Or God could have done it when the sea was under the influence of the wind when the ship nearly sank. He could have done it when the mariners cast lots and they found out that the cause was Jonah; they could have ended him right there! How many times *could* God have finished with you? But He stayed with you. Can you look back at those watersheds in your life, those critical times, when it might have been *all over*? Your life could have gone a different direction and things would never have been the same again; but God stayed with you and guided and protected you across the years.

Thus, the fish! There was more. God pays you a high compliment when He sends the great fish. The chastening may seem to be more than you can bear but God is telling you via the chastening that He is not finished with you yet. He has more for you to do.

There is the story of Luther's standing before the diet at Worms – when he cried out, 'Here I stand'. But did you know what was going on the night before Luther made that heroic stand? Do you know about that? You will know that the day before they confronted Luther, and asked, 'Are these your books?' He replied, 'Yes, they are mine'. They said, 'Will you recant, will you reject, will you say that you don't now believe what is in these books?' Luther asked for a day to think about it. Now it would seem reasonable to think that during those 24 hours Luther would be visited by the angels! Surely, if you were programming that, you would have rewarded Luther – you would have said to him: 'Well, since a great thing is about to happen, I want you to know that we are all proud of you up here in heaven.' Thus Luther would have had a great time for 24 hours – God rewarding him. Surely God would do that for a man that is going to be so mightily used? But, Christian people, the opposite was true. Luther went to his room in utter despair. He wrote down words that have survived to this day – words he addressed to God: 'O my God, where art thou? The devils rage, and thou art not there. The devils hound me, but where art thou? O my God, *art thou dead*?' The next day Luther stood before those men and they said to him, 'Will you reject what you have written in these books?' And Luther replied: 'I do; I reject what I have written – on the condition you prove to me that what I have written is contrary to the Word of God. But if you cannot, here I stand. I can do no other. God help me. Amen.' Those words were carried to every village and every hamlet. The Reformation was well on its way and the world has never been the same again.

Perhaps God is hiding His face at this moment. You cannot understand why. You've confessed your sins, you've done everything you know you should do. But the storm continues. Take courage. You have just told me that God is not finished with you. He had a lesson for you to learn. Remember, God doesn't mete out chastening in proportion to the sin we have committed but in proportion to the lesson we have to learn.

Perhaps God lets the storm continue because he is wanting heaven to become dearer to you. Paul said to Timothy, 'Lay hold on eternal life' (I Tim. 6:19). But we tend not to do that. We make plans for holidays; most of us know what we want to do this summer. We are planning to live a long time, right here on mother earth. God has a way of making heaven dearer to you. God may be letting the storm continue to make you homesick for heaven. As the old spiritual put it:

> This world is not my home,
> I am just passing through.

I spoke about the Puritan who said, 'God deals familiarly with men'. I want to put it a different way this morning: God deals *singularly* with men. He deals with you as though there were no-one else. He doesn't need a precedent. He doesn't have to do anything twice. God deals with you as though there were no one else. And the reason James could say, 'Count it all joy when ye fall into divers temptations' – trials (James 1:2), is that God doesn't grant such trials to everybody. If the continuing storm bewilders you, take heart! God has paid you a compliment. You are special. He has a work for you to do. He is preparing you for something. He deals uniquely with men. Thank God for the continuing storm. Thank Him for the fish.

8 Learning From the Belly of the Fish

Jonah 1:15–2:9

TODAY WE LOOK at Jonah learning in the belly of the fish. You may recall that in my introductory sermon to the series I stated that Jonah is not only analogous to the modern church but a type of the Christian life. Last time we saw something of the doctrine of chastening and today I want us to look at the doctrine of chastening in more detail.

Now I suspect that the first rule for us to grasp with regard to the doctrine of chastening is that chastening presupposes that the chastened person is already a Christian. For the writer to the Hebrews tells us that it is whom the Lord loves that He chastens and that He scourges every son whom He receives (Heb. 12:6). Now, in case you didn't get that point, the writer goes on to put it a different way: 'If ye be *without* chastisement, . . . then are ye bastards, and not sons' (Heb. 12:8). Therefore it is important to realise fundamentally that chastening is the exclusive privilege of Christians.

Implicit in this teaching, moreover, is the doctrine that has been known for a long time as 'the perseverance of the saints'. But in a sense, in a very real sense, this is an unfortunate term. The 'perseverance of the saints' was popularised by Westminster theology (1643–49) and that of the Synod of Dort (1618–19). The idea suggests that saints must persevere as though that perseverance were dependent upon the efforts of the saints. You may be interested to know that the modern father of the teaching that saved people cannot fall away was John Calvin. But he did not talk so much about the perseverance of the saints; he talked instead about the indestructibility of the *faith* of God's elect. In other words, for Calvin it was not the perseverance of the saints but the perseverance of the *faith* in the saints, such faith being utterly the gift of God. Faith is the 'persuasion' that God loves us in Jesus Christ. It cannot be shaken because Christ, the object of the faith, remains the same. *He* is eternal and, as a consequence, faith is indestructible. But eventually the teaching became known as the perseverance of the saints. Of course this is implicit in the perseverance of the faith. But the idea came to suggest that we must work and persevere to prove to ourselves that we are really saved – as if to say that if we backslide we are not saved. Now this has been a common teaching.

Obviously if that is our theology, we will then be deriving our assurance from our having persevered. And so we say to ourselves, 'Well, I am still persevering, therefore I must be saved'. That is a false ground of assurance. That can only lead to more introspection, more checking of the spiritual pulse and telling ourselves, 'I must be all right, since I am still persevering'. This, I say, is a false ground. This point is most relevant for the present subject because Jonah certainly was not doing a good job at persevering. Jonah was far from the ideal Christian.

We must reckon Jonah to have been one of three things. Either he was (1) an apostate, or (2) what the New Testament calls an 'overtaken' saint, or (3) a 'castaway'.

An apostate is one who has fallen away without the hope of ever being restored. The apostate is described in Hebrews 6:4–6 where we are told that those who were once enlightened, who had tasted of the good word of God and the powers of the world to come and were thus made partakers of the Holy Ghost, having fallen away (the correct translation from the Greek), cannot be renewed again unto repentance. There we have a description of some who fell, who cannot be restored. Thus the impossibility of restoration is something that fits only an apostate. Was Jonah an apostate? Obviously not, for we read in the second chapter of Jonah that he was restored. Jonah was not an apostate.

Well then, the second category that I mention is that of an 'overtaken' saint. Now you Bible students already know that I am referring to Galatians 6, verses 1 and following. If a brother is 'overtaken' in a fault, the spiritual are to restore such a one in the spirit of meekness, simultaneously considering themselves lest they also be tempted. It is a teaching in the New Testament that saved people may be overtaken in a fault. One Old Testament expression is 'back-sliding'. One New Testament expression is the 'overtaken' saint. It is the same thing. In either case it is a true child of God that is being described.

Then there is the third category – the 'castaway'. Again, you Bible students will know that I am referring to 1 Corinthians 9:27, where the Apostle Paul says that he keeps his body under subjection, lest, having preached to others, he himself should be a 'castaway'. A castaway is a real Christian but one who has been rejected for Christian service. Now there are those who say, 'Well, don't forget the word "castaway" comes from the Greek word *adokimos*.' *Adokimos* is generally translated 'reprobate' (Cf. Rom 1:28, II Cor. 13:5). And reprobate, being a theological term to many of us, suggests that one could not possibly be a Christian and be reprobate at the same time. Well, logically and strictly speaking that may be true. But Paul uses this word because the word *adokimos* simply means 'tested but not approved'. It merely means one who did not meet the test. *Adokimos* may indeed mean a 'castaway', one who was *rejected* – not because he was not saved but because he became unfit for service. This is also the context in 1 Corinthians 9. Paul talks about rejoicing that the gospel is preached. He says, 'To the weak became I as weak, that I might gain the weak: I am made all things to all men, that I might by all means save some' (v. 22). He is talking about this matter of being 'all things to all men', the type of instrument of God that is usable and of service to anybody. And so he said at the very end, 'I fear lest having preached to others I myself should be a castaway'. Now, was Jonah a castaway? Obviously not, because we read in the third chapter, 'The Lord came to Jonah a second time, saying, Go to Nineveh. And he arose according to the word of the Lord'. And so I want it to be clearly affirmed that Jonah was not an apostate; he was renewed again unto repentance. He was not a castaway; he eventually did what God told him to do and he was used of the Lord. Jonah is to be seen, then, as one overtaken in a fault – the 'overtaken' saint.

Now I think it would be helpful to remember that there is a difference between apostasy and backsliding. There is a difference between the apostate and the saint overtaken in a fault. The first difference is the reality that underlies the experience. There is to be seen a distinction between the grace of regeneration and the grace of illumination. All that have been regenerated have been illuminated, but not all that have been illuminated have been regenerated. And illumination is a grace sufficient to precipitate a change in the outward man so that externally he appears to be a Christian. Inwardly, however, he may not be. The Bible sometimes calls this illumination, such being the description of the man in Hebrews 6:4–6; he had been enlightened, illuminated, but he was not regenerate.

The second difference concerns the nature of the sin. The man who is overtaken in a fault is one who disobeys God's commands or breaks God's law. This means that all of us to some degree, sooner or later, are overtaken saints. Strictly speaking, we all sin every day. Thus breaking the law does not fit apostasy. The apostate is not one who merely broke God's law, he is one who rejected Christ's mediatorship. This is the essential point, and all the difficulty that surrounds the Epistle to the Hebrews can be traced to this very matter, that apostates do not embrace Christ the mediator. It is amazing how many people can read through the Epistle to the Hebrews and never see this. This is the central thing; apostates are those who will not recognise a mediator – and this is what happens: they crucify to themselves the Son of God afresh.

There is a third distinction concerning the apostate and the overtaken saint; and that is the loss involved in the fall. The apostate loses the *hope* of salvation, that is, the hope of ever being saved. Hebrews 6:4–6 says, 'It is impossible to be renewed again unto repentance.' The overtaken saint however loses the *joy* of salvation. And this may be seen in the prayer of David in Psalm 51. David was an overtaken saint. In Psalm 51 he prayed, 'Restore unto me the joy of thy salvation' (v. 12). He had not lost salvation; he had lost the joy of it. And that is the critical difference: the apostate loses the hope of salvation; the overtaken saint loses the joy of salvation.

The fourth distinction is the time involved. Now this is somewhat complicated and I am liable to be misunderstood. But let me say that, generally speaking, the overtaken saint finds himself in a *temporary* condition of having lost the joy of his salvation. The apostate is one who is in a *permanent* state of hopelessness. But, on this point of the overtaken saint being in a temporary state of having lost joy, I would not want to say categorically that it is always necessarily temporary. For if the person isn't undoubtedly restored in the eyes of everybody, that does not mean he is not saved. This is the mistake many people make when they try to understand this doctrine. Many of us who hold to the doctrine of the perseverance of the faith of the saints feel very defensive about it when there are those who say, 'What about the regenerate who have fallen?' And we tend to say, 'Well, they always come back.' Do they? Usually we say this because we are a little bit embarrassed about the doctrine. And I have actually heard the idea expressed that if David had died *before* he prayed Psalm 51 he would have gone to hell! This, dear friends, is sheer rubbish. As if Jonah had been digested by the fish he would have been eternally lost. Again, this is nonsense. Now it is true that in these two cases both were restored. But don't forget that the Apostle Paul said to the Corinthians that there were those unworthy saints who were 'sickly', and some 'sleep' (I Cor. 11:30). You see, there is such a thing as God just taking a man on to heaven. We should never say that a person is not saved because of his outward behaviour. It is so easy for us to judge one another. But I dare say that *you* have had *your* bad moments and you would not want to be judged then and there! Such a bad moment may have lasted an hour, it may have lasted a day, it could have lasted a week. And I do not hesitate to affirm that some could be in the belly of the fish for years. Yet if you saw them during that time you would say there is not the slightest indication that they are saved. We don't have to apologise for the doctrine. It is either true or it isn't. I am prepared to say that it is true and thank God that it is. Thank God that our salvation is not dependent upon our perseverance; it is dependent upon Christ, our substitute, who faithfully intercedes at the Father's right hand.

The final difference between the apostate and the overtaken saint is the punishment involved. For the apostate, says the writer to the Hebrews, the punishment is fiery judgement, indignation, eternal wrath, hell (Heb. 10:27). But to the one overtaken in a fault it is not an eternal punishment, it is a temporal punishment. This the Bible calls *chastening*. Now, in Hebrews chapter 12 we learn some fundamental lessons with regard to the doctrine of chastening. Three fundamental lessons are to be grasped. First, if you are a Christian, chastening is inevitable. Second, chastening is painful. Third, chastening is for our profit.

Chastening is inevitable if you are a Christian. It is a sign of God's love. It is also a feeling of His wrath. Indeed, this is why we need to understand chastening as simultaneous wrath and mercy. But make no mistake about this: chastening is painful and there are degrees of chastening. Furthermore, chastening is not meted out in proportion to our sin – the fault which overtook us. Chastening is meted out in proportion to the work God has for us to do. The greater the pain, the greater the work that lies ahead. Chastening, then, is painful, but it is God's way of preparing us. It is correction for a future task. Chastening is preparation not punishment. It is not God's way of getting even. God is not holding grudges; chastening is not an eye for an eye and a tooth for a tooth. Chastening is a sign that God is not finished with us.

Now, what about this question of being a castaway? Well, a castaway is a Christian who is no longer useful in God's service. It is 'the Christian on the shelf'. And I am prepared to say that Jonah was not a castaway. There are not that many castaways, really. There are some, but I think we need to regard them as faceless people. You need not be too sure precisely who is a castaway. I think however there are some indications as to what a castaway is like. Paul refers not only to the possibility of himself being a castaway but he also mentions Alexander the Coppersmith. Paul says of this man that he had delivered him unto Satan that he might learn not to blaspheme (I Tim. 1:20). Three things are to be seen about a castaway. First, he is out of circulation. Second, he is exempt from chastening. Third, he is past usefulness. So much for that. The castaway is the regenerate equivalent of the apostate but the former is nonetheless regenerate.

Thus I am prepared today to affirm in the strongest possible way this glorious doctrine of the perseverance of the faith of the saints. And I suspect that the depression that besets many Christians and increases their anxieties is often due to the fact that they find that doctrine too good to be true. And I want you to know today that it *is* true! It is the clear, lucid, unmistakable. undeniable teaching of the New Testament. Now I wish I had time to preach on it entirely today. But I shall give you three reasons why I uphold the doctrine of the perseverance of the faith of the saints. Southern Baptists call it 'eternal security', or 'once saved, always saved'. I believe it. The first reason is the nature of the promise. Listen to the Apostle Paul in Romans 4:13: 'For the promise, that he should be the heir of the world, was not to Abraham, or to his seed, through the law, but through the righteousness of faith'. And so it is, our salvation is not contingent upon our relationship to the law. For God knows if *that* were the case there would be *no* hope of persevering! We fall a thousand times a day. But the promise is not with regard to the law but the righteousness of *faith*. That is the first reason. The second reason is because of the nature of atonement. The New Testament doctrine of atonement is a correlation of the Old Testament doctrine of atonement; and that means we need a substitute. And so Isaiah put it like this: 'The Lord laid *on Him* the iniquity of us all' (Isa. 53:6). Or in Paul's words, Romans 5:19: 'For as by one man's disobedience many were made sinners, so by the obedience of one shall many be made righteous'. So it is, our salvation is dependent upon another's *obedience*, even our Lord Jesus Christ who did keep the law that I have just referred to. It's an amazing thing when you realise this. I suppose the most extraordinary statement that Jesus ever uttered was Matthew 5:17: 'I am not come to destroy the law but to fulfil it'. Looking at that verse by itself, not knowing who said it, we would be obliged to say that it is the most arrogant, presumptuous statement ever uttered by mortal man. But our Lord Jesus, God in the flesh, uttered it. 'I am going to fulfil the law.' Do you know what that means? That means that our Lord Jesus was virtually saying. 'I am going to keep the law perfectly in thought, word, and deed until I die.' And so it was Jesus fulfilled the law and it is by His obedience we are made righteous. If my salvation were contingent upon my obedience there would be no hope for me. But it is not my obedience, it is His; and by the obedience of One to the death on the cross many are made righteous.

There's a third reason I affirm this doctrine and that is because of the nature of Christ's continuing intercession. Up to now perhaps many would be in agreement, even many who believe you can actually fall from your salvation. They would say, 'Well, I agree with your first two points.' But what they want to say to me is, 'What if a person ceases to believe?' There are those who say, 'Yes, it is justification by faith, not the law. True, I agree it is through the obedience of Christ, but what if you quit believing? Then what?' Well, I have an answer for that and thank God for the answer. Paul raised the very question in Romans 8: 'Who shall separate us from the love of Christ? If God be for us, who can be against us? Who shall lay anything to the charge of God's elect?' And then came the crucial question: 'Who is he that condemneth?' The answer: 'It is Christ that died, yea rather, that is risen again, who is *even at the right hand of God who also maketh intercession for us.*' What is it you think that Jesus is praying for? He is praying as He once did for Peter. He put it to Peter, 'I have prayed for thee that thy faith fail not' (Luke 22:32). And you see, it is Jesus at the right hand of God praying that my faith will not fail! It is not my faith in the end that ultimately matters. It is *His* faith. Because my faith is in measure, my faith is weak. Many times I am swallowed up in doubting but there is One at the right hand of God who is interceding for me. He is interceding for me that I will not fail, and this is why Paul could affirm to Timothy:

'If we believe not, yet He abideth faithful: He cannot deny Himself' (II Tim. 2:13). And so it is, the substitutionary nature of the atonement continues in heaven. Jesus is there *praying for me*, and for me to say that I could fall would be a mockery of His own prayers. For if Jesus cannot get His prayers answered there is no hope for any of us. But thank God He is there! He is there praying for us and His prayers are offered with perfect faith, without measure. This is why Paul could say, 'I live by the faith of the Son of God' (Gal. 2:20). This is how we know finally that we cannot be lost. In sum: if you've ever had a glimpse of the Lord Jesus Christ and have seen Him dying on the cross, that glimpse is enough to keep you for ever, because then and there He owned you and He will not give you up. O love that wilt not let me go!

Very well then, Jonah is an example not of an apostate or even a castaway but a saint overtaken in a fault. He was not given over to a reprobate mind, a mind void of judgement. God was preparing Jonah for further work. Is there somebody here today – you are saying to me, 'Surely I'm not a Christian. You don't know how much evil I have done. You don't know the sins I have committed. You don't know how far I have wandered, and, most of all, you don't know how long I have been in this state.' It may be that somebody has walked into Westminster Chapel this morning to learn that all that has happened to you is that you have been swallowed by a great fish – and the fish has just kept you a little longer than three days and three nights! You may have been in the belly of the fish for years. And all these years you have been without the joy of your salvation. The fact is, God can keep a man in the belly of the fish a long, long time. So:

> Judge not the Lord by feeble sense,
> But trust Him for His grace;
> Behind a frowning providence
> He hides a smiling face.

You see, behind the storm that came from God, behind the fish that He prepared was the smiling face of a loving

Father. Chastening is painful. Jonah was an overtaken saint who had some lessons to learn. He had to learn some lessons in the belly of the fish. Now there were many lessons, and we shall look into some of the lessons. But I think we can even now see some initial lessons that Jonah needed to learn.

The first was: God's commands are not to be taken lightly. And so it was, God said to Jonah: 'Go'. Jonah said: 'No'. And God said, 'I have a storm for you! I have a fish for you!' And Jonah learned that God's commands are not to be taken lightly. Moreover, when Jesus said to the church, 'Go ye into all the world and preach the gospel to every creature' (Mark 16:15), He meant it. He meant it. God is *determined* indeed that the great commission shall be *carried out*. There may be some of us along the way who think we have learned better. That is because we think we have had a glimpse of some of the secret things of God and we no longer take seriously the plain revealed word, 'Go'. And so we don't go.

Does it surprise you that God raises up others who *do* go? I can think of nothing sadder than a group of people who think they have a monopoly on the kingdom of God because of some of their cherished theological views, and possibly only few of those are right, but they think they all are, and they use them to justify their lack of zeal. It is like some Antinomians who justify their own wicked behaviour by their theology. And many of us have prided ourselves with having upheld the orthodox faith while the world is going to hell. What is it going to take to wake us up? I am prepared to say we may not be castaways but it is obvious we are in the belly of a fish.

A young minister went to Mr Spurgeon and said: 'Mr Spurgeon, I need some advice.' 'What is it, young man?' 'Well', he replied, 'I'm a good preacher. I just don't see conversions in my ministry.' The wise Spurgeon looked at him and said: 'Do you expect to see a man converted every time you preach?' And the young minister answered: 'Oh, of course not.' Spurgeon said: 'That, young man, is your problem.' When God says: 'Go' and we say: 'No', there is one recourse – God puts *us* in the belly of the fish and gets somebody *else* to 'go'. It is as simple as that. And we can continue to justify ourselves in the meantime but we are going to stay in the belly of the fish until we learn the lesson. That is my prediction. The first lesson Jonah had to learn was that the commands of God are not to be taken lightly. I say: God wants His people to take evangelism seriously.

The second lesson is, God has strange ways of teaching a man. You see, Jonah was not learning this lesson in Nineveh or Tarshish but at the bottom of the sea, in the belly of the fish. And you should also see, if you don't learn from Scripture you will learn the hard way! You can learn from Scripture or you can learn via God's painful chastening. He can do it to you as an individual. What form will the belly of the fish take for you? Could it be financial reverse? Could it be failure? Could it be illness? Could it be emotional problems? Could it be a rocky marriage? Could it be exposing your folly before men? Could it be withholding vindication from you? Perhaps you have taken a stand, you want everybody to see you are right. Nobody sees it. God *could* rectify the matter and make you look good. But he doesn't. He just lets them misunderstand you. It's God's way of chastening – by withholding vindication. God has strange ways of teaching us some lessons. If we don't want to learn from Scripture, He has this thing instituted called chastening.

The third initial lesson Jonah had to learn (and thank God for it) is that our disobedience is not enough to make Him turn His back on us. God does not hold grudges. He got even at the Cross, and the wonder of wonders is that despite our disobedience God loves us.

> Depth of mercy! can there be
>   Mercy still reserved for me?
> Can my God His wrath forbear?
>   Me, the chief of sinners, spare?

Thank God He is not finished with you. He may put you in the belly of a fish, but that disobedience is not enough to cause Him to turn His back upon you.

I have long withstood His grace,
    Long provoked Him to His face,
Would not hearken to His calls,
    Grieved Him by a thousand falls.

Now the Lord had prepared a great fish to swallow up Jonah. Have I diagnosed your problem? You are wondering what is happening and what is going on. You are in the belly of a fish. Mark you, the fish is not recognisable for what it is. Jonah did not have a clue that he was in the belly of the fish while it was happening. He lived to tell the story and he told it, and gave his own description of what it was like. He didn't know he was in the belly of a fish. He said that he cried 'out of the belly of hell'. He said, 'Thou hast cast me into the deep, in the midst of the seas'. He said, 'I am cast out of Thy sight; the waters compass me about even to the soul; the depths close me round about; the weeds were wrapped about my head. I went down to the bottoms of the mountains' (Jonah 2:2–4).

Jonah did not know where he was. That which makes chastening chastening is the confusion. The greatest pain of the chastening is that you don't know what is happening. Everything goes wrong; you are not coherent; you cannot see clearly; there is confusion. 'Weeds' are wrapped about your head. And of course the greatest confusion of all is that you don't know when it will end. Three days and three nights seemed an eternity. In fact, that is the very language he used. 'The earth with her bars was about me *for ever.*' Thus the thing that makes chastening chastening is the confusion and the fear that it will never end.

But it *will* end. Thank God, it will end. The three days and the three nights – that was the time Jonah needed. I do not know how much time we need, but I promise you that we will stay in the belly of the fish until we learn God's lesson.

While the world is going to hell and the Lord is having to teach us some elementary lessons God will go to other places and other people and use them. No, I don't think we are castaways. I think we are overtaken saints. And maybe you as a Christian are confused. You don't know what is happening. 'What is this? What's going on?' You are in the belly of the fish but I promise you it will end. 'His anger endureth but a moment; in His favour is life: weeping may endure for a night, but joy cometh in the morning' (Psa. 30:5). 'He will not always chide: neither will He keep His anger for ever' (Psa. 103:9).

The belly of the fish is not a happy place to live but it's a good place to learn. Sometimes we think we have learned the lesson and we have not. It is like when I helped my son recently with his multiplication tables and he said: 'I already know them.' And the next day I said: 'Give them to me', but he couldn't give all of them. We often think we have learned the lesson we haven't. Are you still in the belly of the fish? Well, you are still learning. God will keep you in the belly of the fish no longer than necessary. He doesn't delight in that. 'In His favour is life: weeping may endure for a night, but joy cometh in the morning.'

9 Jonah's Affliction

Jonah 2:1-2

WE RETURN TO the Prophet Jonah and this time find him praying – in the belly of the fish.

I want us to take a look at the word 'preparation'. It is a key word in the book of Jonah. We are told that the Lord had 'prepared' a great fish to swallow up Jonah. It was the Lord who sent out a great wind into the sea and the Lord who prepared the fish. The same Lord who prepared the fish was preparing Jonah. But the object of the preparation of the wind and the fish was neither the wind nor the fish. It was Jonah. God does not delight in chastening; He delights in *us*. St Augustine put it like this (one of the greatest statements he ever uttered), that God loves everybody as if there were no one else to love. This is another way of saying not only that God deals familiarly with men, He deals singularly with men. And so, if *you* know what it is to be in the belly of a fish, realise that God is not delighting in the fish or the chastening. He has gone to great pains to bring you to the place where you will conform to His will. That is how much God loves you, God loves you as though there were no one else to love.

Very well then, chastening is not punishment for its own sake; it is *preparation*. Another way of saying it is this. Preparation, or chastening, is ensurance that you will do His will. Now the primary method God uses with His people to ensure that they will obey is simply His Word, as in preaching. He uses the Word and the Spirit. That is His primary method. Happy is the man who responds to God's beckoning through this primary means – the Word. But there is a secondary means – chastening. Thus if you will not obey the Word directly and immediately, then God uses another method – chastening. But not for its own sake; chastening is always preparation.

Now may I remind you of the three cardinal rules (see Hebrews 12:6-11) with regard to the doctrine of chastening:

1. Chastening is inevitable if you are a Christian.

2. Chastening is painful.

3. Chastening is preparation, 'for our profit that we might be partakers of God's holiness'.

Chastening is simultaneous wrath and mercy. And so all chastening may be called a fish of some kind. You need to discover *your* fish, the fish God uses in *your* life. You will see that God operates upon the malady with the *future* in mind. Furthermore, what may be my fish may not be yours. What may be your fish may not be mine. God deals with each of us as though there were no one else. God needs no precedent. He need do nothing twice. God deals singularly with men. And so, if you have a particular malady that needs operating on, God will deal with it with your future in mind. The fish, then, is not the end; it is the means.

Today we will examine the first in our series concerning Jonah *in* the fish. Keep in mind that Jonah was out of the fish when he wrote the story; he lived to tell it. He puts himself back in the situation so that we can follow what was going on in his mind. And we are brought immediately into the subject of prayer. We are told that Jonah was motivated at last to pray. The words are: 'Now the Lord had prepared a great fish to swallow up Jonah. And Jonah was in the belly of the fish three days and three nights. *Then* Jonah prayed . . .' You may want to ask the question, 'Why not before? Why didn't he pray before he was swallowed by the fish? Why "then"? "Then he prayed." Why not before?' Well, because he was out of the habit of praying. We were told that Jonah rose up early on 'to flee from the presence of the Lord' (Jonah 1:3). That is the quickest way to get out of the habit of praying. Disobedience often leads you to a prayerless life. Do you know what it is like to be out of the habit of praying? Don't adopt that spiritual: 'Every time I feel the Spirit moving in my heart I'll pray'. The thing especially wrong with that spiritual is that it promotes the idea that you just wait till you *feel* like it. Candidly, if I waited until I *felt* like praying, I would pray very little. Prayer is not a natural attribute in man. I find praying the most difficult enterprise in the Christian life. Praying is not easy. It is hard work. And if you get out of the habit of praying it is very difficult to start again. The chances are it may take a fish to swallow you up and bring you to the place of prayer – since you would not likely have prayed any other way. 'Then Jonah prayed.'

We need to have a regular time to pray. There is no-one spiritual enough to go out into the day without first spending fifteen minutes in prayer. 'Well', you may say, 'I don't have time to spend fifteen minutes every morning.' I say to you, 'Take the time. Set your alarm clock fifteen minutes earlier. None of us is spiritual enough to go out into the day apart from a minimum fifteen minutes of praying. If you haven't been doing it, start it tomorrow morning.' 'Then Jonah prayed.' He had been out of the habit of praying.

Another reason he hadn't been praying is that things were happening too fast to pray. He rose up to flee from the presence of the Lord. There came the wind, there came his awakening, there came the disclosure of his true identity, then came his confession, then came his own counsel – 'Throw me overboard'. All this was going on so fast. He didn't pray until he was at the bottom of the sea.

But there is still another reason Jonah had not prayed until then: he had assurance all along that God was with him, and he wasn't really that worried. Now this should not surprise you but it may. Faith, or assurance, is indestructible. Jonah never really questioned God's love for him – even when he rose up to flee from the presence of the Lord – for he knew God was with him. He wasn't that worried about what he was doing. Such disobedience may forfeit a measure of assurance but not all of it. Even in disobedience the true Christian is assured in measure because, according to I John 3:9, 'his seed remaineth in him.' And I would say further that this kind of Christian is the hardest to deal with. There are many Christians today who will not do what they ought to do simply because they *do* have assurance and they take their assurance as the sign that there is no further obedience necessary. I find sometimes that the most difficult man or woman to deal with in a vestry is the one who has the assurance. You can't tell him anything. He thinks he knows it all. And to get a man like that sufficiently motivated to conform requires a fish to swallow him up, until at long last he comes to his senses and sees what he has done. And so, until now Jonah had not been sufficiently motivated to pray.

Now the Lord had a way of getting Jonah to obey. Jonah didn't obey the word of the Lord directly – as I hope you will do as you hear me preach. The word of the Lord had come to Jonah; this should have been enough: 'Go to Nineveh'. Jonah might have gone, but he rose up to flee from the presence of the Lord. Could I be talking to someone like Jonah today? You know already what God's word teaches. You don't need to come into the vestry to have me remind you of what you ought to do, or what God's word says. You don't need to be told that; you already know. But you go on in your disobedience. That is what Jonah did. But thank God for the wind, and for the fish. 'Then Jonah prayed.' I ask you, what is it going to take to make *you* pray? What is it going to take to bring about the obedience in your own life that God's revealed word clearly demands? What is it going to take?

Well then, when God's word by itself fails, chastening often succeeds. When preaching doesn't produce it, God's 'preparation' often works. When counselling in the vestry fails, the fish may do it! God has a way of making you do His will when you would not have done it any other way. Let me give you a warning: God can be ruthless in producing the obedience he wants out of you. 'Then Jonah prayed.' What will it take to get you to conform to God's will?

But there is something else to be seen – the manner of his praying. We are told that he not only prayed but that he *cried*. 'Then Jonah prayed unto the Lord his God out of the fish's belly, and said, I cried.' There is praying and then there is *praying*. There is recited prayer. We pray the Lord's

Prayer every week together. There are also read prayers. We are not concerned about doing that in this place, but it is better than no praying at all. There are public prayers. There is conversational prayer. There is silent prayer. There is praying and then there is *praying*, and we are told that Jonah *cried*.

When is the last time you wept in prayer? There is an interesting insight to be had from the story of Hezekiah in the book of Isaiah, chapter 38. It is the account of when Isaiah the prophet came to Hezekiah and said, 'Thou art going to die. Set thine house in order; thou shalt die and not live.' Then Hezekiah turned his face to the wall, and prayed to the Lord. But the word came to Isaiah again, and said, 'Go to Hezekiah. Thus saith the Lord, the God of David thy father: I have heard thy prayer, I have *seen thy tears*.' 'I've heard your prayer. I've seen your tears.' We may not have the things we want because we have not wanted them enough to cry, to weep. Are you too proud to cry? I feel sorry for people who cannot cry. They take it as a sign of cowardice. But God has a way of making you cry. 'Then Jonah cried.' The interesting thing about this passage in the book of Isaiah is that *tears* apparently moved the heart of God. Imagine that! Thank God – he sees the tears! And they touch Him. And so, after once saying to Hezekiah, 'You are going to die', Hezekiah prayed and the prophet came back and said, 'Thus saith the Lord, I've heard your prayer. I've seen your tears.'

But now to the subject of Jonah's prayer. We are told that he prayed and we are told how he prayed. What then is the subject of his prayer? 'Then Jonah prayed unto the Lord his God out of the fish's belly, and said, I cried *by reason of mine affliction*.' The subject of his prayer was his affliction. God can send an affliction to make you pray. An affliction is physical or mental distress. It can be bodily pain, it can be sickness, it can be mental anguish, financial worries, emotional problems, concern for your children, fear of the future, marital problems. I could go on and on. Affliction can be spiritual suffering, as when God hides His face.

There is a critical distinction to be noted here – between

affliction and oppression. God afflicts; the devil oppresses. God does not oppress us. An affliction is like Paul's thorn in the flesh, II Corinthians 12. Here God actually sent a thorn in the flesh. But an affliction is the means to the end. Oppression is the end. This is why God never delights merely in punishing us. Chastening is always preparation. God's affliction, you see, motivates us. Oppression binds us, and that is something the devil does. You need to discover your affliction, and see it not as the end but as God's means to bring you face to face with your deeper malady.

Now, there are many illustrations that I might use to illustrate this point, how God uses an affliction. I mentioned a moment ago one way that God afflicts us is through financial worries. I might use another illustration that would be just as suitable but I am deliberately choosing the subject of money because I want to kill two birds with one stone, especially since I feel I must mention it at some stage. Some people cannot handle money – even a little money, a small amount.

God wants to teach us to be good stewards, to make money go further. Did you know that God can make 90% of your income go further than 100% of it? Did you know that? 'Mathematically impossible', you say. But it is true! And if you haven't learned the secret, I feel sorry for you. The subject that underlies this mathematical incredulity is called *tithing*. Hold tight, fasten your seat belts! It is giving God 10% – not 2%, not 5%, not 9%, but 10% of your income.

I must tell you how I was introduced to the subject of tithing. I was taught it by my father. The best place to learn is at home. Are you teaching your children? Are you one of those that say, 'Well, I send them to school, I send them to church; I hope they can help them.' *You* are supposed to be doing it. I thank God my father taught me to tithe, and, like most lessons, I didn't enjoy his teaching me. The first job I ever had in order to earn money was when I was ten years old. I sold a newspaper called 'Grit'. You Britishers wouldn't know about it and not many Americans do. It is a small weekly paper that comes from Williamsport, Pennsylvania. My father said that he sold 'Grit' when he was a boy, and what was good enough for him was good enough for me. 'Grit' sold for 10 cents a copy. I made 3 cents every time I sold one, and I went door-to-door. The first week I made 50 cents, and I was so excited. We came to the dining room table and counted up the money that I had to send in to Pennsylvania and I had 50 cents left. I was so glad to see it. But my father put his finger on a nickel – 5 cents – and slid it away. He said, 'This is the Lord's.' I stretched out my finger and brought it back! 'This is mine. I earned it.' 'Son, this is the Lord's.'

When I was twelve I had a bigger job; I sold the *Cincinnati Enquirer*, a great newspaper. And my first week I was in big money. I made $6, and I never will forget it – sitting around the dining table. I found out how much money I had to send in to the office, and there were $6 left for me. My father picked out 60 cents. 'This is the Lord's.' 'But Dad, let's do that *next* week – or wait till I get older. Surely the Lord doesn't care anything about my 60 cents?'

There are two reasons people do not tithe. One is, God has not broken their hearts and they remain stingy and stubborn. The second reason, they simply have not been taught. And maybe you didn't get the teaching at home and maybe you have not been taught it from the pulpit, I don't know.

There are four elementary lessons regarding tithing. The first is this: *the tithe is the Lord's* (Lev. 27:30). There may be some Bible student here who says, 'Ah, that is from the book of Leviticus; we are not under the law.' You are right. It is from Leviticus. But have you forgotten that we are under the covenant of grace, which did not begin with the law but goes back to Abraham? That is one great lesson we learn from the book of Galatians, that the law came 400 years later (Gal. 3:19). The promise that we are under as Christians is not a covenant of works. The promise goes back to Abraham – and do you not remember that Abraham paid his tithe? So don't give me that rubbish that this is legalism. Tithing goes back to the *first* promise under grace! (See Gen. 14:20 and Heb. 7:2.) The Levitical law just spelt it out more clearly. The law was 'added' because of the transgressions of the people (Gal. 3:19). So we are told that the tithe *is* the Lord's. That means that *it is already His*. Now, in case you wonder mathematically what it means – if you earn £100, then £10, the Lord says, is already His. If you earn £10, £1 is already His. Young people, if you earn 80p, 8p is already God's. Rule number one.

Rule number two: God puts you on your honour to pay the tithe. Now I have found out that the Income Tax situation in England is somewhat like what it is in the States, but that you pay more Income Tax over here. In America, Uncle Sam, as we say, does not put you on your honour to pay Income Tax; he deducts it from your wages – as has been happening to me here. I said to the treasurer, 'Wait till the end of the year, and we will see whether I still owe anything to Her Majesty's government.' But he said, 'I am compelled now to deduct this'. They are not trusting me! But God trusts us; He puts us on our honour, and this is why Malachi the prophet raised the question: 'Will a man rob God? Yes, by tithes and offerings' (Mal. 3:8). How much have *you* robbed God? How much across the years? Have you? Yet God puts you on your honour. The tithe is not deducted from your wages, from your pay cheque, from your tips and so forth. God wants you to give it freely, voluntarily. You are on your honour. That is rule number two.

Rule number three: You pay your tithe to the store house (Mal. 3:10). Now I don't want to get into an endless debate here as to what the store house is. If I had time I could convincingly prove that the store house is the place where you get your soul fed. It is the *church*. 10% goes to the church, 'that there may be *meat in mine house*'. Well, there is always somebody who says, 'I give part to the church and part to charity'. Then you are not living according to Scripture. What you want to give to charity – or to any other cause – is fine and good – and I will put Missions in the category. But that should be *above* your tithe. 10% goes to the 'store house'. Now somebody is going to say, 'Well, you can say that because you are an American.' Well, you can decide why I am saying it. You may also say, 'You are a Southern Baptist and we all know about them.' You should know that Southern Baptists have 3,000 missionaries scattered around the world; they are the largest Protestant denomination in the world today. One other thing about Southern Baptists that you should know is that they are tithers. And do you want to know one reason why God blesses Southern Baptists? God is just keeping His word. It is there for you to read in I Samuel 2:30: 'Those that honour me I will honour.'

Rule number four: You cannot outgive the Lord. Do you know something? The Bible never tries to prove God. I have little patience with theologians who spend their time proving the existence of God. It's a sheer waste of time. The Bible doesn't do it – why should we? The same is also true concerning proving the Bible. I love that statement by the great Charles Haddon Spurgeon, who put it like this: 'Defend the Bible? I would as soon defend a lion'. There are those who want to 'defend' the Bible. Therefore when it comes to 'proving God', it is not our task to do so for the Bible doesn't. However, one time, one time only, the Bible mentions 'proving God'. Do you know where it is? It is in the Book of Malachi 3:8–10 under this subject of tithing! 'Will a man rob God? Ye have robbed me. Where have we robbed thee? In tithes and offerings . . . Bring ye all the tithes into the store house that there may be meat in my house, *and prove me herewith,* says the Lord of hosts, if I will not open you the windows of heaven, and pour you out a blessing, that there shall not be room enough to receive it.' Rule number four: you cannot outgive the Lord. 'Prove me and see if I will not outpour a blessing so great you cannot contain it.'

It has been my joy across the years as a pastor to introduce many Christians to tithing. I have not made an enemy yet. I have had people thank me later: 'You have done me a favour.' They are way ahead! They have found out that the 90% goes further than the 100% they had to themselves.

I never will forget a saintly man who was a member of my church in Fort Lauderdale. He told me how he began tithing. You can question the method but here was his story. He was a member of a church in Detroit, Michigan, and he said the pastor made a deal with all the members of the church that they would all tithe *for three months* – and then forget about it. My friend said, 'We went along with it'. He said, 'We started tithing, and after three months we kept it up. We have been doing it ever since. That was twenty years ago.' He said, 'I would be afraid *not* to tithe.' One of my deacons in my church in Florida used to say, 'If you don't give your tithe to God He will have another way of taking it from you.' 'Now it might not go to the store house but He will get it from *you*,' he would say.

I will tell you candidly, I can't 'afford' to tithe. The *only* way to tithe is to take it off the top and make it the number one priority. You say that you can't afford it and I understand for I can't. Let me give you a personal illustration – I am not sure I have ever told this publicly before. Shortly after Louise and I were married we lived in Springfield, Illinois – Lincoln's home. We were deep in debt. I owed everybody, it seemed, and my income was so unstable. But I never will forget one hot August afternoon when I was seeking the Lord's will, and I was asking God to give me a Scripture. And He did. But I didn't like it. It was Malachi 3:8: 'Will a man rob God?' I hadn't been paying my tithe for a year. I couldn't afford it. One day, thank God, I started paying my tithe. I must tell you, things began to work out for us. Sooner than I dreamed, we were out of debt. Rule number four is: You can't outgive the Lord.

Now, I have been saying that Jonah was analogous to the modern church and I have a theory – you can think about it – that the sad condition of the church today in this country is traceable in part to the awful fact that most British Evangelicals are not tithers. I will not speak of the Church of England – I don't know much about it. I gather that they get their money a little differently. But the free churches – which, by the way, lost 85,000 members last year in this country – are dependent upon the freewill offerings of the people. They do not have endowments from the church or from the government. And so, free churches today are dependent upon tithes. You should know that I have visited around this country a bit in the past three and a half years, and I have talked to many ministers. This country is full of discouraged ministers. They are depressed, they are underpaid, and some are bitter. They can't preach on tithing because they are afraid their members will think they are just looking after their own interests. So they never mention it. And people don't tithe. Yet it is God's command and I will preach it – whatever you want to think about my doing so. But it is a pity, it is a pity, that there are ministers in this country underpaid and depressed and discouraged. And some don't preach well because they are not motivated. And if it is true that the church is the salt of the earth, then look at the state of the church in this country! I say, it is traceable in part to the fact that British Evangelicals are not tithing. Many churches today are almost bankrupt. It is a sad story.

Back to Jonah: 'I cried by reason of mine affliction.' What is the church's affliction? No blessing, low attendance, poor financially. Tithing is part of the answer – a real part – and I am going to predict that we will remain in the belly of the fish as a church as long as we are disobedient to God's word. What is your affliction? What is our affliction as a church here? Have I touched a sensitive nerve? I am not here to scold you. As your Minister I am here to help. I urge you to consider this. I do not say, 'Try it because it works'. I say, 'Do it because it is right.'

There are three levels of motivation here, when it comes to this matter of tithing. One is, you give because you *have* to. Well, you *don't* have to, so most don't. And some who do tithe say, 'Well, I guess I must'. That is the lowest level. The second level is, doing it because you know God is going to bless you. That is a rather selfish motive. But there is a third level, the highest of all; you do it for the glory of God. You do it *because it is right*. You don't even think about whether you are going to get anything in return; you must do it because it is God's will. It is like the three Hebrew children in the burning fiery furnace – one of my favourite stories in the Old Testament, one that my father used to tell me as a boy. It is in the third chapter of Daniel where those three Hebrews, Shadrach, Meshach and Abednego, were told, 'Now if ye be ready that at what time ye hear the sound of the cornet, the flute, the harp, the sackbut, psaltery and dulcimer and all kinds of musick, ye fall down and worship the golden image which I have made; well: but if ye worship not, ye shall be cast the same hour into the midst of a burning fiery furnace; and who is that God that shall deliver you out of my hands? Shadrach, Meshach and Abednego answered, "We are not careful to answer you in this matter. If it be so, our God whom we serve is able to deliver us from the burning fiery furnace, and he will deliver us out of thine hand, O King. *But if not*, be it known unto thee, O King that we will not serve thy gods, nor worship the golden image which thou hast set up".' (Dan. 3:15–18). This is the right motive, acting upon a principle because it is right. The three Hebrews knew God was able to deliver them, but even if He didn't they were not going to bow down! 'But if not, we won't bow.' That is operating upon a principle because it is right. Refusing to bow, to disobey.

'I cried by reason of mine affliction.' Let's start praying. Let's start crying. Let's look at our affliction and let's look to God who has promised that He will neither leave us nor forsake us.

10 Jonah's Answered Prayer

Jonah 2:1–7

JONAH'S PRAYER IN the belly of the fish reads like a Psalm of David, or perhaps parts of the book of Lamentations. If you have read the book of Jonah you could not have helped noticing this. Sometimes God seems to compel us to live entirely in the Psalms. Do you know what it is like – not to want to read anything else in Scripture but the Psalms? It is not a bad place to be. We learn how to praise God properly by reading the Psalms. We find as well the experience of feeling left out. For many of us know what it is to feel rejected by friends and to have the fear of enemies plotting against us, and, worst of all, the feeling that God does not love us any more. And so we can read the Psalms and find that there have been those that have felt much the same way.

But do not forget that such a feeling is not permanent or final in the Psalmist. Now when I say that the book of Jonah chapter 2 reads much like a Psalm of David, I mean that you can go through the Psalms of David and virtually see Jonah's prayer in the belly of the fish many times. Look at the 6th Psalm, the 30th, the 31st, the 69th, the 116th –I could go on. But the point not to be forgotten is that the Psalms always show that trials are temporary. For example, in the 6th Psalm the Psalmist starts out by saying, 'O Lord, rebuke me not in thine anger, neither chasten me in thy hot displeasure. Have mercy upon me, for I am weak. Heal me, for my bones are vexed.' But before he finishes he says, 'The Lord hath heard the voice of my weeping. The Lord hath heard my supplication; the Lord will receive my prayer.' Or take the 30th Psalm, verse 5: 'His anger endureth but a moment; in his favour is life: weeping may endure for a

night, but joy cometh in the morning.' Consider the 31st
Psalm. Whereas verse 9 reads, 'Have mercy upon me, O
Lord, for I am in trouble: mine eye is consumed with grief',
do not forget that the Psalm ends by saying, 'The Lord pre-
serves the faithful, and plentifully rewards the proud doer.
Be of good courage, and he shall strengthen your heart, all
ye that hope in the Lord.' Look at the 69th Psalm. It begins: 'Save me, O God; for the waters are come in unto
my soul. I sink in deep mire, where there is no standing: I
am come into deep waters where the floods overflow me.'
It sounds so much like Jonah. But before the Psalm ends
he says in verse 35: 'God will save Zion, and will build
the cities of Judah: that they may dwell there, and have
it in possession. The seed also of his servants shall inherit
it: and they that love his name shall dwell therein.'

Well, I could go on and on to show that the Psalmist
knows what it is to feel rejection, to feel despair. But the
Psalmist consistently ends up on a note of victory. And so
we come now to that place in the book of Jonah that shows
his prayer being answered. 'I cried by reason of mine affliction unto the Lord, *and he heard me*.' Thank God for
answered prayer. Thank God, *we do not have to stay* in the
belly of the fish. Thank God: 'Weeping may endure for a
night, but joy cometh in the morning.' And so today I want
us to see Jonah's answered prayer. Now, the fact is, he tells
us five times in this psalm (Jonah 2:2–9) that God answered
his prayer. He says it five different times in different ways.
The first, verse 2: 'I cried by reason of mine affliction
unto the Lord, *and he heard me*.' Then he says it again:
'Out of the belly of hell I cried, *and thou heardest my voice*.'
Or, look at verse 4: 'I said, I am cast out of thy sight; *yet I
will look again* toward thy holy temple.' And look at verse
6: 'I went down to the bottoms of the mountains; the earth
with her bars was about me for ever: *yet hast thou brought
up my life* from corruption, O Lord my God.' And then for
the fifth time he tells about it in verse 7: 'My soul fainted
within me and I remembered the Lord: and *my prayer came
in unto thee*, into thine holy temple.' So it is, Jonah's prayer
was answered.

Now we have already seen Jonah's motivation to pray.

He prayed because he had nothing else to do. He prayed because he was constrained to do it. 'Then Jonah prayed', being in the belly of the fish three days and three nights. We saw also the manner of his praying: he '*cried* unto the Lord'. We saw the subject of his prayer – his affliction. Now, since Jonah's prayer was answered I should think we would all do well to examine this experience of Jonah. We surely want to learn how to have a prayer answered, don't we? What can be more rewarding than to know how to pray and to have that prayer answered? I would like to ask you: Do you know what it is to see answered prayer? Do you know what it is like to have a prayer answered? Have you ever experienced answered prayer? Well now, if you are a Christian, you have. I remind you that in being converted you asked the Lord to save you. And He did. That is one prayer God answered: He saved you. How many times since have you experienced answered prayer? I want us now to examine more carefully Jonah's prayer – and the circumstances surrounding it. I suggest it gives us all a hint how to know God will answer our prayer.

The first thing to see is that Jonah faced his problem directly. Last time we dealt with the subject of his prayer – his affliction. We will examine that affliction now in more detail. Jonah looked directly at his problem. He did not pray *around* it. He knew his affliction and he knew that God had sent it. He also knew *why* God had sent it. Therefore he did not pray around it. Many of us waste so much time praying around our problem. It is so foolish when we do this because God sees right through to what we are. Now we may succeed in playing games with other people. All of us wear masks with others; we do not want the public to know what we are really like; we don't even want our best friends really to know what we are like. It is like the title of a little book I read some years ago by a Jesuit priest: 'Why am I afraid to tell you who I am?' He concluded that I am afraid to tell you who I am because you wouldn't like me if you really knew who I am. That idea may have been put forward by a Jesuit priest but I submit that he describes all of us. We don't want others really to know us because we are afraid we won't be liked! So we wear a mask. We project upon others the image we want them to see so that we will be liked.

Now it is one thing to do that with people, but how foolish indeed to do it with God. And so many of us pray around our problem and never seize directly upon it. But David learned to pray in Psalm 51: 'Thou desirest truth in the inward parts' (Psa. 51:6). God wants us to come clean before Him. You do not need to play games with God. You may do it with people, and you may have succeeded. But do not try it with God. The writer to the Hebrews put it like this: 'All things are naked and open unto the eyes of him with whom we have to do' (Heb. 4:13). And so, you will be wise if you will come clean in the presence of God. Do not pray around your problem. The modern church has been doing this for years, including Evangelicals. We like to pretend that things are a certain way. We have our conferences, and we pretend and convince ourselves that things are not really too bad. But we go on and on in our folly although we are not really being used of God. It is so foolish.

I wonder sometimes if we really *want* God to answer our prayers. It is much like doing Christian counselling. I have been preaching and counselling people in vestries now for twenty years. I have learned one thing: most people don't want their problems *solved*; they want them *understood*. And I wonder – do *you* really want *your* prayer answered? So many of us are spiritual neurotics who thrive on affliction. We like being just as we are, thank you! We enjoy our neurosis. I never will forget going to a dentist who was to fill a hole in my tooth where the filling had fallen out, and during the time that I waited for the appointment I got so used to that hole in my tooth – I would stick my tongue in it – and I got to like it – that when I went to the dentist I was disappointed to have him fill it up! I liked the hole. We become acquainted with the way we are and don't want to change. I have often been amazed at a verse in the fifth chapter of John. When Jesus went to the man who was by the pool of Bethesda waiting for the troubling of the waters by the angel so that he could be healed, do you know the first thing Jesus said to him? 'Do you *want* to be healed?' Think of that. 'Do you want to be healed?' (John 5:6)

Why do you suppose Jesus put it that way? We can become so used to our condition that we like it that way, and we thrive on a particular neurosis. Many people do not want to get well, or get cured of their neurosis lest they forgo sympathy. So they are comfortable in their malady. I recall reading how the leaning tower of Pisa is in danger; they are afraid that it is leaning so far that it will fall over. And the city fathers are worried. But they laid the instructions down to the architect who was going to try to keep it from leaning any more: 'Do not *correct* the tilt – keep it just like it is.' We don't want our problem to get worse. 'But don't make it perpendicular.' And we are that way, and I ask you: Do you *want* God to answer your prayer? For as long as we pray *around* our problem we delay the answer to prayer. But Jonah did not do that. He faced the problem directly. He knew God had sent this affliction.

Now I want to elaborate upon the distinction that I suggested earlier – between affliction and oppression. Now, an affliction may be defined simply as mental or physical distress. But oppression is different; it is being overwhelmed by a superior power that is continual, cruel, and binding. Such is the critical difference between the two. Yet there are similarities between being afflicted and being oppressed: both are usually accompanied with anxiety and depression, if not desperation. Both affliction and oppression have their origin outside the individual, and both affliction and oppression can happen to a Christian. But there are some differences. The first is in the origin. God may send affliction, as He sent Paul's thorn in the flesh. But God does not oppress us. Oppression is of the Devil. Happy will be the day when you find out that this is really true. God does not oppress us – oppression is always of the devil. Another distinction is this: affliction is God's means of preparing us. As Paul put it, God sent the thorn in the flesh 'lest I be exalted above measure' (II Cor. 12:7). Affliction is preparation; oppression is sheer bondage and cruelty. Oppression is torment, whereas affliction has purpose. But oppression does not. Now then, God sends affliction to motivate us. Satan oppresses in order to bind us and immobilise us. There is that interesting verse II Timothy 2:26: the Apostle

118

Paul warned Timothy of this very problem, of the danger, that some are 'held captive by the devil at his own will'. It is very possible that Christians can be caught up in the snare of the devil. Do you know what it is to be caught in the snare of Satan? It can happen.

Now let me show you how these work. Affliction is a sign of God's mercy and is not meted out in proportion to our particular sin. 'He hath not dealt with us after our sins nor rewarded us according to our iniquities' (Psa. 103:10). Affliction is a sign of God's mercy and is not meted out in proportion to our sin; but only with the future in mind. But Satan oppresses us by taking full advantage of what I should like to call a four-fold weakness. Now these four weaknesses – some of us have only one of them, some of us have all four – make us vulnerable to the devil. Satan by oppression will take advantage of a physical weakness, a psychological weakness, a spiritual weakness and a theological weakness. Moreover, affliction may be laced with oppression. It is often not merely one or the other; it is usually both. You see, when God sends affliction, do not be surprised if the devil is right behind, waiting to seize on some weakness that we have – whether it is physical, emotional, spiritual or theological. Satan will do anything he can to immobilise us, to bind us, to bring us to despair without any purpose. This is because oppression is never the means; it is always the end. And it happens by Satan's taking advantage of one, if not all, of these four weaknesses.

But the question is, how is affliction and oppression overcome? Well, the answer is simply this: when God answers prayer. Answered prayer. Thank God for answered prayer.

But you should also understand how oppression can be avoided. It can be avoided by taking seriously these four potentials of weakness – physical, psychological, spiritual and theological. For example, if Satan is going to take advantage of a physical weakness, common sense would dictate that you ought to take your own health seriously. God does not want us to be unhealthy. I refer now to physical health. We ought to take care of our bodies; we ought to see that we get to a doctor if we are ill. Moreover, we ought to see that we eat the proper food and get the proper sleep. If you are not feeling well physically you are so vulnerable to Satan's oppression. It is very simple. When I feel good physically, often I feel good spiritually! And so if you are behind on sleep, for example, you are so vulnerable to Satan's oppression. Do not live physically in such a way that you become vulnerable to his way of oppressing you.

Or, let us take a psychological or emotional weakness. Now we all have them. What may be your neurosis may not be mine; what may be mine may not be yours. We are all neurotics to some degree. Nobody is perfect emotionally. None of us had perfect parents. None of us had childhood experiences that were without traumas. And it is foolish to think that conversion or regeneration will instantaneously wipe away the memories of childhood. In much the same way, a person who had diabetes before his conversion will have it after – or if a person has gall-bladder problems before his conversion he will have them after he is converted – or if he has high blood pressure before he is saved he will have it after. Surely you do not think that regeneration automatically or instantaneously heals the body? I do not know why it is that some think that regeneration simultaneously cures all emotional problems. Regeneration does not wipe away the memories of childhood. Such memories are like an iceberg submerged in the depth of the sea. We all have emotional problems; we ought to know ourselves. Some of us are given to depression, some to anxiety. Some of us are very sensitive; we get our feelings hurt easily. Others of us tend to project: if we see two or three people talking, we say, 'I wonder if they could be talking about me?' We project. These are emotional weaknesses, and Satan is ruthless in taking advantage of any weakness we have. And so, you will do well to know yourself better. And if you come into the vestry to talk to me about it, the chances are I will ask you first if you have read Dr Lloyd-Jones' book *Spiritual Depression*. If there were only one book that he wrote that I had to recommend it would be that. That book has helped me immensely many times. So we need to know ourselves.

But now let us go to the third weakness – the spiritual

weakness. Satan will take advantage of your lack of praying and your lack of Bible reading. I love that quotation:

> The Devil trembles when he sees
> The weakest saint upon his knees.

And so, if you have been negligent in your prayer life or in your Bible reading or in reading good books, you are vulnerable to the oppression of the devil. He will take advantage of that spiritual weakness. I recommend at least fifteen minutes a day in private prayer alone. Try it.

What is the fourth? Theological weakness. I am appalled at how many people I meet on both sides of the Atlantic who are biblically and theologically illiterate. None of us are as theologically sound as we ought to be. You may think yourself orthodox and yet be theologically illiterate at the same time. We need to discover afresh the great doctrine of justification by faith. This is the importance of studying the book of Galatians. None of us here is so theologically sound that he can do without studying this book. So if we do not understand the doctrine of justification by faith, I cannot exaggerate how vulnerable we will be to the oppression of the devil. For there is nothing that will defeat the devil like a firm grasp of justification by faith!

Well then, Jonah was vulnerable to both affliction and oppression. Physically, he had no food for three days and three nights. I suspect he did little sleeping in the belly of the fish at the bottom of the Mediterranean. And not only that, Jonah was physically weak from the ordeal. He tells us: 'Thou has cast me into the deep, in the midst of the seas; and the floods compassed me about: all thy billows and thy waves passed over me ... The waters compassed me about, even to the soul: the depths closed me round about, the weeds were wrapped about my head.' So obviously Jonah was tired, physically exhausted from this ordeal. He was psychologically exhausted as well. We are told in verse 7: 'When my soul fainted within me I remembered the Lord.' The soul and the mind are often used interchangeably in the Old Testament. This is why the Psalmist again and again would talk about 'fainting' – his soul 'fainting', the spirit being 'overwhelmed'. 'I had fainted unless I had believed to see the goodness of the Lord in the land of the living' (Psa. 27:13). Thus when you are feeling low emotionally you may know why Jonah said: 'Out of the belly of hell I cried'. There is nothing more painful than emotional difficulty. There is nothing more desperate than to experience the pain of a psychological malady. And the Devil will take full advantage of it.

As for Jonah's spiritual weakness, we know all about that, don't we? Long before, God had told him to do one thing – 'Go to Nineveh' – and he did another. And that disobedience shows us Jonah's spiritual weakness. But what about his theological weakness? Could it be said that Jonah had a theological weakness? Well, he tells us about this, too. This should not surprise us. In verse 4 Jonah said: 'I am cast out of thy sight'. Now this was a foolish comment. This was an ill-advised statement. It was nonsense, utterly foolish for Jonah to have spoken like that. In fact, David put it like this in Psalm 31: 'I said in my haste, I am cut off before thine eyes' (Psa. 31:22). What is the answer to this? Well, it is only the man who has a firm grasp of the doctrine of justification by faith who can say: 'Neither death, nor life, nor angels, nor principalities, nor powers, nor things present, nor things to come, nor height, nor depth, nor any other creature shall be able to separate us from the love of God which is in Christ Jesus our Lord' (Rom. 8:39). Thus when we know that God accepts us for Jesus' sake, we know the folly of saying, 'I am cast out'. We know the folly of saying, 'I am cut off'. Therefore David said, *In my haste I said that*'. And Jonah, alive to tell the story, admits to having said: 'I am cut off – I am cast out'. And you need to know, in a time when you are vulnerable to the oppression of the devil, that 'you are not your own; you are bought with a price' (I Cor. 6:19–20). And so the words of John Newton: 'I may my fierce accuser face and tell him Thou hast died'. We are told in the book of Revelation that there was war in heaven, and they overcame the Devil by the blood of the Lamb and by the word of their testimony (Rev. 12:11). As long as you have this going for you, Satan cannot defeat you.

When all around my soul gives way,
He then is all my hope and stay.
On Christ the solid rock I stand;
All other ground is sinking sand.

And many times the darts of the devil may be turned back by having a firm theological grasp of justification by faith. Satan will take advantage of such a weakness and we find Jonah vulnerable to the same thing.

But now we are to see that Jonah's prayer was heard. 'I cried by reason of mine affliction unto the Lord, and he heard me.' Thank God for that. How do you know he was heard? Well, you may say first of all, he lived to tell the story; he got out. But there is more to it than that. Jonah knew that he was heard. He was given assurance at the moment. 'I cried and he heard me.' There is such a thing as knowing God hears you at the moment you are praying. And I suspect now we will be venturing on territory largely untrodden by Christians today. Do you know what it is to pray consciously in God's will? Now we read in 1 John 5:14–15: 'This is the confidence that we have in him, that if we ask anything according to his will, he heareth us.' And someone says, 'Fair enough, if I could just know what God's will is.' John goes on to say, 'If we know that he hears us, whatsoever we ask, we know that we have the petitions that we desired of him.' This is one of the most unexplored areas among Christians – this question of praying consciously according to the will of God. And Jonah was praying according to the will of God. 'I cried' – 'He heard me'.

We like to get the hearing of people. If we can just get somebody else to listen to us! A great deal of my counselling is listening. People just want to be able to say it to me – they want my ear. Many times people will go to high officials in government to lay before them their complaints; they just want to be heard. But what is greater than this, to know that *God* hears us? Jonah knew it – and I am saying today, there is such a thing as praying consciously according to the will of God. Most of us do not know much about this. You know what we do, don't you? We hide behind Jesus' prayer in Gethsemane. What would we do if we did not have that?

We use it to cover for our unbelief. 'Let this cup pass from me; nevertheless not my will but thine be done.' We get up from our knees and go on our way. By the way, do you know why Jesus said that? He said that because He *knew* what God's will *was*! He already had the apprehension of what He had to do. He was acquiescing in it. But we use that to cover for our unbelief and say, 'Thy will be done'. Now I grant, Christian people, we should want God's will pre-eminently, and that is what is behind this whole discussion – how to know we are praying in the will of God.

Assurance in prayer comes by a holy and reverent familiarity with God and His revealed will. I have said that God deals familiarly with men. And now I want to say that we should deal familiarly with God. Does this surprise you? Have you forgotten that the very nature of the Spirit of adoption in our hearts is to cry 'Abba, Father' (Gal. 4:6)? This familiarity – not the undue familiarity with holy things, the sort of thing that got Jonah into trouble originally – is knowing God in the most intimate and familiar way. Did you know that the great prayers in the Bible are not ended with 'Thy will be done'? Read them. The great prayers in the Bible are in the context of having become so familiar with the will of God that the one praying *commands* God to do it – demanding that He keep His promise! I often read with amazement that prayer in the book of Acts chapter 4. When they came to the end they said, 'Now, Lord, behold their threatenings: grant to thy servants boldness that they may speak Thy word.' And the Word says: 'When they had prayed, the place was shaken where they were assembled together' (Acts 4:29-33). They were given great power, and received great witness of the resurrection of the Lord Jesus. Most of us are so remote from this kind of thinking that we have not a clue what it is to pray consciously in the will of God, and ask by claiming the promise.

Most of us have heard the story of George Müller of Bristol – the man of faith as he is called. Many years ago somebody gave me a copy of his autobiography, and it was so powerful in my life at that time. There are many stories to be told about that man. One time he was on his way to America and on the ship he discovered that the captain had ordered the ship to come to a standstill because of a fog that had settled over the Atlantic. George Müller went to the Captain and said, 'I must be in New York on Friday evening to speak.' 'Well,' the Captain of the ship said, 'if we don't leave within an hour you are not going to make it.' Müller said, 'I have got to be there and the Lord has told me I will be there.' The Captain replied, 'I am sorry, but we are not going to make it. This fog will probably last for many hours, and perhaps a day or two.' George Müller said, 'I believe in the God who answers prayer, do you?' The Captain said, 'Well, I don't know.' 'Well', Müller asked, 'do you mind if I pray?' The Captain said, 'Go ahead.' So Müller prayed. The Captain later reported that he was disappointed in Müller's prayer. 'There was not much to it,' he said. When Müller had finished, he looked at the Captain and said: 'You don't believe God is going to do it, and I believe He already has.' They looked out and everything was clear.

I say, most of us haven't a clue what this is, praying consciously according to the will of God. It comes by having a holy familiarity with God and His revealed Word, so that you can claim the promise, claim the promise boldly. *Repeat to Him what He has promised*. Are you afraid to do that? 'I cried by reason of mine affliction, *and he heard me.*' Jonah's prayer was answered.

But I close by asking this, did Jonah have to help God out? Many times we say, 'Well, God has promised that He will help us'. So we then make sure it happens. We help God out. God has promised and so I work things out, and make it come to pass. We know what it is to manipulate things so that our prayer will be answered. Such folly. Consider Romans 8:28. Many people say that since it has got to work together for good, they go around trying to make it work together for good. But the more we do that the worse it will get! Romans 8:28 is a promise that *God* will make things work together for good. We must stand back and watch God do it.

So it is when it comes to answered prayer. It is *God* who answers. Jonah was helpless – in the belly of the fish. Do you think that he was saying, 'Well now, God has heard me, so I must make this sea monster eject me on dry

125

land'? It was hardly that. Jonah's prayer was answered because the answer was outside himself. God did not speak to *Jonah* and say, 'Make the fish eject you'. We are told in verse 10: 'The Lord spake unto the fish and it vomited out Jonah.' Answered prayer is not something psychological or something we imagine. Neither is it a case of our manipulating things. God does it. He does it by a transcendent power, so that all human capabilities and expectations are overruled. Do you know what this is like?

I ask you, do you *want* your prayer to be answered? Or are you just enjoying being in the belly of the fish? Three days and three nights in Jonah's case. How long is it going to be in your case? Do you want to stay there? Do you want to be healed? Are you happy nurturing your own neurosis, your own weakness? Do you want to be out of the fish? Very well then. God sent the wind, God sent the fish, and God spoke to the fish. God was at the bottom of everything. The book of Jonah shows how God came miraculously – all the way through. He will deal with you like that. God deals singularly with men. He loves you as though there were nobody else to love and deals with you in a particular way because He has got something you can do that nobody else can do.

But you will say, 'I do want God to answer my prayer. When will He come?' I answer: there has no trial taken you but such as is common to man. God knows how much you can bear. But perhaps you have not become that desperate. There is the story of a farmer out in the Mid-West in the United States, who was watching all of his crops go to nothing because of a drought, a near famine. There was no rain for weeks. So what was he doing in the mean time? He had a well; so he would go to the well several times a day, drop down the bucket, bring the bucket up full of water, and go out into the corn field to pour water on the crops to keep them moist. He did this hour after hour every day for weeks, until one day he looked into the well and said to his wife: 'There is now just enough water for us to live on. If God does not send rain in the next day or two, we can just kiss everything good-bye.' For all those weeks he had done nothing but take buckets of water and pour them on the crops and the corn to keep the ground moist. But now all he could do was to sit on his back porch in his rocking chair and just watch. He looked toward the West and noticed a big, black nimbus cloud – the first he had seen in days and weeks. It got bigger and bigger and it came closer; and the wind began to blow. He called to his wife: 'Just look at that! Do you suppose it is going to happen?' And a drop of rain hit the dust, then another drop; and then another, and another. Within a minute or two it began to pour and the rain fell all over his field. The farmer took his rocking chair out in the middle of the field, set it down, sat himself in the rocking chair and looked up into the skies while the water beat in his face. His wife looked out and said, 'Have you gone mad? What are you doing?' He said: 'I am just enjoying seeing God do so easily what was impossible for me to do.'

As a young preacher I went to an older evangelist, as I was wanting some advice. That day Evangelist C. B. Fugett shared something with me that I pass on to you – I have never forgotten it. He had me sit down while he pulled up a chair. He looked me in the eyes, took hold of my lapel and said: 'Remember – God is never too late; He's never too early; He's always *just on time.*'

Three days, three nights – that's all Jonah could take. He was desperate.

'I cried because of mine affliction, and He heard me.' The same God who had chastened him answered him. And He will answer you.

Do you want to stay in the belly of the fish?

11 Some Lessons Learned Well

Jonah 2 : 1–9

MOST OF US have to learn lessons the hard way. The greatest university in the world is neither Oxford nor Cambridge, neither Harvard nor Yale. The greatest university in the world is not even the 'university of hard knocks' because most people go through a world of suffering and never learn to succeed, much less do they discover the secret of abundant living. The greatest university in the world is the university of the Holy Ghost. For all who enter here, pass. Not all get first-class honours, but all pass. This is why Paul could write to the Philippians, who included some weak Christians as well as strong Christians : 'He that hath begun a good work in you *will perform it* until the day of Jesus Christ' (Phil. 2 : 6). In the university of the Holy Spirit we have two options : one way is to learn directly from the Word, the other is to learn the hard way – in the belly of a fish by chastening. The latter is simultaneous wrath and mercy; it is God's way of preparing us for a future task.

Most of us don't learn directly from the Word apart from having had first to live in the belly of a fish. Most of us are like Jonah. We have seen by now that Jonah is an example of one who had to learn the hard way. Jonah tells us moreover that he *did* learn. He learned some lessons and he learned them well. I want us to see today some of the lessons Jonah learned in the belly of the fish. Now, he tells us at the beginning about the chance he had to go to Tarshish. He wanted to go; the ship was going, it looked providential. It was so easy for him to rise up and flee from the presence of the Lord. Then he tells us about the wind; he tells us about being awakened by the mariners, about his exposure before them, his confession and then the solution to the problem: to throw him overboard. Then he tells us about the fish. But he does not end the story there. For a lot transpired in the belly of the fish. He prayed as he never prayed in his life, and God heard him. God answered his prayer and he winds up this section by saying, 'When my soul fainted within me I remembered the Lord' (Jonah 2:7). 'I prayed to Him; He heard my prayer.' Then immediately he tells us what he learned, namely, three things in the belly of the fish.

First, he learned that those who live in disobedience do not magnify God's mercy; they rather dishonour it. The first thing he said was this: 'They that observe lying vanities forsake their own mercy' (Jonah 2:8). The second lesson was, God wants our gratitude even though we are not saved by it. Jonah learned this well and so he said, 'I will sacrifice unto thee with the voice of thanksgiving; I will pay that that I have vowed' (Jonah 2:9). The third lesson he tells us he learned is that salvation in any case is out of his hands: 'Salvation is of the Lord' (Jonah 2:9b).

Jonah learned these three lessons in the belly of the fish and he learned them well. This is another example of the truth of Romans 8:28 being carried out: 'And we know that all things work together for good to them that love God, to them who are the called according to his purpose.' Our problem is that when we find out that we do learn lessons through adversity we tend to justify such adversity. Shakespeare said, 'Sweet are the uses of adversity.' True, but does it follow that all adversity was right and necessary? In other words, the greatest lesson we have to learn from Romans 8:28 is this: merely because something is *made* right does not mean it *was* right. But if it *is* made right then everything *is* all right. But we tend to justify ourselves and the temptation is to say that our disobedience was justified simply because we profited.

Well, thank God we do profit from adversity and thank God for the truth that all things work together for good to them that love God, to them who are the called according to his purpose. It is true and thank God it is true. It is *so* true that we are tempted to justify everything happening exactly as it did. Take David, for example. I have often marvelled at the story of David. Most of us, I am sure, are aware of David's heinous sin of adultery; and to cover up that sin he murdered the husband of Bathsheba, whose name was Uriah. Yet when we come to the first Gospel in the New Testament, in the first chapter where we have that long series of the 'begats' (leading up to Christ the Messiah) we are told that 'Jesse begat David the king; and David the king begat Solomon *of her that had been the wife of Urias*' (Matt. 1:6). The immediate conclusion might be that because it worked together for good that made it right. Thank God it can be *made* right! But that does not mean it *was* right.

Or, again, take the example of when Israel wanted a king, and the prophet Samuel went before the people and told them: 'It is not best for you. God does not want you to have a king' (1 Sam. 8:9). Samuel indeed warned them. They said, 'We want a king like other nations.' Finally God said to Samuel, 'Acquiesce in their request; let them have a king' (1 Sam. 8:19–22). It was never God's will for them to have a king in the first place. But God accommodated them so that even when Jesus the Messiah came He fulfilled the prophecy of Zechariah, 'Behold thy King cometh, sitting on the foal of an ass' (Zech. 9:9; Matt. 21:5). And so it worked together for good – so much so that we are tempted to look back and to say, 'That is the way it was *supposed* to be.'

Still another example is to be seen in the very fact that our Lord could use Jonah as an example! In Matthew 12:39 Jesus said: 'An evil and adulterous generation seeketh after a sign; and there shall no sign be given to it, but the sign of the prophet Jonah: For as Jonah was three days and three nights in the whale's belly, so shall the Son of Man be three days and three nights in the heart of the earth.' Here Jonah's disobedience and chastening became a paradigm, as it were, of our Lord's death, burial and resurrection. And so there is the immediate temptation to justify what happened. I say to you that we must learn the lesson that merely because something is *made* right it does not mean that it *was* right. Yet, thank

God, it can be made right, even to look so good that we are tempted to say that it was meant to have been that way.

And this is what I am putting to you today. Thank God for the lessons Jonah learned. But he learned them the hard way. And Jonah learned his obedience through suffering. Now, we are told that Jesus learned obedience also through suffering (Heb. 5:8), yet Jesus learned such obedience without sinning (Heb. 4:15). We learn our obedience as sinners saved by grace. Let us be thankful for the lessons we have learned, without justifying our disobedience. God's grace gets us through. *All eventually pass.* But that process may be a long one and we are reminded of the first lesson Jonah learned. He was virtually saying, 'It wasn't worth it'. I say this to anybody here today who may be contemplating something that is manifestly wrong. Are you playing fast and loose with some moral principle? Are you on the brink of some financial deal that is very shady? Are you taking lightly the fact that you are created in God's image, and that your body is the temple of the Holy Spirit? The first thing Jonah said when he looked back was: 'It wasn't worth it.' He learned a lesson and he learned it well. Thus lesson number one was this: 'All that I did *did not* extol God's mercy. I dishonoured grace by what I did.' So Jonah was out of the fish telling the story. Jonah gives us the whole story as one who had been through it all. And this was the first thing that he said he learned.

Now, the abuse of God's mercy does not extol God's mercy. The Apostle Paul laboured to make this point clear. After treating the glorious doctrine of justification by faith Paul was forced to say this. You see, Romans 6:1 was necessary because all that Paul said logically led to the question, 'Shall we continue in sin that grace may abound?' Now Paul asked the question because he assumed you would ask it if he didn't. May I remind you of Dr. Lloyd-Jones' famous statement that if our gospel does not make us vulnerable to the charge of Antinomianism, then the chances are we haven't preached the Gospel! And so Romans 6:1 had to be put because all that Paul was saying with regard to the doctrine of justification by faith led him to realise that others would say, 'Well, if that is true we might as well sin on and on that we might have more and more grace.' And so Paul had to say, 'No! God forbid! How shall we that are dead to sin live any longer therein?' (Rom. 6:2). And in Romans 6:22 he put it like this: 'Now being made free from sin and become servants to God *ye have your fruit unto holiness* and the end everlasting life.'

This is what is going on in the Book of Jonah. Jonah 2:8 reads like a proverb. Yet if you look at that verse out of context it makes almost no sense. It only makes sense when you realise that it is the first thing Jonah uttered after he realised that God had heard him and he was ejected from the fish. 'They that observe lying vanities' – that is what Jonah had done – 'forsake their own mercy'. Jonah 2:8 is another way of saying that a child of God cannot ultimately get away with flagrant disobedience. Now, we have seen already that Jonah was a man who had assurance. Failure to see this will mean that you will never see the depth of the Book of Jonah. Jonah was a man who did have assurance. Because we do have assurance we are sometimes all the more vulnerable to disobedience because we know we are kept by grace. This is why Paul said to Titus, 'I will that thou affirm constantly, that they maintain good works' (Titus 3:8). Do not forget good works. It is an easy thing to do, and assurance sometimes makes us vulnerable to living disobediently. And this partly explains why Jonah could rise up to flee from the presence of the Lord. He simply wasn't that afraid! And I say to you again, the hardest type of Christian to deal with in a vestry is one who has assurance and is living in disobedience. You can hardly get through to them, they will not take counselling; they already know it all. The only thing which works is when a fish swallows them up and brings them to a place where they too will pray as they never prayed before! God gives such special attention to His own people. God's fish alone can reach a person like that. God thus must sometimes go to extremes. This is the reason Paul had to be ruthless in his dealing with that man in Corinth who was guilty of incest. 'Deliver him unto Satan that his spirit may be saved in the day of the Lord Jesus' (1 Cor. 5:5).

Very well then, while Romans 8:28 is true, it is never

given to us in an *a priori* sense, as if looking ahead we can do as we wish. It is an *a posteriori* promise, that all things in the *past* fit into a pattern for good. Therefore *looking back* you can see the marvellous grace of God! But the warning for us today is this: Jonah, now out of the fish, said, 'It was not worth it!'. May I remind you that however true it is, and thank God it is true, that 'as far as the east is from the west so far hath he removed our transgressions from us' (Psalm 103:12) – and how thankful we are that God has 'not dealt with us after our sins' (Psalm 103:10) – I want you to know this, that *it is no sign of God's mercy that you get away with flagrant disobedience*. Now there is always someone who comes forward and says, 'Well, sin is sin and we all sin, and since we are going to sin I might as well pick a good one.' Let me tell you something. There are some sins more serious than others. Any sin that affects God's witness in the world provokes His anger! God is jealous for His Kingdom and when you sin in such a way that it affects His witness you had better watch out. God is serious about His own witness in the world. And the fact that you get away with sin is no sign of His mercy; it may be a sign rather that you are being given over to a reprobate mind. And that is a painless transaction. You may never consciously know that it has happened. God just gives some over to a mind void of judgment. And if you live in bold disobedience, and go on and on doing things that you know are wrong and you say, 'God hasn't touched me yet', you had better fall on your face and pray that He will! It could be that God is just setting you aside and moving on. God sometimes does that.

But if God has put you in the belly of a fish be thankful. Thank God for it.

Let us look again at Jonah's first lesson. The sin wasn't worth it. Another way of putting it is this. Jonah was once an Antinomian. He was one of those who had a taste of God's free grace, but concluded that the way he lived did not matter. God said, 'Go to Nineveh.' Jonah said, 'No, thanks', and rose up to flee. But listen to him a little later: 'I cried by reason of mine affliction ... Thou hast cast me into the deep, in the midst of the seas. Thy waves passed over me. I said, I am cast out of thy sight . . . The waters compassed me about – the depths closed round about me, the weeds were wrapped about my head . . . When my soul fainted within me, I remembered the Lord.' It is much like the Prodigal, who 'came to himself' (Lk. 15:17).

What will it take to bring you to yourself?

Jonah immediately concluded, then, that when he thought he could take God's commands lightly, he was deluded. It was a 'lying vanity', this idea that God was extolled by his disobedience. When God tells us to do something, he means it. And when God commands something in His revealed Word we had better take it seriously. He does. He gave it to us because we need His Word; it is His Truth. It reflects His holy character, and He demands worship before Him. He demands that we follow His Word. The fact that we have a taste of His free grace, the fact that we know forgiveness does not mean that God is inviting us on to live as though there were no God in the world. Such was the first thing that was on Jonah's mind after he was rescued from this traumatic experience. 'They that observe lying vanities forsake their own mercy.' He had not extolled God's mercy by the way he lived; he had forsaken it.

There is still another way of putting it. They that live in such open disobedience tempt the most high God. In the fourth chapter of Matthew we have the account of how Jesus was dealt with by Satan. Satan came to him and said, 'If thou be the Son of God, cast thyself down.' Jesus was then high up on the pinnacle of the Temple. It was a height of over 100 ft. Satan's reasoning was this: 'God is all-powerful and you are the Son of God. God is surely not going to let anything happen to you. Prove God's power; jump off.' And then Satan, who can quote the Bible better than any of us here today, quoted a Psalm to Jesus to support this reasoning. The Psalm reads: 'He shall give his angels charge concerning thee, and in their hands they shall bear thee up, lest at any time thou dash thy foot against a stone' (Mt. 4:6; Psa. 91:11). This, you see, is Satanic reasoning. The Devil knows how to reason with one who has got a fairly sound theology. 'You're a Christian, aren't you? God is going to take care of you. Claim His word, go on and do it. Jump off the cliff; you are a child of God; He will pick you up. Romans 8:28 is true: it will work together for good, so go on.'

What was the answer our Lord gave in reply to this kind of reasoning? 'Thou shalt not tempt the Lord thy God' (Mt. 4:7). Have you been doing this? Have you been a victim of this kind of reasoning – that says, 'Well, I am a child of God. He must look after me. He will take care of me, and it is all right if I do this. I am sure, mind you, that it is against God's revealed word, but, after all, God is powerful. If I jump off the cliff, He will pick me up.' That is Satanic logic and reasoning, and if you fall prey to it you may live in the belly of a fish for a long, long time. It does not take away the truth of Romans 8:28. You simply may wait much, much longer before you are allowed to look back with any kind of relief.

Jonah, then, was once an Antinomian. I ask you: Are you flirting with anything that is dangerous to the witness of God's glory in this world? Satan wants you to prove God's grace by your disobedience. God says you are to prove Him by your obedience. And I don't mind telling you again – it is like that verse in Malachi 3:10, where the only time we are commanded to prove God was to prove Him by giving Him what is already His. He promises: 'I will prove it back to you by pouring out a blessing that is almost too much for you to contain.' Satan says: 'Exalt God's mercy by disobedience.' God says: 'Exalt it by obedience.' Let no-one be deceived; the word of the Lord to Samuel is still true: 'Them that honour me I will honour' (1 Sam. 2:30). We do not extol God's mercy by tempting Him, or by an unholy and undisciplined life. This is to observe 'lying vanities'. We magnify God's mercy by faithfulness – by living in such a way that men see something different in us. How many of us pride ourselves on the preciseness of our well-thought-out theology, and we suppose that God is going to bless us merely because we understand things that many people don't. That is sheer nonsense. I remind you that the world out there couldn't care less about our theology. The world out there doesn't care about those things that may seem important to us. It is like the words of that poem:

For me 'twas not the truth you taught; to you so clear, to me still dim;
But when you came to me, you brought a sense of Him.

The first thing, then, which Jonah wanted to say after being ejected from the fish was: 'It wasn't worth it.' I say to you: If you are on this side of being swallowed up, that is, if it hasn't happened yet, then it doesn't have to happen! Be careful.

But Jonah also learned that God takes gratitude seriously. Lesson number two was that God wants our gratitude even though we are not saved by it. Thus after giving us the first lesson he learned he went on to say: 'But I will sacrifice unto thee with the voice of thanksgiving; I will pay that that I have vowed' (Jonah 2:9). This was the second lesson Jonah claimed to have learned. It is really stating the first lesson in a slightly different way. If the first lesson was that disobedience is not exalting grace but forsaking it, the second was that God wants us to show gratitude – not merely by our words but by the way we live. 'I will pay that that I have vowed.'

There is a tendency in us to suppose that since we are saved by grace it does not matter whether we show gratitude for this. Since we are saved by grace and kept by grace, God is not interested in our response to grace; we are not saved by gratitude, therefore the flesh in us suggests that gratitude is unnecessary. Well then, this was the way Jonah had looked at the matter. But he learned differently. He promised God in the belly of the fish that, if he ever got out, he would live differently: 'I will pay that that I have vowed.' It took the fish's swallowing him up to bring him to this realisation. This is why I said earlier that most of us seem not to learn from the Word directly; we need God's fish to demonstrate to us. The Word of God on the matter of our sanctification is clear enough, but most of us require God's chastening first-hand before we see this soberly.

The doctrine of sanctification may be called the doctrine of gratitude. Sanctification does not save us – or even contribute to our justification; it is God's ordained way by which we may say, 'Thank you, Lord, for saving my soul.' Sanctification is a way of saying 'Thank you' to God for His marvellous grace. Lest we think however that sanctification is not important, the Apostle Paul put it to the Thessalonians: 'This is the will of God, even your sanctification, that ye should abstain from fornication... For God hath not called us unto uncleanness, but unto holiness' (1 Thess. 4:3, 7). Not only that; God has chosen us in Christ from the foundation of the world 'that we should be holy and without blame before him in love' (Eph. 1:4). God is serious about this matter of our personal holiness and obedience, not only because of our witness in the world but because we are His adopted children. We are predestinated 'unto the adoption of children by Jesus Christ' (Eph. 1:5).

Jonah made a vow in the belly of the fish. It is not that God is particularly pleased with our vows and our promises. 'Better is it that thou shouldest not vow, than that thou shouldest vow and not pay' (Eccl. 5:5). I'm not so sure God takes our vows all that seriously. But He accommodates us by letting us make vows in desperation by which we may measure our gratitude. If we take too much comfort from having made a vow we border on deriving our joy from the wrong source. God wants our source of joy to be Himself. Yet He sometimes accommodates us by letting us make vows, even if only because we further condemn ourselves if we don't keep them. But Jonah made a vow – and kept it.

Finally, there is a third lesson: 'Salvation is of the Lord' (Jonah 2:9b). Although Jonah had to abandon his Antinomianism, he didn't have to abandon the greatest truth of all – that salvation was out of his hands. How did Jonah know that salvation was out of his hands? Well, he knew that only a loving God would take him back after doing what he did. He knew that he had nothing to do with the wind, he had nothing to do with the way he got exposed before the mariners, and he knew he had nothing to do with the fish that swallowed him up. What is more, he was all the more helpless in the end. He didn't know whether God was going to end his life in the fish or eject him. God has a way of bringing us to the place where we are willing to be completely in His hands, even willing for the outcome to be entirely His prerogative to do what He pleases. The best thing one can do then is to watch God work – to watch God do it. 'Salvation is of the Lord'.

Are you trying to bring something to pass? Are you trying to manipulate Romans 8:28, so that since it is promised that 'all things work together for good' you must help the promise along by making it work together for good? Has God promised you that something is going to happen, but now you think you must guarantee that it works out – so you begin to manipulate things? When Jonah could say, 'Salvation is of the Lord', he was saying many things of course, but the ultimate point is that *his own deliverance was out of his hands*.

It is much like the way David Brainerd was converted to the Lord Jesus Christ. Do you know who David Brainerd was? Had he lived he would have become Jonathan Edwards' son-in-law. David Brainerd died in Edwards' home. Jonathan Edwards was in the bedroom at the moment Brainerd died. Said Edwards, 'A sense of the glory of God came into the room and then left.' But before his conversion this man David Brainerd had a quarrel with God. He read the Bible and didn't like what he read. He read that the Bible teaches that God requires perfect righteousness, and he couldn't produce it – and it made him angry with God. It meant that he would have to have a substitute. He went on and on in his quarrel, thinking that surely there must be another way. But the more he read the more frustrated he became. He saw that if he were ever saved it would be because God gave him a Mediator. He went on reading. He learned a second thing, that God demanded perfect faith; and he couldn't produce it. It meant that if he had any faith at all God would have to give it to him, and this made him all the more angry with

God. He walked the floor, he walked in the fields, angry with God that there should be such a way of dealing with men. And then he went on reading the Bible and found something else – that God could give faith or withhold it. This brought him into a greater debate with God, as he saw even further that salvation was completely out of his hands. He saw that the God with whom we have to do is the same one Moses met. God said to Moses: 'I will have mercy on whom I will have mercy and will be gracious to whom I will be gracious' (Ex. 33:19; Rom. 9:15). Brainerd saw that God could give mercy or withhold it. Then Brainerd saw that God could save him or damn him, and that God could be justified either way.

Does it surprise you, Christian people, that a man could learn this about God? Or have you been guilty of projecting upon the back-drop of the universe the kind of God that coheres with your natural idea of what He ought to be? The God with whom we have to do does not have to save anybody. If He wants He can pass over a whole generation without saving the first soul. If God gave us what we deserve we would already be in hell.

Have you learned that salvation is of the Lord? Perhaps you are like Brainerd, quarrelling with God at such an idea. Maybe God will put you in the belly of a fish to teach you that. 'I will have mercy on whom I will have mercy.'

But I end on this note – that He is 'rich in mercy' (Eph. 2:4). He is rich in mercy and He promises, 'Whosoever shall call upon the name of the Lord will not be confounded – will not be ashamed – they will be saved' (Rom. 10:11, 13). And maybe you are an unsaved person here this morning, and you have been trying to save yourself. Perhaps you, prior to your conversion, have been put in the belly of the fish to bring you to pray when you wouldn't any other way, and thus force you to call upon the only true God. God can do that.

Jonah learned some lessons. He learned them well. 'It wasn't worth it. In my disobedience I didn't magnify God's mercy. I abused it. I dishonoured it. I can see that God wants my gratitude, and He is going to get it.' And, best of all – at the bottom of this whole experience – was a God of mercy who loved Jonah so much that He went to such pains to give him this kind of attention. 'Salvation is of the Lord'. Thanks be to God.

12 Jonah's Ejection

Jonah 2:7–10

'OH THAT THOU wouldest rend the heavens, that thou wouldest come down . . .' When Jonah learned some lessons in the belly of the fish, this did not immediately solve his problem; more heart-searching had to take place. He was still in the belly of the fish and he learned some lessons well. But now the fear emerged that he might not live to tell what happened. The first lesson, you may recall, was that he did not magnify God's mercy by his disobedience but dishonoured it. He was once an Antinomian; he was once of the opinion that it did not matter how he lived. And his first comment when he came to himself was: 'They that observe lying vanities forsake their mercy.' In other words, he saw that what he did was foolish; it wasn't worth it. He also saw that gratitude, although we are not saved by it, is something, nonetheless, that God wants. And so, he was in a state of readiness – 'I will pay that that I have vowed.' Then there was the third lesson: that deliverance, salvation, was completely out of his hands. He exclaimed, 'Salvation is of the Lord.'

Now while he is obviously telling all this after the whole episode is over, we must keep in mind that he wrote this story as though he were still in the belly of the fish. Thus we live through the ordeal with Jonah. The point, however, to be seen today is that merely learning the lessons did not solve his problem. He had the knowledge, he saw clearly certain marvellous things. The question follows: Would he live to tell what happened? He may well have felt much like Isaiah the prophet: 'Oh that thou wouldest rend the heavens, and come down' (Isa 64:1). That same Isaiah saw that, 'Thou art a God who hidest thyself' (Isa. 45:15).

141

We must not underestimate the possibility that God could have taught Jonah these lessons and let him die in the belly of the fish. God could have done it and been just – and I suspect that God has done it many times across the centuries. There have undoubtedly been those who learned lessons but did not live to tell anyone what they had learned – God took them. Jonah's new fear was of dying in the belly of the fish and not being able to tell what he had learned. It is much like when we see something that is remarkable, or extraordinary, and we say, 'I must tell this.' But then we stop and think: 'Nobody would believe it.' And many times things are never told – for various reasons. Perhaps because they would not be believed; or perhaps because their incredibility is such that no-one would ever believe us. In any case, Jonah's fear at this stage was not knowing whether he would live to tell what had happened.

Now, you may think God would be most anxious for everybody to know what had happened to Jonah – and, obviously, God did permit us to know. Obviously, God let Jonah live. But we need to see something at this point and learn this lesson well. And that is that one thing which makes God most unlike man is that God is not a pragmatist; God is not a man, a being who needs to prove Himself. Pragmatism is the philosophy that what works is true; if it works it is right. Utilitarianism holds that doctrines are right and true if they are useful; otherwise they are not right. But God is not like that. God is true, not because His truth is useful but because He *is* truth in Himself. God does not need approval outside Himself, and this makes Him most unlike man. Man grows up needing approval outside himself. We grow up wanting the approval of our parents. My daughter, Missy, came into our sittingroom this morning to have me look at her, waiting for me to comment on how she looked. And my son, T.R., wanted to wear one of my ties again today; he is getting to the age when he wants to be like me. We grow up needing the approval of parents, and then we reach a certain age when we want even our peers to like us. Contemporary psychology stresses building one's self-image by learning what others say about us. There is group therapy, encounter groups. One person may say to another, 'You make me sick every time you open your mouth.' The latter suddenly discovers how he looks to somebody else. But another says, 'I like you when you are that way.' 'So,' he thinks, 'perhaps I am not so bad.' The idea is that what we learn about ourselves is based on what others say about us.

But God does not learn about Himself by what anybody says about Him. God does not learn more about Himself by what we say *to* Him or *about* Him. When God made a promise to Abraham, 'because He could sware by no greater *He sware by Himself*' (Heb. 6:13). For God is sufficient within Himself. Behind all the promises of God lies this unchangeable axiom: It is impossible for God to lie (Heb. 6:18). And that which makes God God is that He is independent of all things. He needs to do *nothing* in order to glorify Himself. In terms of time, one wonders how long it was before God created the first thing. The first announcement of our Lord to John on the Isle of Patmos was: 'Fear not, I am the first and the last' (Rev. 1:17). For our Lord Jesus Christ is the eternal God. Beside God there is no other. 'Even from everlasting to everlasting thou art God' (Psa. 90:2). Before there was ever a star in Bethlehem, God was there. Before sin lifted up its ugly head in the Garden of Eden, God was there. Long before Lucifer, son of the morning, said 'I will be like God', God was there. Long before the sun was made to shine in creation's morning, God was there. If there had been one speck of dust in remotest space apart from God's creation, He would not have been first. But God was the first. 'In the beginning was the Word, and the Word was with God' – showing the trinitarian relationship between the Father and the Son – and 'the Word was God' (John 1:1). God is *independent;* with and by Himself He gets all the glory He needs. That which makes God God is that He does not need to *do* anything to glorify Himself. For that reason, God may be pleased to reveal Himself without there being a precedent for what He does, or how He does it, nor does He have to repeat it even once.

Jonah discovered this in the belly of the fish. He learned these three great truths, then, without any promise that he would live to tell what he had learned. For he saw that God does not need to have people see what happened to Jonah. Jonah saw the glory of God – but in doing so he realised that God didn't need to have anybody see what he saw. This, perhaps, was the most painful part of the ordeal – to see clearly certain truths and to think that nobody would be told about them. After all, the truth of God is already known in hell. This was the point that the rich man in hell was trying to make: 'Send Lazarus, that he may tell my five brothers about this place.' The word came back: 'Your five brothers have the Bible, let them believe the Bible.' But the man in hell said: 'You don't understand, my five brothers do not believe this place exists. My five brothers won't believe the Bible' (Luke 16:27ff). The truth of God is known in hell. Sometimes God will give men a glimpse into the deepest insights of His truth on this earth; but God does not need to have men tell it in order to glorify Himself.

And Jonah knew this; he saw that God, who is all-powerful, could show anybody and everybody what is known in hell, even the things Jonah discovered in the belly of the fish. But God is not a pragmatist. He is not even enriched by His creation. He is not more pleased with Himself by what He does or by the approval of others. God does not learn by experience. God receives all glory in Himself alone. To state it another way: God can get as much pleasure by revealing Himself to one person as to many. So again, Augustine: God loves each person as though he were the only one to love. He loves everybody as though there were no one else to love. And thus God can reveal the deepest insights of His Word to one man and nobody else. The Psalmist learned it: 'The secret of the Lord is with them that fear him.' Consequently, God can reveal the deepest insights to the most insignificant person. God can reveal the deepest truths to the most simple man. 'The secret of the Lord is with them that fear Him' (Psa. 25:14) – not the mighty, not the noble, but them that fear Him. And it shouldn't surprise us that some of the greatest theological truths have been disclosed throughout the ages to some of the simplest minds who never have opportunity to tell what they saw. And not only can God get as much pleasure by showing Himself to one person and no-one else, He can reveal himself in one era and no other. Or, He can reveal Himself in one place and nowhere else. God does this. I heard this past week of a great revival going on right now in a remote island in the Pacific and people are genuinely afraid the press will find out about it and come in there and exploit it. Some remarkable things are going on right now – a genuine, authentic awakening. God can get as much pleasure by revealing Himself to one person as to many; or in one era and no other; or to one place and no-where else.

Jonah knew this. Jonah knew that seeing the glory of the Lord did not guarantee he would ever get out. And thus it is, God reveals Himself to those who fear Him. However, sometimes God does show deep insights to a great mind in a strategic place and, when that happens, the world is never the same again. What Athanasius saw concerning the Person of Jesus Christ had no doubt been seen by others before him and has been since by those who never heard of Athanasius. But when Athanasius saw it the whole world was affected by it; the Christian church was never the same again. What St Augustine saw concerning the grace of God and the depravity of man may well have been seen by many before and since, but when he saw it the whole world was affected and the church was never the same again. What Luther saw may well have been seen by others throughout the 1400 years of church history that preceded him. But when Luther saw it, God using his personality in that situation, and with perfect timing, the whole world was affected by it and the church was never the same again. And thus we pray that God will do it again. He can do it and yet He can get as much pleasure *if He does not*. But Isaiah summed it up: 'Oh that thou wouldest rend the heavens and come down.'

That was the prayer of Jonah. But a great part of Jonah's chastening was now having to see the glory of God in the belly of the fish combined with the fear of never getting to tell it; that is, never getting to share what he had seen and learned. You see, these were truths worth sharing – and you may think that if God gives a truth to somebody surely God needs to get it out. God is not a pragmatist. God can by-pass a whole generation if He wants to.

Very well then, Jonah was in a state of readiness. He knew one thing: 'I will thank Him if I am ever out of this place! I will sacrifice thanksgiving to Him if God lets me live.' There was one thing for certain: 'I will pay that that I have vowed...' But something was holding things up: 'Deliverance, or salvation, is of the Lord.' *Jonah knew there was not a thing more he could do.* He must wait in a state of readiness. There was no 'guarantee' he would ever be ejected from the fish. He must wait; only wait.

The greatest kind of consecration at this point in time was for Jonah to be willing *not* to be used! At the beginning of the story it was his unwillingness to be used. 'Go to Nineveh, that great city and cry out against it.' Jonah rose up to flee from the presence of the Lord. But now, God had worked on Jonah until he was *so* willing that he had to become willing *not* to be used. Only God can do a thing like that; only God can turn a man's affections and make him do what he thought he never wanted to do. God can do that. And now such a time had come. Jonah had to wait.

What if God doesn't use us? After all, God can use somebody else. The most humbling experience we can ever have is to discover that God does not need us. He can pass us by so easily. He has done it before. All Jonah could do was to wait.

'I will pay that that I have vowed.' God sometimes puts His own, including the church, into the belly of a fish to make us yearn for a universal manifestation of His glory. It is one thing to be willing to do what God wants you to do, when you are unwilling and then it is another thing to be willing not to be used when you are ready. To some people the greatest act of consecration is merely being willing to do what God says; to others of us, who have come to that place long ago and who are so anxious to be used, it can be even more painful to become willing not to be used. All Jonah could do was to say: 'I will offer the sacrifice of thanksgiving, I will pay that that I have vowed. Oh that thou wouldest rend the heavens and come down.'

But Isaiah went on to say: 'Eye hath not seen nor ear

heard what God hath prepared for those that wait for him'
(Isa. 64:4). 'Oh that thou wouldest rend the heavens and
come down.' God did come – six hundred years later: 'Behold, I bring you good tidings of great joy which shall be
to all people' (Luke 2:10). 'Oh that thou wouldest rend the
heavens and come down.' God can make us yearn, like Job,
who said: 'Oh that my words were now written, that they
were printed in a book . . .' (Job 19:23). It is much like the
way Paul felt when he was waiting for Silas and Timothy at
Athens. He looked around and saw the idolatry, and his
spirit 'was stirred within him' (Acts 17:16). Oh, for a
chance to say something about it.

Do you know what it is like to see something clearly,
something that is viable and worth while, and not be able
to tell it? It is great pain. Perhaps you are not articulate
and you can't; perhaps you do not have the platform
necessary in order to get your point across; perhaps you
don't have the credentials the world expects, and so you are
not going to be taken seriously, or perhaps your time has
not come. You must be willing *not* to be used. God's timing
makes all the difference as to whether or not one's voice is
truly heard. It was the literary genius, Victor Hugo, who
said: 'More powerful than the tramping of an army is the
force of an idea whose time has come.' And the psalmist
could only say: 'My times are in thy hands' (Psa. 31:15).
It takes more grace or effort for our consecration many
times, then, to be willing not to be used. This we recognise
when we also see that it takes no more grace or effort for
God to show His power to thousands than to one soul, or
to the ages than to one era, or to the whole world than to
one locality. Those that have seen the glory of the Lord
know this; they recognise this; they know that God may do
it and He may not. That is the remarkable thing about the
leper who went to Jesus and said: 'Lord, if thou wilt, thou
canst make me clean' (Matt. 8:2). And there was that
centurion who came to Jesus and said: 'I am not worthy
that thou shouldest come under my roof: but speak the
word only, and my servant shall be healed' (Matt. 8:8).
Those who have had one glimpse of God's glory know that
this is true.

The thing we need to remember is that what God does He does by His word. God demands that we believe His word. He often refuses to accommodate our unbelief by giving us proofs, signs, a system of ethics, or even intellectual ability to reason well. What God does He does by His word. Thus, in creation He spoke: 'Let there be light.' And there was light: His word did it (Gen. 1:3). In providence we are told that He upholds all things 'by the word of His power' (Heb. 1:3). What God does He does by His word. We read that Jesus was asleep on a boat with the disciples when there was a great storm of wind; the waves beat into the ship so that it was now full of water. We are told that Jesus was in the back part of the ship, asleep on a pillow. They woke Him and said: 'Master, carest thou not that we perish?' Jesus arose and rebuked the wind; He said: 'Peace, be still' (Mark 4:37–39). It was His voice, His word. You will recall the occasion when Peter said: 'Lord, if it be thou, let me walk on the water.' And Jesus said: 'Come' (Matt. 14:28–29). It was His voice. God always speaks through His word.

Thus with Jonah, the Lord spoke to the fish. Does it surprise you that God should talk to a creature? To a fish? The same Lord who brought the wind prepared the fish. The same Christ who rebuked the wind and calmed the sea now spoke to the fish. It was outside Jonah's hands; there was nothing he could do.

But God spoke; *and the fish ejected Jonah!*

But, prior to that supernatural event Jonah knew there was nothing he could do. Frequently this is the very way God deals with all of us. He brings us to the place where there is, humanly speaking, absolutely no way of escape. He brings us to the utter end of ourselves. He does this so that we can see positively that the deliverance was completely out of our hands. In other words, as long as there is some chance that we can pull a string or two by manipulating things, we will always be haunted by the fact that deliverance was traceable to our efforts. But God has a way of showing us that salvation is entirely of Him.

This is true with regard to our initial conversion to Christ. 'You hath He quickened, who were dead in trespasses and sins' (Eph. 2:1). While it happens sometimes that the process of conversion appears to be by our co-operation, we can clearly see, when looking back, that the whole thing was of God – from start to finish. Sometimes it takes a keener theological understanding to make one appreciate this fact. If one's conversion was of such a nature that it seemed as though one's will played an active part all along, one should never assume that such a conversion was false. Oftentimes a genuine conversion is like this. On the other hand, there are those conversions that are so extraordinary that the person converted can clearly see from the start that such a change was out of his hands. In any case, true conversion is always out of the hands of man, even if in some cases it appears that man was helping it along.

But God has a way of making one see that salvation is of the Lord. Take, for example, the case just described, in which the initial conversion appears to be by man's co-operation with grace. God has a way of bringing such a person later on to the place where he is as dependent upon divine grace as Jonah was in the belly of the fish. I will go further than that. If someone's initial conversion appeared to have revolved around man's co-operation with grace, God will sooner or later bring that very person to the point where he *will* see God's glory in a time of desperation. It is His way of teaching us how to give due honour to Him. He brings us to the utter end of ourselves that we may see without doubt that the only way out was by God's miraculous intervention.

This is precisely the way it was with Jonah before the fish ejected him. God brought Jonah to despair, to desperation, that he might see God only. 'When my soul fainted, I remembered the Lord.' 'I will come to Him.' 'I have learned something: my folly wasn't worth it. God wants my gratitude.' 'I will pay that that I have vowed. Salvation is of the Lord.' 'Moreover, God can deliver me and get glory, or He can keep me here and get glory.'

But the Lord spoke to the fish, and out Jonah came! For when God speaks He liberates, because His word is truth. 'Ye shall know the truth, and the truth shall make you free' (John 8:32). Are you wanting emancipation today? Are you wanting release? Are you wanting to be freed from all of those things that bind you? Emancipation comes one way: via the word of God, which is Truth. You can look elsewhere for ever! 'Ye shall know the truth and the truth shall make you free.' Have you been playing games with yourself, thinking you can by-pass the truth? Don't be deceived. 'Ye shall know the truth, and the truth shall make you free.' There is no other way. 'I am the truth,' said Jesus, 'no man cometh unto the Father but by me' (John 14:6). When God speaks, He liberates. The reason that God's word liberates is because all things are subservient to that word which created all things, and consequently Jesus rebuked the wind. And God spoke to the fish. Jonah at last was set free.

'Oh that thou wouldest rend the heavens and come down.' 'Eye hath not seen, nor ear heard, neither have entered into the heart of man, the things which God hath prepared for them that love Him' (I Cor. 2:9). And when the Apostle Paul, quoting from Isaiah 64, put this down he added a commentary: 'But God hath revealed them unto us by His Spirit' (I Cor. 2:10). And so it is, these things that God has prepared are revealed *now*. That verse is often used as a text to prove what heaven is going to be like; but you are missing a great blessing if you do not see that it is rather what 'heaven on earth' is like; what God has prepared *now* for those who wait on Him. God may reveal to you the profoundest insights since the mind of Paul explored the deep things of God. 'Eye hath not seen nor ear heard...' 'Oh that thou wouldest rend the heavens and come down.' He may come to you and to no-one else. 'Oh that thou wouldest rend the heavens and come down.' God did come. 'Behold, I bring you good tidings of great joy which shall be to all people.' 'Lo, I am with you always, even to the end of the age' (Matt. 28:20). 'Oh, that thou wouldest rend the heavens and come down.' 'God hath in these last days spoken to us by his Son, whom he hath appointed heir of all things, by whom He also created the ages' (Heb. 1:2).

Jonah was at the end of himself. He saw there was not one thing he could do. He waited. He was ready. 'If God saves me, I will pay that that I have vowed. But only He can deliver me. For salvation is of the Lord.' But up until the moment of the ejection Jonah could only wait. Would God do it? Would God bring deliverance? Will God allow me to tell others what I have seen? 'Oh, that thou wouldest rend the heavens and come down.'

In much the same way the church cries for revival. Can any deny that we are presently in the belly of a fish? Once before the church was in such a state; God sent Athanasius. Once again the church was in such a state; God sent Augustine. And again in a time of despair, God sent Luther. One of the most moving scenes in the history of the Christian church was at the time of the desperate state in Scotland in the middle of the sixteenth century. In England there were those being persecuted under the reign of Mary Tudor – 'Bloody Mary', as she is called. It was hardly better in Scotland with Mary Queen of Scots doing everything she could to stamp out the Reformation. But there was no man available. The one man that might have been used was in Geneva – sitting at the feet of John Calvin and learning all he could from his master. But one day Calvin called young John Knox into his vestry and said: 'It is time for you to go to Scotland.' In the meantime the people in Scotland were praying, praying most earnestly that God would somehow deliver them. Soon John Knox embarked on a ship and headed for Scotland. When that ship touched the shores of Scotland, Knox was spotted. Word spread: 'John Knox is come, John Knox is come.' From village to village and from hamlet to hamlet the people were electrified. 'John Knox is come, John Knox is come.' Scotland was inflamed with joy and hope. The day came when Mary Queen of Scots was heard to say that she feared the prayers of John Knox more than an army of ten thousand men. The rest of that story is standard history. The crucial element was God's timing.

I suspect the church will remain in the belly of the fish today until we learn some lessons. We once needed to be told to go. Perhaps the time will come when we will have to test our consecration by our willingness not to go. You may be sure of one thing: God will eject us in such a way that He alone, not man, will get the glory. The question I put is this: Have we become so desperate that we are like Jonah – 'I will pay that that I have vowed'? Have we reached the place where we yearn that God will rend the heavens and come down?

Jonah was ejected.

When will it happen to us?

13 Jonah's Second Chance

Jonah 3:1

WE NOW COME to the high watermark of the book of Jonah.
We see what I believe is one of the sublimest phrases in all
holy writ and which puts in bold relief the profoundest
principles that underlie God's dealings with men. I can
think of other great passages that parallel this verse – Jonah
3:1 – 'the word of the Lord came unto Jonah the second
time', but I know of no passage that illustrates so perfectly
and so tenderly and so clearly the way God deals with man.

There are other scriptures that suggest this same truth. I
think of the book of Lamentations. The writer there is in
the dungeon and he cries out that God would rescue him,
and suddenly there comes the realisation that 'It is of the
Lord's mercies that we are not consumed . . . Great is thy
faithfulness' (Lam. 3:22f). Then I think of Ephesians 2:3–5.
The Apostle Paul states that by nature we are 'children of
wrath, even as others. *But God*, who is rich in mercy, . . .
quickened us together . . . (by grace ye are saved)'. Or I can
think of the climax of Romans 8: 'Who is he that condemneth? It is Christ that died' (Rom. 8:34). Great texts in
scripture these certainly are, but to me none surpasses this
text: 'The word of the Lord came to Jonah *the second time.*'

God always comes the second time. I recall that hymn of
John Newton, I think his greatest: 'In evil long I took
delight.' There is that phrase which mentions our Lord's
'second look', when Newton cries out:

> Where shall my trembling soul be hid?
> For I the Lord have slain!
> *A second look* He gave which said:
> 'I freely all forgive.'

153

Our God is the God of the second look. He doesn't hold grudges. God came to Jonah 'a second time'.

Now Jonah had learned some things. We have seen the lessons that he learned. He did not extol God's mercy but rather dishonoured it by his disobedience. He was placed in a state of readiness – 'I will pay that that I have vowed'. And he saw that deliverance was outside himself – 'Salvation is of the Lord'. These lessons Jonah learned in the belly of the fish. Jonah also learned that God is independent of all things. God does not need to *do* anything in order to glorify Himself. Jonah found out that God can glorify Himself by doing nothing. And Jonah also knew that he might not live to tell what he had learned. God may show us things and we just have to keep those things to ourselves – that sometimes happens. Jonah saw that God may be pleased to reveal Himself without there being a precedent for such a disclosure and that God does not have to do it again. He saw that God can reveal Himself to one person and no other; to one era and no other; to one place and no other. This Jonah learned. But we saw that God sometimes in His mercy – for the sake of His church and for the sake of the world – lets that one person be an Athanasius, or an Augustine, or a Luther; and the world is never the same again. This is why the church must again cry out with Isaiah: 'Oh that thou wouldest rend the heavens and come down' (Isa. 64:1). For when God is pleased to speak to an Athanasius or a Luther, the world is never the same again.

But Jonah knew that God might not let him live to tell what he had experienced. And so, Jonah did not have all of his problems solved simply by learning these lessons. He still needed to be delivered from the fish.

I think, however, we must also see that merely being ejected from the fish would not solve all of his problems. It is one thing to be delivered; it is another thing to be called to do something. And I suspect Jonah feared that his place of usefulness was over. So I say to you again, that Jonah no doubt felt like Isaiah – 'Oh that thou wouldest rend the heavens and come down.' He felt like the leper who came to Christ – 'If thou wilt, thou canst make me clean' (Matt. 8:2), or like the centurion who said, 'Say the word and my servant shall be healed' (Matt. 8:8). It was now the question whether or not God would act further. He had acted so far, but would He do more? Would there be another chance? That was the question. And so I think of Newton's great hymn:

> In evil long I took delight,
> Unawed by shame or fear,
> Till a new object struck my sight,
> And stopped my wild career.
>
> I saw One hanging on a tree
> In agonies and blood,
> Who fixed His languid eyes on me
> As near His cross I stood.
>
> Sure never to my latest breath
> Can I forget that look;
> It seems to charge me with His death,
> Though not a word He spoke.
>
> My conscience felt and owned the guilt,
> And plunged me in despair.
> I saw my sins His blood had spilt
> And helped to nail Him there.
>
> Alas, I knew not what I did,
> And now my tears are vain,
> Where shall my trembling soul be hid?
> For I the Lord have slain.
>
> A second look He gave which said:
> 'I freely all forgive:
> This blood is for thy ransom paid;
> I died thou mayest live.'

He is the God of the second look. 'The word of the Lord came to Jonah the second time.'

Let us back up a bit. Jonah had been delivered from death. He says, 'Thou hast brought up my life from corruption, O Lord my God' (Jonah 2:6). Now if learning deep theological lessons did not serve to solve all of his problems, neither did his being vomited up by the fish entirely soothe his heart or give him complete satisfaction. For Jonah had had a taste of being used of the Lord. Do you know what it is like to be used of the Lord? There is no greater consideration than this, to think that God should use us in some way – when we discover that God could use frail servants like us. It is a great feeling to know that God really uses us.

Jonah had a taste of that. Jonah also knew that his disobedience might cause him to forfeit ever being used again. It is a painful matter when we see that we have grieved the Lord, or brought disgrace upon His name. And to one who has once been used of the Lord there is nothing more painful than this – the very thought of never being used again. This is why the Apostle Paul could say – and if Paul could say it, how much more should you and I – 'I keep my body under subjection, lest having preached to others, I myself should be a castaway' (I Cor. 9:27).

Jonah, between the end of chapter 2 and the beginning of chapter 3, lived in a state of wondering. Would God use him again? God certainly did not have to. God would have been justified in never coming back to Jonah. So I say there is nothing more painful than having had a taste of usefulness, but having the fear that God has finished with us, that we will never be used again because of our previous sins and foolish mistakes. It is the feeling of being ill-equipped, the feeling of having let everybody down – the feeling of failure. And don't forget, God is not obligated ever to come a second time.

Jonah knew this. Jonah had learned this lesson well.

But the Lord came a second time.

It should give us all great comfort to realise that the best of God's servants have made foolish mistakes, but were used again. It gives me no small comfort to realise that there have been those that have gone on before me that have failed to do as they ought to have done. Yet God did not hold a grudge. I could give you a list that would occupy an hour of those who have sinned and yet were used again. Look at

Abraham. He was willing to pass off his own wife as his sister. On another occasion he actually capitulated to Sarah's bad advice. Since he had been given the promise that God was going to bless him and multiply his seed, he was actually going to use Hagar as the one through whom the promise would come. But God came to Abraham a second time. Look at Jacob. Here was a man who wickedly deceived his father, yet look at the subsequent history of Israel. The Apostle Paul would quote the Prophet Malachi and say that God in mercy was behind the whole thing! 'Jacob have I loved, but Esau have I hated' (Rom. 9:13; Mal. 1:2–3). Look at David, whose unthinkable sin began with Bathsheba and ended with Uriah. Yet God used Bathsheba to carry on the blood-line of Messiah. What better example is there than Simon Peter, who in a cowardly moment said, 'I know not the man' (Matt. 26:74). Jesus had said, 'Peter, I know thou art going to deny me, but I have prayed for thee, that thy faith fail not; and when thou art converted, strengthen thy brethren' (Luke 22:32–34). Yet on the day of Pentecost God came to Peter a second time, and he loudly proclaimed, 'This is that which was spoken by the Prophet Joel' (Acts 2:16). Three thousand were converted. If God can use men like that, He can use me. He can use you. God doesn't hold grudges. He therefore came to Jonah the second time.

Now, there are to be seen in this story the profoundest principles that lie behind God's dealings with man. What are these principles? The first is that God is obligated to no man. Let us be clear about this. God is not obligated to any man and, insofar as Jonah is concerned, God did not even have to send the wind! But He did. He did not have to prepare the fish. But He did. He did not have to eject Jonah from that fish. But he did.

And He certainly did not have to come to Jonah the second time.

But He did.

God doesn't hold grudges against His own. This should comfort us all. But let us keep in mind this fundamental principle – that God is obligated to no man. You see, the reason for this is simple. In Jonathan Edwards' language:

'Man is God's natural enemy.' Oh, how the Christian world needs to discover this truth all over again! We as men are God's natural enemies. Does this surprise you? You see, by nature we are all that God is not. Look at the way the Apostle Paul described man in the third chapter of Romans. Here is a description of man as God's natural enemy. 'Their throat is an open sepulchre; with their tongues they have used deceit; the poison of asps is under their lips: their mouth is full of cursing and bitterness: their feet are swift to shed blood: destruction and misery are in their ways' (Rom. 3:13–16). Jesus said that men loved darkness rather than light because their deeds were evil (John 3:19). And for this reason God is obligated to no man. Yet the Christian church needs to rediscover this truth. For the average man today, when he gets a taste of religion, or if he even darkens the door of a church, gets the idea that he is doing God some kind of favour. Men today have the idea that, if they do any kind of pious act, they are doing something for God. Christendom today witnesses the shabbiest Gospel ever known. Men have the idea that they become Christians because of what they do for God. This is nonsense. The Bible says the very opposite is true, that we become Christians because of what God does for us. And when God comes in mercy, it means *He did not have to do it.* So we need to be reminded that God is obligated to no one. We are his natural enemies, and God would be just in sending the whole world to an endless hell. Some people say they cannot sleep at nights at the thought that God should send men to hell. May the truth get hold of us to make us stay awake at nights wondering how God could save *anybody*! When we realise we have rejected Him; when we live in disobedience; and when we live according to the flesh, the miracle of miracles is that God should come to us at all! God can give mercy or withhold it. He can save or He can damn. God is not obligated to any man.

There is a second principle here that underlies this great statement, that God came to Jonah 'the second time'. It is this, that God voluntarily obligated Himself to faith. This is a remarkable thing to see. God did not have to do

this. But God voluntarily obligated Himself to faith.
Consider again the story of Abraham and Isaac. We
have already dealt with it once in this series on Jonah; we
are going to look at the same story again and see something else. We find that this man Abraham (who, as you
know, was Paul's chief illustration of the doctrine of
justification by faith) was given a series of promises.
For example: 'Look now toward heaven, and count the
stars, if thou be able to number them: and he said unto
him, So shall thy seed be. And he believed in the Lord;
and he counted it to him for righteousness' (Gen. 15:5).
This became the foundation of Paul's doctrine of justification by faith. But what may be overlooked is that the Lord
not only gave such promises to Abraham but also came to
Abraham *the second time*. God's coming the 'second time'
followed Abraham's sin of haste in capitulating to Sarah's
suggestion that he go into Hagar's bed (Gen. 16:2-4). But
God came to Abraham a second time. The occasion is
when God told Abraham to sacrifice his son, Isaac. And
Abraham was ready to carry it out. But at the moment
he began to slay Isaac the voice came from heaven and
said, 'Lay not thine hand upon the lad, neither do thou any
thing unto him: for now I know that thou fearest God,
seeing thou hast not withheld thy son, thine only son, from
me' (Gen. 22:12). In Genesis 22:15 the word says that the
angel of the Lord called unto Abraham out of heaven
'the second time'. And this time it was by an oath. First
came the promise, now came the oath: 'By myself have I
sworn, saith the Lord, for because thou hast done this thing,
and hast not withheld thy son, thine only son: in blessing
I will bless thee, and in multiplying I will multiply thee'
(Gen. 22:16f). Thus we have the basis of the oath. God's
coming the second time brought the oath: when God swore
in His mercy (Cf. Heb. 6:13-18). This was the occasion
when God tied Himself to faith, when God saw the persuasion of Abraham – that Abraham was willing to sacrifice
Isaac, and yet knowing he had been given the promise that
in *Isaac* his seed would be blessed and multiplied. This
oath, this coming the second time, was God voluntarily
obligating Himself to faith. This is of great comfort to us

all. For we know that, if we believe Him, God has obligated Himself by His oath to save us.

This leads us to the third principle: God ties Himself to faith because it is He who gives the faith. Are we clear about this, Christian people? Faith is God's gift. 'Of His own will begat He us with the word of truth' (James 1:18). Faith is *seeing* that salvation is of the Lord. Faith is *seeing* that what God requires has already been accomplished outside ourselves. Jonah saw this. But does this surprise you – that faith is the gift of God? We have in America a very famous preacher who was once known as a faith healer. His expression is, 'Turn your faith loose' – a silly, nonsensical utterance. This implies that all men have faith; they only need to 'turn it loose'. But the Apostle Paul said, 'All men have not faith' (II Thes. 3:2). For by nature man is 'dead in trespasses and sins' (Eph. 2:1). Now, when a person is dead he cannot move, he cannot speak, much less can he hear. Something must take place in order for him to hear, and for this reason faith is something that God alone supplies. And so it is, we by nature could never have believed. Do you think for a moment that you believe because you are more clever? Surely not. Do you think for a moment you believe because you are better? Surely not. Faith is God's gift. Jonah had to learn this lesson all over again. Sometimes Christians must be put into the belly of the fish to be taught certain principles that are so obvious in Scripture. Jonah came to himself and the ultimate lesson that he learned is: 'Salvation is of the Lord'.

But that leads us now to a fourth principle. It is one that we tend to forget, that God accommodates us with language on our level. To put it another way: God communicates His word to us by way of accommodation. This is because of our frailty. The Lord meets us on our own level and speaks to us in a way that we, as simple people, can understand. For example, Genesis 22:12 implies that God learns something. But this was the language of accommodation. Genesis 22:12 says: 'Lay not thine hand upon the lad, neither do thou any thing unto him: for *now I know* that thou fearest God', as if He did not know until then. But this is God accommodating Abraham in this simple talk. And so it is, when we preach the Gospel, God tells us to tell people to do something that they cannot do. We are told to tell men to believe, to repent; but they cannot do it. And yet, when they *do* believe and repent their first reaction is to think it is something they themselves have done.

But God confronts men initially on their own level. It is as we grow in grace we learn the family secret. Still another way of putting it is this: God at first uses 'baby talk' with us. He talks to us in simple ways. When God said to Abraham, 'Now I know you love me', what God was really saying to Abraham was, 'Now *you* see what *I knew* – that you love me. I have let *you* see it.' But what a pity that some Christians never move beyond the baby talk, even after they have been Christians for years. Once I actually heard a man in his late sixties give this testimony – that when he was sixteen years of age he 'gave his heart to the Lord'. And he said: 'That was over fifty years ago and I have never been sorry.' Now, only a babe in Christ could talk like that. We would expect somebody who had only been converted for a year or two to say: 'I gave my heart to the Lord and I have never been sorry.' But we need to move beyond this grasp to see that God is at the bottom of conversion.

Jonah saw this. Jonah saw that God did not deliver him because of anything in himself. Thus God at first meets us on our level and later we learn the family secret: we are saved by grace. Later we learn we have been adopted; later that we were chosen from eternity. Blessed thought! But God always confronts man initially by using this language of accommodation.

We must see, then, that God always comes the second time. When did God come the first time? Well, all of us should know. We find it in the book of Genesis. God came to man in the Garden of Eden and said: 'Of every tree in the garden thou mayest freely eat: but of the tree of the knowledge of good and evil, thou shalt not eat of it: for in the day that thou eatest thereof thou shalt surely die' (Gen. 2: 16–17). After man's Fall came the promise: 'I will put enmity between thee and the woman, and between thy seed and her seed; it shall bruise thy head, and thou shalt bruise his heel' (Gen. 3:15). The Lord came the second time. And this is the way He always works. God always comes the second time. This second time could be called the ratification of His promise. It is that which makes His word effectual. As Jesus said to Peter: 'I have prayed for thee that thy faith fail not.' Or, as Jesus said to all of His disciples: 'If I go not away the Comforter will not come unto you' (John 16:7).

God always comes the second time, and the second time is effectual.

Now, applying this to ourselves, the first time God comes is simply through His Word. The first time is simply the fact that the preaching of the Gospel comes to us. Jesus described the preaching of the Gospel in Matthew 22:14 like this: 'Many are called'. For example, I am preaching to a large number at this moment. All of you are being called now and you can look back upon times when you heard the preaching of the Gospel before. You were called. But there must be the second time. 'Few are chosen.' This is when God gives hearing ears and you come to *see*. It is the break-through. Long you withstood His grace, long provoked Him to His face. Again,

> Where shall my trembling soul be hid?
> For I the Lord have slain.
> A second look He gave . . .

God always comes the second time. What if the first time you heard preaching it was also the last? What if? The chances are, you would never be here. Most of us know what it is to have God go after us. God goes to great pains to secure the response that He wants.

Now this expression 'second time' also suggests to some 'second best'. The Lord in coming the 'second time' leads some sincere souls to think that if only we had obeyed the first time we would have had the 'perfect will' of God. I don't know whether you have ever come across this idea before. I can recall as a young student in college hearing a sermon preached by some well-meaning minister. He stressed: 'Don't miss God's first best.' And I immediately began to worry when I heard it that I had already missed God's 'first best'. So, I thought, this sermon is no comfort to me. For I could think of many naughty things I had done, therefore it was too late for me to get God's 'first best'. Moreover, if I had not missed His first best then, I surely did within a few months because I did more things that I knew had disqualified me for the 'first best'. And I was long haunted with this idea that I didn't want to miss God's first best.

Christian people, God's first best was in the Garden of Eden. Now this raises the question, What if man had not sinned? This opens the way to but unprofitable speculation. The point is, ever since the Fall all things have been His second best. The best, then, is His second best. And the second best is good enough. For that is what we all have. For by nature we are enemies of God. 'All we like sheep have gone astray'; we have offended Him; we have grieved Him by a thousand falls. And the best any of us will get is second best. But the second best is good enough. Many of us can look back across the years and say, 'Well, we missed it, we missed God's will.' Or we see how we have wasted time – or have done such foolish things. I will never forget one evening walking out of my church in Fort Lauderdale, Florida. I stood behind a man who was looking at the moon and stars with tears rolling down his cheeks. I just watched him for a moment. That particular man had been converted to the Lord Jesus Christ about two months before. I walked up beside him and I said: 'George, what are you thinking about?' He said: 'I just wonder what I have been doing all these years.' He was a man of 50. He said: 'Why didn't I become a Christian sooner? I had no idea a man could be so happy. I had no idea things could look so good.' And he began to feel guilty about the wasted years. But I said: 'George, God came to you; and when He came, it was soon enough. Some are never saved.'

And that leads me to the most comforting thought of all in this connection. When God comes a second time it seems none too soon. But it is always soon enough. You may feel guilty that you wasted so much time. You may feel so depressed that you could have done such awful things. You ask: Why didn't God come sooner? As Mary put it to Jesus who came to the tomb of Lazarus: 'Lord, if thou hadst been here, my brother had not died' (John 11:32). But when He comes the second time, it is soon enough.

We may cry out: 'Oh that thou wouldst rend the heavens and come down!' 'Have mercy upon us.' 'Say the word, and we shall be healed.' And you may be saying today, 'Oh, but I have grieved Him. I have withstood His grace. I have not obeyed Him.'

> Where shall my trembling soul be hid?
> For I the Lord have slain.

But He is the God of the second look:

> A second look He gave which said:
> 'I freely all forgive . . .'

Away with the doubting! Quit murmuring about the past! Away with thinking of the wasted years! We can all think about things we have done that are so foolish. If only God had not permitted this to happen – 'If thou hadst been here, my brother had not died.'

For Jonah, the second time came none too soon. But it was soon enough. God knows when you must hear that word from beyond. God knows how much you can bear. God knows how much you can take. He is aware of all the foolish things you have done. He knows the things you have done that nobody else knows about; but you know. He knows these things and you don't like to think about them because when you do you feel worse. But He comes a second time.

You may say, 'But how can I know that He has come again to me?' I ask you: Do you see that any deliverance is outside yourself? And do you see that God is King, that He is sovereign? Do you see that His way is the right way – and that you must do things His way? Do you see this? He is coming to you now, the second time, with a second look. You who have been rebellious, disobedient. You have been in hiding. He has come again. It is none to soon, but it is soon enough. His second best is good enough. 'All things work together for good.' And 'good' is good enough: and the second time, soon enough. He comes now.

14 Jonah's Obedience

Jonah 3 : 1–4

WE ARE NOW clearly in the second half of the Book of
Jonah. In many ways this is the more interesting half. I
have long been more attracted to the second part of Jonah
than to the first. I might say that the second half of Jonah
is also more painful for us because it exposes the motives
of the human heart in even sharper focus. This may cause
us to blush, even to tremble. Now if the first half of
Jonah may be seen as being analogous to the modern
church, so is the second half. And if the first half of the
Book of Jonah is a type of the Christian life, I think we
will see that the second half shows a type of Christian that
all of us know too well – that which we see in ourselves.
While the first half of Jonah shows us how God chastens
His own and how He keeps His own, the second half of
Jonah shows how carnal men can be, even after they see
clearly what God is doing in and through them. It is an
appalling thing to think that Jonah, having seen the glory
of the Lord, could still be so carnal. We sometimes like to
think that when we have moved up a little closer to the
Lord this rids us of all our maladies. Jonah could not
have seen the Lord work more clearly or closely; it exposed his sinfulness in sharp focus.

And so, 'The word of the Lord came to Jonah the second
time'. I know of a minister who made famous a statement
which was quoted far and wide: 'No one has the right to
hear the Gospel twice till all have heard it once.' Now that
statement is more clever than it is accurate. And it is really
rather superficial. It became a slogan for a vast missionary
enterprise. I think it is far more accurate to say that most
people haven't heard the Gospel once until they have heard

it twice. Most of us would never have been converted if our destinies were determined by our response to hearing the Gospel the first time. And thank God He comes again and again. He comes the second time. This is the way God works. This is the way He always deals with men. God comes the second time. He gives us the second look. And when He comes the second time it is soon enough. God knows how to deal with His own – how to manoeuvre us and how to guide us. He knows our frame. He knows our nature. He knows our emotional make-up. He knows everything about us and He knows what it takes to secure the needed response in every man. God can do that. And God did it. The word came to Jonah the second time.

Now in this section of the book of Jonah there are some lessons for us to learn. We have already seen some lessons Jonah learned. But I speak largely now to the church; for I suspect that the church too has lessons to learn from this story as to the way in which God came to Jonah the second time. Lesson number one is: God's orders to the church remain the same. The first time that God came to Jonah He said: 'Arise, go to Nineveh ... and cry against it.' God said: 'Go.' Jonah said: 'No.' Jonah had other thoughts. Now, Jonah may have thought that by taking a holiday on a Mediterranean cruise God would forget about those orders. Jonah may have thought that if God had a little time to think about it He would change His mind. And so, Jonah said: 'No' – and he boarded a ship going to Tarshish. But God sent a wind and put fear into the mariners. God even used the casting of lots by the mariners to bring about Jonah's exposure. The only choice was to throw Jonah overboard. But God prepared the fish. Then Jonah prayed. Jonah learned some lessons. Jonah said: 'I will pay that that I have vowed, if ever I get out of this fish'. God ejected Jonah from the fish and saved his life. He came to Jonah the second time and the message was the same: 'Go to Nineveh.'

Some like to think that God outgrows His word. There is in this country and in America a theory known as 'process philosophy', or 'process theology'. The idea is this, that God grows, that God is enriched by His creation, that God learns from us, that God has made us co-creators with Him. This philosophy claims that God speaks in different ways at different times, even if it comes to repudiating what He may have done once before. And so this philosophy would suggest that what God was doing in the sixteenth century is one thing – when He was using Calvin and Luther; but today God is doing other things. Today it may be ecology, it may be dealing with racial issues or speaking mainly on social issues. The idea then is that God is not interested in the same things He was interested in at a previous time. This philosophy posits that God is growing and we grow with Him and He grows with us: thus God today is saying different things than before. Some 'process' thinkers even claim that God is behind the feminist movement today, or that He is behind revolutionary activities in the world.

Now, at first glance this is a very clever notion. It suggests, you see, that there are no absolutes, that there are no eternal verities by which the church is to be guided. The fact is that theology today, and I speak largely of contemporary theology, has moved so far from the simplicity of the New Testament that it is absurd; it is truly ridiculous. There is a saying that theology is concocted in Germany, corrupted in America, and corrected in Britain. But I have looked at some of the corrections – and they look awfully like the corruptions in America! The corruptions in fact that began with the concoctions – the idea of trying to be vogue, to be clever, to be 'relevant'. And so, the modern church has fallen victim in many places to this idea of 'process' thought. The modern church today, wrapped up in the Ecumenical Movement, is saying, 'We will have unity at any cost' – even at the expense of truth. Consequently the modern church is largely concerned with philosophy and reason. The modern church is preoccupied with earthly concerns – food, shelter and clothing, and dealing with the hunger of the world, the poor. These, some say, are the issues that matter, and they sometimes even scoff at preaching aimed at making the calling and election of men sure.

And so the modern church is involved in everything, it seems, but the Great Commission of the New Testament.

Once we hold that it is crucial to be 'contemporary', to be vogue, to be relevant at the expense of the rugged truth of the Gospel, then our days are finished! God is sure to overthrow us and begin anew with a people, perhaps, we never dreamed of. The interesting thing is that when you examine church history you notice that when God comes in great power, there is always the reappearance of the cherished truths He used before. Look at the highwater marks in church history: the times of Athanasius, Augustine, Luther, Calvin, Whitefield, Edwards, Spurgeon – and you see a main-stream of thought. And when God comes in great power, although He may come in a slightly different way each time, there is this recognisable line, this common denominator that brings us back to the very simplicity of the Gospel. And so, if God comes to our generation we may be sure that He will bring us back to the same message.

The lesson to be learned, then, is that the orders which God gives to the church remain the same.

Very well then, I think there is also a lesson to be learned in the so-called reformed movement on both sides of the Atlantic. We need to learn the lesson that when God said 'Go', He meant it. Jonah found out that God meant it. 'Go to Nineveh that great city.' Jonah had other thoughts. And now, after all Jonah had been through, the Lord came to him the second time with the same message: 'Go'. And I say there is a lesson for us who are a part of this reformed movement. I believe that many of us have grieved the Holy Spirit by not going, by not doing those things He has plainly told us to do. We have not taken seriously, for example, the Great Commission: 'Go into all the world' – that includes Nineveh – 'and preach the Gospel to every creature' (Mark 16:15). And so many of us have been hiding behind the doctrine of predestination in order to justify our lack of zeal. We have said, 'God has His elect; His elect will be saved.' We continue holding to this while God uses everybody else to save His elect but us! While we are going our way, justifying ourselves for our orthodoxy and toeing the line on some of these biblical truths, God has been using the Pentecostals, the Pelagians, Billy

Graham and the Arminians – while we continue to hold to 'the faith' and criticise everybody else's methods.

You see, God meant it when He said 'Go'; and He may set us aside – if He hasn't done it already – using others to save His elect. I say, it ought to be us who are used! We who claim to be orthodox ought to be the ones being used. But we are not being used. If the Lord sent a William Carey to us today most of us would reject him as a fanatic and would identify with that moderator in that Association who hammered with his gavel and said: 'Sit down, young man, sit down. When God is ready to save the heathen, He will do it without your aid or mine.' We need to re-discover for ourselves that God meant it when He said 'Go'. But it is embarrassing for many of us to see that God can use a crooked stick to draw a straight line; He has used many to save His elect whose methods we can pick to pieces. But God has used them and we should be thankful that God can do that. I repeat, if we are the ones holding to the truth, if that is true, then it ought to be us whom God is using. The Lord has said 'Go'. We have said, 'No', and justified it. There is a lesson for us here. God takes the Great Commission seriously. And I will tell you something else: He blesses those who do. Forgive me if I come back to the subject of tithing again. I use it only as an illustration. But I made the point a few weeks ago that you can't outgive the Lord and God blesses those who honour Him. And I referred to the Southern Baptist Convention which now has over 3,000 missionaries all over the world because the people tithe. God has also blessed that movement, because there is a denomination that took seriously this Great Commission. You will possibly question the theology of some of their ministers, but God has used them. God is serious about this matter of 'going'. I referred to a certain minister a while ago and I made light of his famous statement, but do you know that God has blessed that very enterprise about which I was talking? God has blessed it. And so, *we who go* will be blessed. How much better if, indeed, when we go, we are equipped with the message, the truth. It ought to be us, then. There is this lesson to be learned.

The second thing to be seen is this. Not only are God's

orders the same – 'Go to Nineveh' – but so is the *method: preaching.* 'And the word of the Lord came unto Jonah the second time, saying, Arise, go unto Nineveh, that great city, and *preach* unto it . . .' We might wish there was another way God would save men. We might wish He worked through a different method. We might wish that He had chosen to save men by wisdom, by reason, by signs, by proofs, by demonstrations, by gimmicks, by cleverness, by organisation, by flashy personalities, salesmanship, entertainment, high-level conferences. We might wish God would use things like this. I Corinthians 1:21 seems to suggest that God considered other options. Paul says that 'in the wisdom of God the world by wisdom knew not God'. That was an option. God might have taken that route. But in the wisdom of God the world by wisdom knew *not* God. Therefore God has decreed that men are to be saved by preaching. Sometimes it is foolish preaching. This I grant. But that is not what He really wants. He works through the foolishness *of* preaching. But God *can* even use foolish preaching. We who pride ourselves on our orthodoxy do not like to think that God would do that. But He does. In any case, the method is the same. And if ever God visits us again He will do it through the phenomenon of preaching. This is painful for us. We may like to think there could be another way.

But I think I hear someone saying to himself, 'Well, I am glad to hear what you are saying, because I like good preaching. I will just come and hear preaching.' But I am going to have to disappoint you. Preaching is something *you* are to do. Preaching is every Christian's business. I would not want to embarrass you, but I want to ask you a question. Have you led a soul to Jesus Christ in the past six months? Have you led a soul to Jesus Christ in the past year? Have you led a soul to Jesus Christ in the past five years? I think I can hear somebody say, 'I witness with my life.' God *could* have sent Jonah to Nineveh and told him to 'walk godly' before them all. But He said 'Go to Nineveh and preach'. You are to give the *word*. When you say, 'I witness by my life', I grant that God can use that as a testimony. But when you say that, I fear it is an excuse. You ought to be so equipped that you are able to talk to anybody. You

171

ought to know the Gospel so well that you may share it with anybody you meet – whether you sit beside him on a bus, or in the Underground, or somebody you know that lives across the street from you. You do not have to be an orator. You don't have to be articulate. You don't need a university degree.

One of the things that has amazed my family and me since we have been in England is how the British can get so excited about football. I have never seen anything like it in my life! If it were not for that, I might say that all of those things I have heard concerning the 'reserve' and 'conservatism' of the British would be true. It just so happens we lived for three years in Oxford about six blocks from the football stadium. That myth about 'British reserve' needs to be demythologised! Don't tell me that it is not in you people to get excited and noisy about something. May God hasten the moment when you can get excited about Jesus, and what He has done. Learn to tell it in your own way. God is serious about this matter of going to preach the Gospel to every creature. Well then, there is the lesson. The method is the same. People are not going to be saved *until they are told*. 'How can they hear without a preacher?' (Rom. 10:14).

The next lesson for us to see is that God only owns one kind of preaching: and that is, the preaching that He has given. 'Go to Nineveh, that great city, and preach unto it *the preaching that I bid thee.*' You see, we are not given a choice of what to preach. I can tell you candidly, I do not have a choice what I am going to preach from week to week. Sometimes I tremble when I think what God has told me to say to you. But I have got to say it. The pulpit is not a private platform for a person to propagate his peculiar views. The only kind of preaching that God owns is *that which He gives*. Thus the message to Jonah the second time was: 'Go to Nineveh, preach the preaching that I bid thee.' God is only going to own His own preaching. The modern church has occupied itself with its own concerns. So many of us have been intimidated by the spirit of the age. We seem to be afraid to let some sophisticated person know that we actually believe the Bible. We are often afraid to admit to some intelligent man, 'Yes, I believe in the simplicity of the Gospel. I even believe the Book of Genesis.' It seems to me that we are sometimes intimidated because there are those who are saying that the Gospel, the Bible, is for a pre-scientific age, a pre-Freudian age, a pre-*Formgeschichte* age, but now the Bible is irrelevant, it is 'all past'. We have wanted to be respectable, to be vogue, to be relevant, to be clever, to be contemporary.

But I suspect that God has the modern church in the belly of a fish. He is trying to show us things. May God help us to see what these things are that He is showing us. Look at the situation! We might as well talk about it – small crowds, very few converts, little money to do things with. Low morale. There is always someone who says, 'Crowds are not everything.' We always say that when we are 'down'. But it was important on the day of Pentecost; Luke told us 3,000 were converted. If God ever saved 3,000 nowadays we would be telling it! Small crowds are a sign that God is *not* blessing, let us face it. Little money to do things with, that is a sign God is *not* blessing, and nearly every church I know of in this country has that problem. There is something wrong. We can justify ourselves if we want to but God help us to see we have been chastened! Oh, that God will come to us a second time!

But the word of the Lord came to Jonah a second time; and he obeyed. 'Jonah arose and went to Nineveh according to the word of the Lord.' Someone has put it like this: 'Some people are made *by* the times. Some people are made *for* the times.' I think a better statement would be, 'Most people are made *by* the times, few, very few, are made *for* the times.' But all God's people are made *for* the times! The problem is that we as a church have been swallowed up by the spirit of the age. We are not setting any trend, we *follow* the trend. The church is to be the salt of the earth. The church is to be the light of the world. But we are not seasoning government. We are not seasoning society. We are not giving a clear light to the world. We are generally going along with the trend of the times. As a church, we give every evidence that we have been made *by* the times. The church by God's authority deserves the right to counsel men in government. Members of Parliament should bow before the church and say, 'What do we do now?' You can read history and know that in this country it was once that way. God has used the church and His prophets to influence Parliament. But who today would ask the church for any advice? Can you blame government, can you blame anybody? We are just following trends.

Jonah was a man *for* the times. He was made for the times. God selected him to do a work nobody else could do, and God has something for you to do that nobody else can do. If you are His child He will help you to do it. You may be miserable, however, until you have learned the lesson well. He has a way of making you obey. Haven't we seen that by now? There is something for you to do that nobody else can do. You do not need to be afraid when God says, 'Go'.

We have sometimes made this subject of obedience far more difficult than it is. I do not preach on Jonah's obedience today to make you feel guilty. Not at all. Obedience is not an act of the will whereby we prove to ourselves and to God that we can do it. No. Obedience is *by faith*, and faith is the persuasion of what His will is. And when God gives the persuasion, what we do is the most natural thing we ever did! It is like when a person is converted to the Lord Jesus Christ. When he is actually converted by God it is the easiest thing he ever did. Before his heart was softened, before his heart was moulded, he rejected the Gospel, resisted. But when the day of salvation came it was the easiest thing he ever did to believe on Christ. And God does it this way. God gives the faith, the persuasion, by which we do His will and we do it naturally.

To put it another way, God does not promote us to the level of our incompetence. Now, perhaps you know that I am referring to a best-selling book in America some years ago. It spoke of the 'Peter principle'. The idea is that every man is promoted to the level of his incompetence. It is a very clever book. The author put forward the thesis that many people today have jobs they ought not to have; they should have kept their previous position; many people you meet have jobs they are not able to do. And so you have people in management, in government, in business, who were determined to have a certain job and got it, but now are not doing things very efficiently. They should have just stayed where they were. There is one thing worse than no ambition, and that is too much ambition. Maybe you are dying for that promotion, or to get ahead.

In any case, when it comes to the things God has asked us to do, He does not ask us to be what we are not. He does not ask us to do things we can't do. In the words of John, 'His commandments are not grievous' (I John 5:3). Whatever God asks us to do He gives us the grace to do. Look at the very message of the Gospel itself. We are told that we must be perfect to get to heaven. No unclean thing shall enter therein. But God provided a Substitute; we are not saved by our righteousness but are judged by His. And for everything that God asks us to do there is the supplying grace to do it. And He has a way of making His call the easiest thing we ever did.

Jonah learned this. I suspect his journey to Nineveh was the happiest journey he ever made in his life. There is something happier than being on a Mediterranean cruise; that is going to Nineveh in the will of the Lord. Have you been running? Have you been suppressing what the Holy Spirit has made clear He wants you to do? The happiest pillow on which you may rest your head is the knowledge of God's will. I cannot imagine a more miserable situation than consciously to be out of God's will.

Jonah went. I say it was the happiest journey he ever made. And God today says to us the second time, 'Go'. 'Go.'

There is not much with which I agree in the writings of Harry Emerson Fosdick. But I love the title of one of his books, *It's a Great Time to be Alive*. We are often said to be in a 'post-Christian era', but the time has never been riper to reach the masses for the Gospel. There was once a day when men could say they could go to foreign lands and spread the Word with success because the heathen had not heard it, and they received it. I know the situation is different here because in our own land men are hardened. But do you know something? There is a sense in which the

175

people you meet every day here in Britain have not heard the Word. It is totally new to them.

It's a great time to be alive.

God has told us we are not made by the times but for the times. Jonah was obedient. Are we? Jonah arose and went. Will we?

15 Jonah's Message

Jonah 3:4

AND JONAH BEGAN to enter into the city a day's journey, and he cried, and said, 'Yet forty days, and Nineveh shall be overthrown.' We have been following Jonah for quite a while. We have seen his initial disobedience; his confirming himself in that disobedience; the way in which God went after him by sending the storm and the wind, even controlling the mariners' casting of lots, which exposed Jonah. We saw the solution; Jonah had to be thrown overboard. And then we found Jonah praying as he had never prayed in his life, in the belly of a fish. We have also seen that God came back to Jonah the 'second time'. The orders from heaven were the same: 'Go to Nineveh, that great city, and preach unto it the preaching that I bid thee.' Well, we have indeed become well acquainted with Jonah.

But I think the book of Jonah tells us more about God than Jonah. This book is unexcelled in all holy writ in giving us a clear and composite portrait of the God of the Bible. This we find in the book of Jonah. We see God in His anger, God in His tenderness. We have seen the God who hides Himself. We have seen the God who shows His face. We have seen the God who controls nature; the God who answers prayer; the God who uses evil in such a way that we are tempted to justify it – as in the case of the mariners' conversion. And we have seen how God singles out His own and deals with His own as though there were no-one else in the world. We have also seen how God gets His way and goes to great pains to accomplish His purpose. Jonah won the battle by getting on the ship to Tarshish. But God won the war.

Thus Jonah now is doing what God first told him to do.

God must have been very earnest about this. One of the most wonderful things to me is to see how much God really cared, that God was so earnest in getting this message to Nineveh and that He went to such pains to make sure Nineveh heard the message. Thus we see the trouble God went through to accomplish this. It also gives us a hint as to how jealous God is for His prophets, and how jealous God is for the message He wants told. And consequently God invests much in His prophets: He prepares them; He teaches them; He chastens them; He refines them.

You see, prophets are God's sole vehicles for communicating His word. This is why we have those words: 'Touch not mine anointed and do my prophets no harm' (Psa. 105:15). For when people harm God's prophets they do a very dangerous thing. For one thing, God has invested too much in His prophets and He will not let men get away with touching His anointed ones. When anyone harms a prophet of God it can back-fire in one of two ways. It may be that the person who harms God's prophet will soon be struck down. I could stand here and talk for a good while about cases of certain men and women who have hurt God's men and how unthinkable consequences came to them. But that is not always the way it happens. Sometimes when people harm God's prophets the consequence is a general famine of the word of the Lord. And that is the greatest judgment of all. I cannot help but wonder if this has happened in the United Kingdom. I have begun to get acquainted with some of the ministers of the Gospel over here and have understood their hurt, their woes and how they have been mistreated. And then I look around. I look at the condition of the church, of the nation. It can be partly traced to the way men have treated God's messengers. Thus one of the wisest things men can do is to respect God's prophets. 'How beautiful are the feet of them who bring the gospel of peace and preach glad tidings' (Rom. 10:15). And so it is: 'Them that honour me, I will honour' (I Sam. 2:30). And this may be done by honouring God's prophets. To summarise: God has invested much in His prophets. God is jealous for his word, for His prophets. And so He has given all of this attention to Jonah to deliver one message.

One message. We should be particularly interested in Jonah's message. After all, when God went to such pains to see that it was delivered, one should eagerly want to see what the message is. We have heard so much about this which God was wanting to get over to Nineveh – surely it must be some message! Do you know what it is to hear a lot about something, and then the moment comes when you see it, and you say, 'Oh, is that it?' I remember when my wife and I were in Paris a couple of years ago. We insisted that my son and daughter see the Mona Lisa. I never will forget waiting in the queue for an hour. T.R. said: 'This must be something to see.' And we waited and waited and finally came the moment. I put my arm around the shoulder of T.R., who was then eight, and said, 'Son, look at it. Some day you will say to your friends back in America, "I saw it." ' I said, 'This is it, this is it.' He said: 'That is the ugliest woman I ever saw in my life.' 'But, Son, that is the Mona Lisa.' 'Dad, I'm hungry. Let's go get a hamburger in MacDonald's.'

So we come to the message itself. God went to such pains. What kind of preaching would this be? Do we look for a Whitefield? Do we look for a Spurgeon? Do we look for another Chrysostom? The message is summarised in eight words: 'Yet forty days and Nineveh shall be overthrown.' That is it.

God is jealous for His word, however brief, however simple. And today many reject the Gospel because it is so simple. Brilliant men say it is too simple – the idea that God became man; was born of a virgin; died on a cross; and that we are saved by His substitutionary death. Such simplicity! The idea of a heaven, of a hell – such simplicity! But God is jealous for His word, however simple, however brief, however clear to the simplest mind. Thus we come to the point in time when the message that God wanted brought to Nineveh is made known. 'Yet forty days and Nineveh shall be overthrown.' But these eight words to the people of Nineveh were of immense importance to the most high God. And we had better learn a lesson from this, that God is serious about His word – and we must not be

179

ashamed to preach it in its utter simplicity. For this word is true. It shall not be broken.

Now let us examine this text – Jonah 3:4: 'And Jonah began to enter into the city a day's journey, and he cried, and said, Yet forty days and Nineveh shall be overthrown.' We find contained here the mark of a true prophet. Many people often want to know how to tell the difference between a true prophet and a false prophet. There were opinions circulating in the early church concerning how to tell the difference, for prophets came and went. The church needed some sign, some clue.

We can find right here what is the mark of a true prophet. Five marks I will give you. The first is, God's prophet is an ordinary man. You may be disappointed to learn that. There is nothing extraordinary about the man God uses. God uses ordinary men. Most of us stumble at this. We like to think that if a man is going to be used by God Almighty he must be an extraordinary human being, almost a semi-divine person. And many people need to know, or think they do, that God's ministers are flawless and perfect; but when they find out that they are mere ordinary men, will have little to do with them. This is why Jesus said, 'No prophet is without honour, save in his own country' (Matt. 13:57), because in Nazareth they said, 'Oh, is this Joseph's son? We know him' (John 6:42). By nature people need to feel there is something mysterious about a prophet of God. You may remember what Paul and Barnabas had to say to the people. 'We are men of like passions with you' (Acts 14:15). The people thought they were gods. And when James was motivating Christians to pray he reminded us that Elijah was a man subject to like passions as we are (James 5:17). So by now we know, don't we, that Jonah was an ordinary man. We know Jonah well. We understand him. We should have no illusion about him, no wild fanciful dream or silly projection that makes him quasi-divine. We have seen Jonah, we have seen him in the wrong; we have seen him laid open. And yet God could use Jonah. I do not know of anything more encouraging than this. When I think that God can use Jonah it strengthens me to know He can use me. And I know if God can use me,

He can use anybody. The first mark of a true prophet, then, is that he is an ordinary man.

Second, he is an obedient man. Now, not that Jonah had always been. We remember the original message – 'Go to Nineveh'. Jonah rose up to flee from the presence of the Lord. But *now* Jonah is an obedient man. The Lord came to him a second time and said, 'Go to Nineveh'. And he arose and went according to the word of the Lord. Now while it is folly to think God uses extraordinary men, not ordinary men, it is equally foolish to think He will consistently use rebellious men to deliver His word. Let us see both sides of the coin. God uses ordinary men. He also uses obedient men, and Jonah obeyed. We saw the details of this in a previous sermon.

A third characteristic of a true prophet is that he is a man who does not speak for himself. The word he gives is not his own. The prophet is like an ambassador, who simply delivers the message; he is the representative. Furthermore, he does not take it personally when his message is rejected. Nor does he take it personally if his message is accepted. Thus a true prophet is a man who does not speak for himself. This is why Paul could say to the Ephesians, 'We wrestle not against flesh and blood but against principalities, against powers' (Eph. 6:12). Paul knew, when he had opposition, not to take it personally. He also knew when there was hostility toward him, that the people were really angry with God. The mature prophet is one who has learned not to take it personally when he has opposition. He knows who men are really angry with. A true prophet, then, is one who does not speak for himself.

Fourth, a true prophet is a man who recognises that his true role is completely out of his own hands. His calling, in the first place, is from beyond. His message is from beyond. Now, I grant you that Jonah must have felt like a fool, walking into Nineveh with this message. But he would have taken great comfort from Paul's words: 'We are fools for Christ's sake' (I Cor. 4:10). And many times we feel that we are being so irrelevant, that we are doing things the world laughs at. But, as servants of God, we must see that the role we have to play is out of our hands. And so, success

181

or failure will not be ultimately charged to us. When the true Gospel is preached to men as they are it will save some and condemn others, but it will accomplish God's purpose.

Finally, a true prophet is impartial in his administering the word. He becomes like God, who is no respecter of persons. He is one who cannot be bribed to change his message, as was Balaam, 'who loved the wages of unrighteousness' (II Pet. 2:15). Jonah could not be bought. I don't believe that the Mayor of Nineveh gave him the key to the city, or met him on the outskirts of the town, saying: 'Now, go easy on us; we have people of different backgrounds here. There are some who are this way and some who are that – and some with certain psychological problems; so just tone it down a bit.' The true prophet is impartial in his administering the word of the Lord. This is why Paul said: 'If I yet pleased men, I should not be the servant of Christ' (Gal. 1:10).

Well then, Jonah began to enter the city a day's journey. One interesting thing about it is that he did not procrastinate. He knew what he had to do. It is so easy for us to say, 'I know what my duty is. I am going to get around to doing it.' How many of you have said, 'I am going to start reading my Bible'? How many of you have actually begun to get up fifteen minutes earlier in order to have more time in prayer? You keep saying, 'I am going to do that'. How many of you, when I preached on tithing, said, 'Well, I know eventually I ought to get around to doing that.' Why wait when it is so obvious what the word of the Lord says? How many of you have said: 'I am going to get around to inviting my friends to hear the Gospel'? Why wait?

We are dealing with a man now who did not procrastinate. Nineveh was a city, a province of three days' journey. But Jonah began to enter the city a *day's* journey and cried. He did not wait until he understood the whole town. He was not there as a tourist. He was not sight-seeing Nineveh. He was not there to survey the whole province and to get to know the people, to know what were their needs. He had a message. There was no use waiting. He did not have to find out who was the right one to know. He preached it because the message was from God. Here was a man who learned his experience in the belly of the fish and he was not playing games now. He was like Noah, who 'moved with fear, prepared an ark to the saving of his house' (Heb. 11:7). He knew that God meant to have the message delivered. He wasted no time. He trembled because he spoke for the most high God.

Perhaps the saddest commentary on the Christian ministry today on both sides of the Atlantic is the utter absence of the sense of urgency in the message. Jonah did not procrastinate. But that is not all. He *cried*. He began to enter into the city a day's journey *and he cried*! Now this was not anything Jonah had recently learned. He had learned to cry in the belly of the fish. 'Then Jonah prayed unto the Lord his God out of the fish's belly, and said, *I cried* by reason of mine affliction unto the Lord, and he heard me; out of the belly of hell *cried* I, and thou heardest my voice' (Jonah 2:1–2). Now Jonah transferred that desperation he felt in the belly of the fish to the people he confronted. He learned to cry when he was alone; He now brought it out into the open with the same urgency, with the same fervour, the same sense of desperation. Hence anybody could see that Jonah was authentic, that he was no phoney. We tell what we are by what we do when we are alone. When Jonah was in the belly of the fish he cried. And when he came to Nineveh he was the same person publicly. It is like when Jesus said: 'When you pray in secret the Father will reward you openly' (Matt. 6:6). Jonah was a transparent man; anybody could see he was not a phoney.

Jonah came into Nineveh with *one message*. He was not ashamed of that message. The reason is that he was persuaded of it. Men are ashamed of things when they are not persuaded. And the reason that there is little preaching today on God's wrath and judgment and eternal hell is this: the average minister is ashamed to preach it. Some are ashamed to admit they *do* believe in eternal hell, some that they do not. We are ashamed only when we are not persuaded. And what is missing in the modern church is this inner testimony of the Spirit that the Bible is the Word of God. When the world once again sees that the church is *not ashamed*, then the world *will be awakened*. Our problem is, we do not believe the simple statements of God's Word. Jesus is the author of the doctrine of hell.

But what are the marks of a divine message? The marks of a divine message, first of all, will always reflect the true character of God. Do you want to know whether a man has a message from God? The first thing to look for is whether that message transparently reflects the character of the God of the Bible. We are told that the God of the Bible is a God of wrath, justice, holiness. We are also told that the God of the Bible is love, mercy, compassion, pity. We may know whether a man delivers a divine message by whether it reflects the true character of God.

Second, a divine message will always be clear and definite. Any child could understand Jonah's message: 'Yet forty days and Nineveh shall be overthrown.' You do not have to have finished 'O' levels or High School to understand that. Any child can understand that message. A divine message is always clear and definite, lucid and unambiguous. All can understand it. One cannot help comparing the simple Gospel with most contemporary theology. If you turn to most theologians of the twentieth century you may not get past the first page. And then, after you think you understand them, you probably don't. You can read through these men for ever and ever and still debate what they really mean! Why is it that theologians today have to be so mysterious and vague? The divine message is always definite.

The third mark of a divine message is that it calls attention to the message, not the messenger. Jonah did not call attention to himself. He made men see *God*. Furthermore, the chief function of the Holy Spirit is to point men to *Christ*. This is why the Holy Spirit is the only perfect preacher. He is the only One who never calls attention to Himself. And God's prophet is not mastered by his cleverness or his witty sayings but by the One whom he represents. He is mastered by the *truth*.

The fourth mark of a divine message is that it is authoritative; not because it is learned but because it so obviously comes from *beyond*. One problem men in the world have today is that they don't really believe the church is speaking for God. The consequence is that the world outside is unimpressed; we have no authority. We have cowered to the times, we have capitulated to the trend of the age, even to the secular spirit of the day; and yet we wonder why the men of the world will not come inside the church. Can you blame them? We have no note of authority. And it seems we have spent our time trying to be learned and clever and 'relevant'. But a divine message is one that obviously has its origin beyond what you see; it is undeniably from heaven and that is what makes it authoritative; not because of any charisma in the speaker, not because he is learned or even 'orthodox', but because it is from God and all men see it.

Finally, the divine message can be recognised as such because it is given without alternatives. The divine message is not a pragmatic presentation of a set of options, as if one can take one's choice on what is true. It shuts men up to one option. This is why Peter could say to the Sadducees: 'There is no other name given among men whereby we must be saved' (Acts 4:12). We are weak Christians indeed when we do not know how to answer somebody who asks: 'Will the Buddhist be saved if he is sincere?' The divine message is, there is one way, there is no option! Thus Jonah goes marching into Nineveh: 'Yet forty days and Nineveh shall be overthrown.' Jonah not only spoke for God and not for himself but his message was clearly from beyond. It gave no alternative. He did not call attention to himself.

In fact, it is very interesting to look at Jonah 3:5, where we read these words: 'So the people of Nineveh *believed God*.' It might have said that they believed *Jonah*. But no. It had not occurred to them that it was Jonah's philosophy, that it was his theory. They believed God.

Yet I can hear someone say: 'But wait a minute. You said that God is not only just, that He is not only righteous, that He is not only holy, that He is not only a God of wrath, but you said that He is a God of mercy and love. Where do you find that in these words? "Yet forty days and Nineveh shall be overthrown." Where is the love of God there? Where do you find mercy in words like that?'

I answer: That is the wonderful thing about this message. It is full, absolutely bubbling over with God's love and mercy. Why? *God never talks like that when there is no hope.* Whenever God gives a warning in this life, that is the best sign of all! He is not mocked. In Romans 1 we do not find that there was a warning; God just 'gave them up'. He just 'gave them over to a reprobate mind.' It just *happened.* And there is no hint at all that God ever went into Sodom and Gomorrah and foretold what was about to happen. There was no warning – God rained fire and brimstone upon Sodom and Gomorrah. And, I remind you, in hell there is no warning at all. Men in hell are not told what is going to happen. That is the end.

Why do you think God went to such pains to give His message to Nineveh? The very warning presupposes hope. The very fact that God should send a prophet and talk like that meant there was hope. When God's anger is visible in the world it is a happy sign. And so, the sign of mercy, as I have been saying, is when God said, 'Their wickedness is come up before me'. 'Go to Nineveh, their wickedness is come up before me.' That is the greatest thing that can ever happen, when the wickedness of a nation is discovered by God. The problem is, God may pass us by, God may give us up. It was a sign of mercy when God took note of Nineveh's wickedness. The way we had better spend our time in our prayer meetings or when we are up before dawn or whenever we pray, is in asking that God will discover the sin of our country. For if He discovers it – thank God! It means He is going to deal with us now and not abandon us. There is no warning in hell. Pray for the warning in the here and now! What tenderness, what mercy, what love that God should do this.

But there are those who say the church should avoid the world. Others say the church should not get involved in contemporary issues. Nonsense. We are to invade the world. We are the salt of the earth. We should be the ones setting the pace. We are the ones made for the times. Do you think Parliament or Congress will by nature come up with a solution? Never. Solutions come by *grace.* The church must point the way. Then the world will be awakened and all flesh shall see it together. We are charged to go into the world. We are charged to confront men. God help us not to run but to see the heathen around us and pray that in mercy God will discover and uncover our wickedness, that He will raise us all up wherever we find ourselves – in our jobs, in church, in our neighbourhood, to have that word that has a note of authority – a word from beyond.

16 Nineveh's Repentance

Jonah 3 : 5–8

WE HAVE SEEN the pains that God went to in order to make Jonah obedient. God sent the wind, prepared the fish, then came to Jonah the 'second time'. Thus we can readily see how much trouble God went to in order to accomplish Jonah's obedience. This is an amazing thing when you stop and think about it, that God should invest such time in and give such attention to one man. But God loves each of us as if there were nobody else to love. God gave Jonah this great attention.

But I think we need also to see that when God goes to such pains with a man, it is a twofold sign: not merely of His singular love but because there is a deeper motive. God does this for us because there is a great work for us to do. I hope that by now you have learned this lesson, that God's chastening is not His way of 'getting even'. God does not chasten us merely because He wants us to compensate for our lack of obedience; it is not 'getting even'. God 'got even' at the Cross: 'He hath not dealt with us after our iniquity.' 'As far as the east is from the west' – that is 'how far our transgressions are removed from us'. Only Christ can satisfy God's justice, so let us never for one moment think that our disobedience is punished so that we are simply to be objects of God's chastening for its own sake. Instead, we must see God's chastening as preparation for a future task. So God's chastening is His hint that there is something more for us to do.

In fact, the circumstances of the chastening indicate the magnitude of the work that is there for us to do. God does not chasten us in proportion to our sin but He chastens us in proportion to the work that we have to do. Thus if you have been through deep waters, or if you *are* in deep waters – if you are going through the fire at this moment – do not take it as a sign that God is mad at you; see it rather as His hint that there is something great ahead. God got even at the Cross. He is not trying to get even with you because of what He puts you through. Instead, it is His way of letting you know there is something around the corner for you to do. And so I say to you that if God's chastening has been extraordinary, then there is an extraordinary path ahead. It should be the ground of great comfort. William Cowper put it:

> His purposes will ripen fast,
> Unfolding every hour;
> The bud may have a bitter taste,
> But sweet will be the flower.

Well then, we have seen the extraordinary circumstances of Jonah's chastening. And now we come to see this task for which Jonah had been prepared. I remind you again that this is not the first time God used Jonah. You can read about it in II Kings 14:25, when the Lord dealt with Jeroboam and a prophecy was fulfilled that Jonah had given. Jonah knew what it was to be used of the Lord. Many times we can look to the past and recall when God has used us; and there is a tendency sometimes to live in the past, and say, 'Well, I know when God *once* used me.' And you may think that was the end. But if you are being chastened now it means God is *not* finished with you. God has something more for you to do and, in the case of Jonah, his greatest work was just ahead. And so I repeat, chastening ought to be the ground of the greatest kind of encouragement. It is a clear hint that God is not finished with you.

At this point we pick up our Lord's own commentary on the Book of Jonah. Now, whenever our Lord Jesus refers to something in the Old Testament this should cause us to take particular note. Jesus did not refer to the Old Testament in its every point, so when He does, we ought to take particular heed. And He refers to Jonah, and it is interesting that to Jesus the extraordinary thing about Jonah was not merely that he was swallowed up by a great fish. To our Lord the real thrust in the message of the Book of Jonah is in this section we are studying right now. He said that Jonah was a 'sign' to Nineveh (Matt. 16:4). And it is in this way that Jesus Himself was to be a sign. I want us to examine this because our Lord referred to an evil generation, so called because that generation sought after a sign.

Now this should give us a strong hint that God wants us to be careful what signs to look for. There are signs and there are *signs*. And many Christians need 'signs', they think, to prove to themselves that they are in a state of grace. Well, that is to align yourself with the evil generation that looks for a sign. But God's sign is always the same: the preaching of the Gospel – the message of Christ and Him crucified (I Cor. 2:2). We need no other sign but the Lord Jesus Christ as He is held up in *preaching*. And so it is to this very day, there are unregenerate men who say, 'I will believe if I have a sign. Give me a miracle, or give me intellectual proof. Give me the evidence that I may see with my own eyes – the tangible, the logical, the proof.' And to such men our Lord said, 'There shall be no sign given except the sign of Jonah the Prophet.' And so, 'The Jews require a sign, the Greeks seek after wisdom' (I Cor. 1:22). The only sign that God gives is preaching. This was the important thing to our Lord about the book of Jonah. And God came to Jonah the second time: 'Preach the preaching that I bid thee.' Jonah went to preach. And as Jonah was a sign to Nineveh, so is the Son of Man to this generation. This is why the Apostle Paul said that 'in the wisdom of God the world by wisdom knew not God'. 'It pleased God by the foolishness of preaching to save them that believe' (I Cor. 1:21).

So Jonah, who had undergone that experience of being swallowed up by a great fish and then ejected on dry land, was now given the commission again. 'Go to Nineveh and preach the preaching that I bid thee.' He entered the city crying 'Yet forty days and Nineveh shall be overthrown.'

We find now the moment that Jonah was being prepared for. Jonah had at last found his niche. It was not in being disobedient; it was in doing the will of the Lord. Could it be that there is somebody here still struggling with this problem? God has said one thing, you are doing another? God has made it clear what is His will because He has shown you in His Word. But you instead have been like Jonah. God said, 'Go'. Jonah said, 'No'. And you too are going on and on? But I can tell you this: it will only get worse. Go on and on in your rebellion and in your disobedience. Things will get worse. For God is determined that His people conform to His revealed will.

And so now we see the moment Jonah was being prepared for. God did not misfire. He did not miscalculate. There was one man He needed for this task. It was Jonah. God stayed with Jonah until Jonah was obedient. And there is a task for *you* that nobody else can perform. God wants you to do it. He will equip you. He will enable you to do it. He will not ask you to impute to yourself more faith or wisdom or knowledge or grace or gifts than is there. He will give you the grace that is equal to the task. 'As thy days so shall thy strength be.' You may be afraid at first, and you may rebel. And you, like Jonah, may be swallowed up by a great fish. But God will stay with you. He is serious about the command He gives. He is jealous for His own word. Finally, Jonah obeyed and we find him going about the task. 'Forty days and Nineveh shall be overthrown.'

And what do you suppose happened? The people of Nineveh believed! God had a plan for Nineveh. This is why God chastened Jonah. It was not chastening for its own sake. Never. God had a plan for *Nineveh*. And when God brings you through fiery trials it is not merely to make you more pious for its own sake, or to make you more godly or to make you some kind of trophy for people to look at. No! There is a work for you to do and chastening is always preparation for something else – to be of service.

I think there are some lessons for us to learn at this point. Two dangers I see of which we should take heed. The first is introspection – the danger of introspection, and thinking that piety is an end in itself. I know people who have great prayer lives but who have never won a soul to the Lord Jesus Christ. I know people who know the Bible well but who do not know how to lead a soul to Jesus Christ. I know people who have the reputation of being holy and godly, but no unsaved person would ever want to come around them. Introspection has its dangers. Another danger is isolation. We are called 'from' the world and we are not to be 'of' the world. Indeed, John did say, 'Love not the world, neither the things that are in the world. If any man love the world, the love of the Father is not in him' (I John 2:15). But do not forget, we *are* in the world God loves and we are thrust out *into* that world. And when God elected a people, He elected a people not only to salvation but to service. Don't forget that great verse – John 15:16 – 'Ye have not chosen me, but I have chosen you . . .' Now we Calvinists stop there. And of course the Arminians love to keep on going and they say that this is the proof-text that we are only chosen for service. *But it is both.* God has chosen us to salvation but also that we are to bear fruit. And there is this danger of introspection and isolation. God wants a people to move out into the world, to invade Satan's territory, to carry out the Great Commission.

Jonah had to learn this the hard way. Many of us are learning it the hard way. You see, Israel championed the belief that they were God's chosen people, the elect nation. Assyria, of which Nineveh was the capital, was the 'enemy'. Never was it regarded as the object of God's mercy. And this was one of the major problems Jonah had to reckon with. Why this call to go to Nineveh? *They* are not of the elect! Jonah found out that God meant what He said. God had a task and a work for him to do. We must not forget the song of the twenty-four elders: 'Thou hast redeemed us to God by thy blood out of *every* kindred, and tongue, and people, and nation' (Rev. 5:9). God has told us to go.

But there is something else to be seen concerning this verse, and that is the casual way this is written up. Nineveh was a great city – of 'three days' journey'. Jonah began to enter into the city and he cried: 'Yet forty days and Nineveh shall be overthrown'. And very casually we read: 'So the people of Nineveh believed'. It does *not* say: '*But* the people believed.' It says, 'So they believed.' I think we could say that our natural expectation is that the people of Nineveh would *ignore* the message of Jonah. It was not an eloquent sermon. It was not a learned sermon. It was plain, it was clear, it was definite. 'Yet forty days and Nineveh shall be overthrown.' Who would expect anybody to act on that? There is, I say, something in all of us that does not really expect to see God work. We are in such a rut that we don't expect to see the unusual. Many have been surprised to see converts in this place of late. This should not surprise us. Most of us are like that very humorous commercial that I can recall being popular in the States several years ago. A well-known corporation had this very clever advert on radio to sell Nash Ramblers. They featured 'Elmer Blurp, the world's lowest pressured salesman.' Elmer Blurp would go up to the door and knock, saying to himself: 'Nobody home, I hope, I hope, I hope.' And then the door would open and, to his astonishment, he would say, 'Well, I don't suppose you want to buy a Nash Rambler?' As he would start to walk away a man would say: 'Yes!' – much to Elmer's surprise. Well, many of us are like that.

But if we unsuccessfully invite somebody to church we often say, 'Well, I invited them – they didn't come. You know they are so interested in everything else. But I did invite them.' You did it once? You did not want to invite them *twice* or a third time lest you save some of the non-elect? But if we could only see that it is almost a natural thing, if I may put it that way, that men believe when *we* are persuaded.

I suspect Jonah was not at all surprised that they believed. Jonah's surprise was not that they believed. His surprise was that God passed over them and did not punish them. Jonah pouted about that. He was not surprised that they believed him. He expected them to believe. And when we too are persuaded, as we ought to be, of the revealed truth of God, it will be so contagious that we will overpower people. Our problem is that we go around not expecting anything. It comes down to this matter of being persuaded. Are you persuaded of what you believe? Are you unshakable in the things that have been revealed to you? Because, if you are, you will mediate that to everybody you meet. It was like Peter on the day of Pentecost when he preached with a persuasion. It was no great surprise that men believed. In the very same way, Peter and John went to the Gate Beautiful and said to that man who was lame: 'Silver and gold have I none; but such as I have give I thee: in the name of Jesus Christ of Nazareth rise up and walk' (Acts 3:6). And he did. They were persuaded of what God would do. So it was, Luther turned the world upside down because he would not budge. 'Here I stand, I can do no other.' So it was when Jonathan Edwards preached that sermon 'Sinners in the hands of an angry God' and said to them: 'It is by the very mercy of God you are not in hell at this moment.' Before sundown 500 were converted. It is a question of whether *we* are persuaded. We do our friends no favour when we take our doubts to them. But when we are persuaded it will be mediated to everybody we meet.

And so, we find the people believed what Jonah had said. One other thing. It does not say the people believed in Jonah. It says they 'believed God'. Isn't this interesting? So the people of Nineveh believed *God*. It is not enough merely for men to believe in *us*. We must have credibility, we must have sincerity, we much have integrity, of course. But men can believe in us and be lost. I never will forget a very powerful preacher who was once my pastor. This man, after he left the area and went on to another church, had many people who fell away from their profession of faith. It suggested how much they were followers of *him*. He was a remarkable man, a powerful personality, a tremendous presence, and when people were around him they almost succumbed to the very things he would say. And this was borne out by the fact that after he was away a year or two and was invited back to this church to preach, many of those who had fallen came back to hear him and they were converted all over again. They would last perhaps a month. So it is not enough to believe in a man.

Jonah was an example of this truth. He was detached from the situation. He didn't have an axe to grind. He was not trying to build a following. Success or failure were not in his hands. Jonah had no vested interest in Nineveh. He had no stock there, he had no money in a savings bank there, and I doubt very seriously whether Jonah was preaching with a view to a call! He was going to deliver God's message and that alone. And he did it with conviction, partly because he knew what he himself had been through. This should be your hint. If God has chastened you and you have seen God work in your life, that should be sufficient conviction for you to get on with the task. Look back on how God has guided your life, how He has spared you, how He has protected you. He has brought you through these things. Jonah was conscious of what he had been through, and so when he marched into Nineveh he did it with conviction. He had no doubt that God was on the throne. He preached with clarity, with lucidity, with definiteness. He preached with simplicity. Everybody there could understand, they got the message. It was very simple. 'Forty days and Nineveh shall be overthrown.'

And, I must also say, he preached without partiality. He would do no-one a favour not to tell the whole truth about the wrath of God. Listen, you do your friends no favour when you try to be less than candid concerning the wrath of God. Why are we coy about this? This is the clearest teaching concerning God in the Bible – His justice and wrath. There can be nothing clearer than this, but it is the very truth we try to cover up. Jonah went into Nineveh and preached God's wrath. And they believed. They believed because they grasped the most offensive but definite truth to be known about God – His justice in punishing sin. The folly of the present generation is that we think we are going to attract people to the church because we say, 'Ah, we no longer believe those things that were preached a hundred years ago such as hell fire and damnation – that has gone. Come, try us out. We are a great group of people. We don't believe things like that any more.' And for a generation the church has been saying that and the churches are empty. The curious thing is that every time a great awakening occurs it is accompanied by the preaching of the wrath of God. Are we going to wait around? Are we afraid? Do we have to apologise? 'Forty days and Nineveh shall be overthrown.' And these people believed.

Moreover, the people of Nineveh were not really surprised at the message. Let me tell you why. Because there is implanted in every heart the knowledge of God. There is in every man a conscience on which is stamped the knowledge of a holy and just God. And when we confront men with Him it brings to their conscious awareness what they already know. And we will get no converts by trying to make God something that the Bible says He is not. And so, when these people of Nineveh heard this message they were not surprised because they were living wickedly, they were living licentiously, they were living in sin, and when they heard this message it struck a chord. They knew what they were doing. And so it is today, men living in wickedness know it; they know it. We do them no favour when we condone what we see.

We are told, moreover, that this truth was not only grasped by simple people. Look: 'So the people of Nineveh believed God, and proclaimed a fast, and put on sackcloth, *from the greatest of them even to the least of them.*' There are those supposedly clever people who say, 'Only simple, unlettered, unlearned people believe in a doctrine like hell, God's wrath and the final judgment.' Listen, all men are created in the image of God. Jesus tasted death for every man, and the Holy Spirit transcends intelligence, education, culture, biases, background, prejudices, differences in taste, colour. All these things are transcended when the Spirit of God works because there is implanted in every conscience the awareness that God is just and holy and will punish sin.

But now let us go a step further. I want us to examine the quality of their faith. The people of Nineveh believed God and proclaimed a fast. These words do not in themselves prove a saving faith, regeneration. I say that because James reminds us that one can believe in God and that the devil also believes and trembles (James 2:19). And I think it needs to be said that belief in God is commensurate with common grace. Now, the repentance of Nineveh might well have been an unusual operation of the Spirit in the sphere of common grace, for we are simply told that they believed God, that is, the message – 'Forty days and Nineveh shall be overthrown.' Whether some were regenerate as a consequence of believing Jonah's message is an open question.

We do know that the mariners were converted but we also know that they feared the Lord – *Yahweh*. The mariners feared God the Redeemer, the Holy One of Israel. We are simply told that the people of Nineveh believed the warning. It may be true that some of the Ninevites knew of God the Redeemer and it could be that some turned savingly to God. And it is also possible that Jonah said more than the mere eight words and perhaps true conversions did follow.

But I want to say that if Nineveh's repentance was but an operation of the Spirit in the realm of common grace it was no less extraordinary an awakening. 'Righteousness exalteth a nation, sin is a reproach to any people' (Prov. 14:34). Nineveh was a wicked city. God was prepared to let it prosper if it ceased its wickedness. It may well be that this was an awakening largely in the realm of common grace, when 120,000 were spared and saved from God's immediate wrath upon the city – from destruction then and there, and that they were given years to live on. It could be that that is all it was. If so, it is no less extraordinary. How wonderful it would be if this kind of thing would take place in London. How wonderful if men were so moved that the word reached far and wide and a general fear of the Lord settled everywhere, that men respected decency and law and order and righteousness!

In any case, what we find here is the proclamation, first of all, by the people. Notice this. 'So the *people* of Nineveh believed God.' The people, the masses. Now, the masses are usually wrong. Jesus said, 'Enter ye in at the strait gate: for wide is the gate, and broad is the way that leadeth to destruction, and many there be which go in thereat' (Matt. 7:13). The masses are usually wrong. And what an extraordinary thing that the people, on this occasion, were right. Look at the contrast. 'Broad is way that leadeth to destruction.' If you think one man can be sinful, get two people together, then three, then four; sin becomes compounded. And when sinful masses move, sinfulness is multiplied many times over. There is a book by Reinhold Niebuhr, *The Nature and Destiny of Man*. It wants in many things but it is a classic treatment that illustrates the depravity of society, collective society. How rude and cruel men can be when they are together. It's an interesting book. In any case, the masses are usually in the wrong. When you consider the minority groups today, saying this and that, we know oftentimes they reflect the wave of the future. How extraordinary it would be if there should be people today who, like these Ninevites, would proclaim a fast and they themselves, as a whole, as a group, should for once be *right* ! Not merely having an issue, not merely trying to vent some hostility, not having an axe to grind so that they can be heard, for we find here that the people were right. The people, the *people* believed.

But there is more. Word reached the king. The tidings reached the king 'and he arose from his throne and he laid his robe from him, and covered him with sackcloth, and sat in ashes.' How interesting this is, that the people were moved and the word went to the top. Leadership. This story discloses the general pattern of how to influence the leadership of a nation. The word went not from the leader to the people but from the people to the leader. It seems to be a fact of life, dear people, that most leaders are followers. Did you know that? Most leaders follow the people. Leaders usually just have stronger personalities. Maybe they are more educated, have sharper minds, are great manipulators and have high ambition. Someone once asked John F. Kennedy, 'Why do you want to be President?' He said, 'Because that is where the power is.' And most leaders just want to be where the power is. But most leaders are followers. Few leaders have a sense of destiny, that is to say, a conviction that they have been raised up to give light in a dark hour. Most leaders follow the 51%. They will follow a Gallup poll. They say, 'Come back and tell me which way the people are going and that is where I will be.' That is where leaders usually are today. 'Most people are made by the times, a few are made for the times.' And this is also true, not only are leaders followers but almost invariably lag behind. Most laws are made because the practice preceded it. They legalise what has already been done, and this often happens, especially when there is a greater emergence of a lawless society; when law and order are pushed aside, and the only thing left to do is to legalise things. And so you have the legalising of homosexuality, the legalising of pornography, the legalising of prostitution, because it was already going on. So laws try to catch up. This is the way the pattern generally works. An American magazine recently made this astonishing comment: 'Of the total population of San Francisco, 680,000, an estimated 120,000 are homosexual, and officials reckon that 28% of the voters are homosexual. One political consultant said that to be elected to office in San Francisco you have to devote one third of the campaign to homosexuals. Go to homosexual bars, have homosexuals on your staff and be photographed with them.' And so here is what happens, a leader follows what is advantageous, how to get the vote. There are few that will stand against the tide.

I am saying that when the people are moved, we can reach the top and this is the way the dominoes fall. *We* must be moved. We are the Jonah in the world. The church, the salt of the earth, must begin to influence the *people*. And so, when the people are moved then the leaders will take notice. And this is the way it always is. It is not a question of legalising righteousness. It is simply that the law is commensurate with nature. Look what Romans chapter 1 says: that these who had the knowledge of God embedded in their hearts 'glorified Him not as God, neither were thankful; but became vain in their imaginations, and their foolish heart was darkened ... They changed the truth of God into a lie, and worshipped and served the creature more than the Creator, who is blest for ever ... And for this cause God gave them up unto vile affections; for even their women did change the natural use into that which is against nature: and also the men leaving the natural use of the woman, burned in their lust one toward another ... And as they did not like to retain God in their knowledge, God gave them over to a reprobate mind' (Rom. 1:21–28). It is a pity when law condones what is against nature and against decency and the dignity of man.

And so we today, in the twentieth century, whether in America or England, are having to face Nineveh, wicked, vile, corrupt. It is a question of whether we are made *by* the times or whether we are made *for* the times. Jonah, I say, is a type of the church going into the world. He was persuaded of God's word. He reached the people; the people influenced leaders; and, I say today, we must not only identify with Jonah in the belly of the fish, for all of us know about that – for we have all been Jonah in the belly of the fish – but we must be Jonah crying out before Nineveh! We are the salt of the earth. We are the ones that must witness daily. Do what you can; witness to your friends. Let's see them converted, and more and more and more the word will get out. God could send an awakening to this country. God knows, I hope something like that happens.

'Ah', but you say, 'Jonah's message was only a message of doom – "Forty days and Nineveh shall be overthrown".' But wait a minute! The warning presupposed *hope*! God is not mocked.

Not only that; a greater than Jonah is here! A greater than Solomon is here! The Queen of Sheba came to hear of Solomon's wisdom but thank God we are 'in Christ Jesus who of God is made unto us wisdom, righteousness, sanctification and redemption' (I Cor. 1:30). A greater than Jonah is here. 'For God so loved the world that he gave his only begotten son that whosoever believeth on him should not perish but have everlasting life' (John 3:16). We have the Word! We have the message! There is hope. It is a dark hour, but a greater than Jonah is here. And we are the ones that must tell the world.

17 Does God Change His Mind?

Jonah 3:6-9

WE COME NOW to the most difficult part of the Book of Jonah, a section that presents a theological difficulty. It is verse 9, the words of the king of Nineveh: 'Who can tell if God will turn and repent, and turn away from his fierce anger, that we perish not?' We are immediately confronted with the question, Does God change His mind? The question demands our examination in the light of certain well-established truths. For example, we know that God cannot lie. The writer to the Hebrews said so – it is 'impossible for God to lie' (Heb. 6:18). Paul also wrote to Titus and referred to God who 'cannot lie' (Titus 1:2). Yet we find, nonetheless, in this particular chapter – 'Forty days, and Nineveh *shall be* overthrown' (Jonah 3:4). There was no 'if' clause. It was a statement. And, lest we think such preaching was merely Jonah's subjective judgment, we are told in Jonah 3:10 that 'God repented of the evil, that *He said He would do*.' So obviously Jonah was delivering *the* message. 'Forty days and Nineveh *shall be* overthrown.' Yet God cannot lie.

We thus see the difficulty. We know that God knows everything; 'all things are naked and open unto the eyes of Him with whom we have to do' (Heb. 4:13). And the writer of the book of Acts states: 'Known unto God are all his works from the beginning of the world' (Acts 15:18). God already knows everything, including the future. How do we reconcile these verses, 'Forty days and Nineveh *shall be* overthrown . . . and God repented'? (Jonah 3:4, 10). The Bible teaches that God wills all things from the beginning. 'I am God . . . declaring the end from the beginning and from ancient times the things that are not yet done, saying,

My counsel shall stand, and I will do all my pleasure' (Isa. 46:9–10). This may be combined with another attribute of God, namely, that He does not change. James said: 'Every good gift and every perfect gift is from above, and cometh down from the Father of lights, with whom is no variableness, neither shadow of turning' (James 1:17). Malachi 3:6 tells us: 'I am the Lord, I change not.'

Does God change His mind? I can give you some verses in the Bible that suggest one answer and other verses that suggest another. Now, a situation like this is what some theologians seize upon in order to show that God contradicts Himself in the Bible. Many non-Christians rest their case for unbelief upon this kind of difficulty. Now I ask the question: Does God change His mind? We know there are verses that say He doesn't. For example, you can read in Numbers 23:19, 'God is not a man that he should lie; neither the son of man, that he should repent'. See 1 Samuel 15:29: 'And also the Strength of Israel will not lie nor repent: for he is not a man, that he should repent.' And so if you take these verses, you build the case that God does *not* change His mind. Most of us in the reformed tradition are quite happy there. We tend to build our case on that view alone. But we face difficulty when we look at a verse, for example, like Genesis 6:6: 'And it repented the Lord that he had made man on the earth, and it grieved him at his heart.' Take Exodus 32:14: 'And the Lord repented of the evil which he thought to do unto his people.' And, of course, there is the classic story told in II Kings 20, 'In those days was Hezekiah sick unto death. And the prophet Isaiah the son of Amoz came to him, and said unto him, Thus saith the Lord, Set thine house in order; for *thou shalt die*, and not live' (v. 1). But Hezekiah turned his face to the wall, 'and prayed unto the Lord, saying, I beseech thee, O Lord, remember now how I have walked before thee in truth and with a perfect heart, and have done that which is good in thy sight. And Hezekiah wept sore. And it came to pass, afore Isaiah was gone out into the middle court, that the word of the Lord came to him, saying, Turn again, and tell Hezekiah the captain of my people, Thus saith the Lord, the God of David thy father, I have heard thy prayer, I have seen thy tears: Behold, I will heal thee: on the third day thou shalt go up unto the house of the Lord. And I will add unto thy days fifteen years' (vv. 3–6).

Does God change His mind? 'No.' 'Yes.' Our problem is that we tend to approach this question with our minds already made up. We are so much like a friend of mine who used to say, 'My mind is made up, don't confuse me with the facts.' Most of our theological difficulty hinges upon an *a priori* approach. We have already embraced a particular truth and we have defended it. We have perhaps gone on record as having defended it. Then we become even more defensive when we face a difficulty. I often watched the common case in which an Arminian becomes converted to Calvinism. I know a case, I am not particularly proud of it, in which I convinced an Arminian to be a Calvinist. And this particular chap was a very argumentative type. When he was an Arminian he was a strong one. He knew all the 'Arminian' verses and he was very argumentative, even hostile and it was all he could think about. And I changed him. Within twenty-four hours he was just as argumentative in the other direction; he was going around saying the very opposite. He actually embarrassed me. He had adopted a new position and now had to make all those verses fit into it.

And most of us do this. We think we have got to defend a particular view so that we can have an answer to make ourselves look good. We don't want to lose face. I never will forget when one particular individual heard my lecture on John Cotton at the Westminster Conference in which I showed that John Calvin did not believe in the traditional doctrine of limited atonement. One soul, dear man, found out where I was staying and came to the hotel to see me. There were tears in his eyes. He said, 'You know, it took me eleven years to come to see the truth of limited atonement and for a year I have been preaching it. And now, must I go back to my people and tell them I have been wrong?' I felt very sorry for the man, for I knew exactly how he felt. And what happens is, we see a position that seems logical and we succumb to it because of its logic and then make other verses fit in. We *make* them fit even if it is a case of making a square peg fit into a round hole. That is what we often do. But we hardly solve the problem by merely adopting one theological view, then supporting that view with selected proof-texts.

We solve the problem only by becoming empty before the Lord. And who is there among us who will do that? To become empty. To go to the Bible like a child. If only we could be open because we *don't* know. God's ways are higher than our ways and we don't like that. We think a certain way and expect God to come down and fit into our mould. We do not like to lose face. This was also Jonah's problem. The secret is to be found not by adopting one view and getting proof-texts to support it but by becoming empty. I might remind you, this was the method John Calvin used when he wrote the *Institutes of the Christian Religion*. And this method of Calvin is one I think many Christians need to learn. We must become empty. It should not be a matter of being defensive for a particular view. Thus this question, Does God change His mind?, is one about which many of us have already made up our minds and we do not want to be confused with contrary evidence.

Believe it or not, the king of Nineveh followed the very principle, the hermeneutical principle, that *we* ought to follow! A heathen king in this case had the right attitude; and may we Christians today sit at his feet. He said: 'Who can tell?' He did not know. He asked the question, 'Who can tell if God will repent?' 'Who can tell if God will turn away from his fierce anger?'

Jonah had been given a second chance. He preached, the people believed. The word reached the king. The king believed and made a decree. And we are going to look at that decree. 'The king caused it to be proclaimed and published through Nineveh, saying, let neither man nor beast, herd, nor flock, taste anything: let them not feed, nor drink water: but let man and beast be covered with sackcloth, and cry mightily unto God; yea, let them turn every one from his evil way, and from the violence that is in their hands' (Jonah 3:7-8).

It is a great triumph when a head of state, the leader of

a nation, or those in authority, in government, will acknowledge the sovereignty of God. It is a great triumph, a weighty factor when we have the sanction of the authorities. Now, there are those who say, 'I don't care what the authorities say. Let the King, let the Queen, let the Prime Minister, let the President, let the leader do as he pleases. It doesn't matter to me.'

But it should. For to have the sanction of the powers that be is a remarkable thing. It is no small matter when a head of state acknowledges God. And so the sanction is weighty, if only because it is weighty with men. And after all, if the authorities make it official its effect increases a hundredfold! This is why our vision should be vast, not merely trying to do something small as a congregation, but to reach out and work to affect the destiny of a nation. Do you know one of the differences between Luther and Calvin? Luther was a bit of a mystic and Lutheranism was limited in its growth partly because it tended to be very pietistic; it was interested in individual salvation, emphasising justification by faith. It was, for the most part, an *individual* matter. With Calvin, the issue was not merely to save souls; it was to save *nations*. Calvin aimed for the top and turned civilisations upside-down, one nation after another. And that is why the reformed phase of Protestantism went so far throughout western Europe; it affected this country and America. And so it is a marvellous thing when one influences a whole nation. Let us not have such a narrow vision. After all, there are the lobbyists. I suppose you have them in Parliament. We do in America, those who are outside the wings of Congress trying to get this passed, that passed, because they know it makes a lot of difference if something becomes *law*. And it is the duty of the church to try to affect government, to give direction. Not by lobbying however but through preaching. We do our leaders no favour when we isolate ourselves. It should be the church calling out to leaders, reminding them that they are stewards of God and His instruments in the world!

And so, the king accomplished two things. When the word reached the king and moved him, he gave it his own sanction. He caused it to be proclaimed and thus it became official policy. It was published throughout all the region because the leaders have the advantage of the media, getting the word out. And so, from the top down, now, everybody knew. It is no small matter when a head of state is moved to recognise the sovereignty of God.

It is weighty, not merely because of what it can do with men but, more important than that, it is weighty with God. We are back now to a phase that is so neglected, this area of common grace. God is the Ruler of all nations. I have been reading of late how it is that Her Majesty Queen Elizabeth II does not rule; she reigns. But God *rules*, and do not ever forget it. Moreover, God is jealous for His creation. 'The earth is the Lord's and the fullness thereof' (Psa. 24:1). Every nation is under Him. The Apostle Paul said that the authorities that be are ordained of God and whosoever resists the authorities resists God (Rom. 13:1–2). And don't forget that it was Caesar in power when Paul said that. God is jealous for every nation, He rules every one of them. And the leaders are His stewards. As leaders go, so goes that nation. Even if it is true that most leaders are followers, it is nonetheless a general pattern that as the leaders go so goes that nation. It makes a vast difference when that leader recognises God. For then all heaven takes notice. God Himself takes it seriously. And I speak freely when I say that the United Kingdom under the Queen is a Christian nation. And so is America, a 'nation under God'. We have a covenant which we may invoke. We have a distinct advantage over a heathen nation. May God have mercy upon us, that the church will influence the leadership and bring to mind this fact.

Thus to have a head of state acknowledge the sovereignty of God is no small matter. And when government proclaims law that reflects the glory of God, God cannot but take notice. While I was doing my thesis at Oxford I spent many, many hours reading through the sermons of the Westminster Divines who drew up the Westminster Confession. Nearly every one of those sermons that I read had on the title page words similar to these: 'Preached on the day of a solemn fast, April 21st 1641.' And in those years from about 1640 to 1647 time and time again Parliament would call a day of fasting for the nation. What remarkable days. When is the last time that our nation was called to a day of fasting and prayer? It can make a lot of difference when a nation by law recognises the sovereignty of God. And the moment Divine law is swept under the carpet, pushed aside, then (because of the depravity of man) things get worse and worse and worse. This is why we must have law, law that reflects the glory of God. When a nation ceases to be stewards of God's law that nation will degenerate beyond imagination. I ask you, Does this concern you? Do you care about the direction government takes? Or do you want to draw back into your shell and say that things like this don't matter, that we are merely living in a wicked world and we just want to carry on? God help us if we think like that. Very well then, it makes a lot of difference when the head of state and then law recognises the glory of God. It can change the complexion of everything.

The king of Nineveh received Jonah's message and made a decree reflecting unfeigned piety. He asked all men to pray, to cry mightily to God. It was not a pompous prayer, as if one was just doing one's part. No; he said: cry 'mightily' to God. He also asked men to *quit their sinning*. 'But let man and beast be covered with sackcloth and cry mightily unto God: yea, let them turn every one from his evil way, and from the violence that is in their hands.' Now, the decree reflects in some measure the kind of sinning of which the Ninevites were guilty – violence. It may have been violation of human rights. It may have been violation of sexual practices. It may have been a violation of conscience; but it was violence. And violence is inevitably the result of lawlessness. When law is swept aside, violence follows. It is inevitable because we are sinful creatures. There is enough hell in the most godly man to make him blush. Yet think what can happen when masses of ungodly men are unbridled and have no law. But this is what is happening today. Our Lord Jesus, speaking of the last days said: 'Because iniquity shall abound, the love of many shall wax cold' (Matt. 24:12). The Greek word translated 'iniquity' here means *lawlessness*. When lawlessness abounds, the love of many shall wax cold. And when Paul referred to the last days in

2 Thessalonians 2:7 he referred to the 'mystery of lawlessness'. Christians ought to be the first to see the validity of this. I repeat, it was a great thing when the head of state saw the sovereignty of God.

Furthermore, when Jonah preached this message it became obvious to all that Jonah was right. I cannot emphasise this point enough. Jonah's message *made sense to them*. Why do you think they believed him? Because they knew what they were doing! They knew they were lawless and when he said, 'Forty days and Nineveh shall be overthrown', *they knew why*. They knew. And yet the church today wants to apologise for preaching the wrath and justice of God. Do not forget that the light of man's conscience is universal. The true light 'lighteth every man that cometh into the world' (John 1:9). And so it is, we must realise that when we declare the truth of God it does not come as any great surprise to wicked men. Men know; it is embedded on their consciences. And immediately the people of Nineveh knew *why* the message was coming: they knew they were guilty; they knew they were wicked. It came as no surprise to them. And God help us never to apologise when we see the ominous signs in our time.

But there is one more thing. Not only did the king make it official and send out the decree but the king led the way by setting the example. He was not like one of these leaders who say: 'Don't do as I do, do as I say.' He set the example. Verse 6: 'The word came unto the king of Nineveh, and he arose from his throne and he laid his robe from him, and covered him with sackcloth, and sat in ashes.' Leaders are not exceptions to law. It is also true with church leaders; we cannot say one thing and do another. If we are leaders, let us set the example. Oh, how God will bless us. The king, then, set the example; he covered himself with sackcloth and sat in ashes. Sackcloth was a garment of goat's or camel's hair and was a symbol of mourning. Ashes, we all know what ashes are – the substance remaining after combustion, worthless. And the king knew there was nothing to live for. The king might have taken the attitude – 'Let us eat, drink and be merry, for tomorrow we die.' The king might have believed

Jonah's message and said, 'Well, we have got forty days to enjoy ourselves, let's live it up!' But the opposite was true. He made a decree; he made it official, which included not only human beings but the whole of God's creation. For, after all, after forty days no one was going to be around anyway. The whole would be destroyed. The king set the example.

But he had this hope: 'Who can tell if God will turn?' The king was not a theologian. The king was not in a theological strait-jacket. Sometimes God can very effectively use a non-theological mind, especially when theologians or theologically-minded Christians are so arrogant that He cannot break through to them. Our problem is, we don't say: 'Who can tell?' Because we already know. It is all cut and dried with us. Oh, I wish I could get this over to people. So many of us don't even expect to see anything happen. Many of us have a view of God that is in practice no different from the strictest Muslim who believes in absolute predestination. Whatever happens, the Muslim religion teaches, 'Allah wills it.' How many of us are like the man who said, 'What is to be will be whether it happens or not.' We don't seem to ask the question the king asked, 'Who can tell?', because we already know everything. But God is not using us. He seems to be passing us by while the world is going to hell.

The king saw through Jonah's message and hoped that God would not give a warning like this if there were not hope. After all, Sodom and Gomorrah's sin was so great that God destroyed them without telling them He was going to do it. The king of Nineveh said, 'Who can tell?' The king emptied himself like a little child. He didn't know the answer to the question. 'Who can tell if God will turn and repent, and turn away from his fierce anger, that we perish not?'

Who can tell? Can you? Do we know? Are we so sophisticated that we know in advance what God is going to do? Who can tell? Will God save your neighbour next door? Who can tell? Will God save your husband, your wife? Who can tell? Will God save your best friend? Who can tell? Can you tell, or do you know it all? We seem only to think with one, closed dimension in our outlook. Take the man who was walking north towards Scotland; that is, he thought he was going north but he was on a train which was going south. So which way was he going, north or south? But wait a minute. While he was walking north, going south, the earth was rotating in an easterly direction every twenty-four hours. Which way was he heading? But all this time the earth is rotating it is in an orbit going around the sun; so in what direction is he going now? But even while the earth is orbiting around the sun it is regularly tilting a little bit, making summer, autumn, winter, spring. So now in which direction is he going? But there is more. The sun is the supposed centre of our universe but we may be a part of a galaxy that is moving in the vast regions of the infinite. In what direction are we going? 'O the depth of the riches both of the wisdom and knowledge of God! How unsearchable are his judgments, and his ways *past finding out*! For who hath known the mind of the Lord?' (Rom. 11:33f). His ways are higher than our ways (Isa. 55:9).

Let's follow the king of Nineveh. The king was a wise man. He feared God, he was like a child. 'Who can tell?' God's judgments are *past finding out*. Yet most of us don't get beyond the man walking north, going south on a train. We consider just one or two options and there are so many more ways of thinking that are beyond our comprehension. How silly are these theologians who try to show contradictions in God's word. How silly are we when we try to prove our ideas to make everything fit. God is determined that we do *not* know everything. His judgments are *past finding out*.

God is not meant to be fully understood.

He is meant to be worshipped. When we cease to wonder, we cease to worship. 'To whom will ye liken God? or what likeness will you compare unto Him?' (Isa. 46:18). Who can tell what God will do? Can you?

18 Does God Reward Works?

Jonah 3:10

BACK TO BACK in this section of the Book of Jonah are two of the greatest and most difficult theological issues ever known. We have dealt with Jonah 3:9 and raised the question: Does God change His mind? Now, verse 9 reads: 'Who can tell if God will turn and repent and turn away from his fierce anger, that we perish not?' And thus the question: Does God change His mind? I did not answer that question. Perhaps you were disappointed. I did not answer the question because I do not know the answer. I prefer to leave it with the question of the king, who asked 'Who can tell?' The Apostle Paul claims not to know either. For he exclaimed in Romans 11, 'O the depth and the riches of the wisdom and mercy of God ... His ways are past finding out.'

Our problem is that we want a simplistic Yes or No to so many theological questions. Some, who are essentially humanists, project their humanism upon the backdrop of the universe and see a God like that; but we must not forget that God is not a man that He should lie, neither the son of man that He should repent. But on the other hand there are those who are most comfortable with a deterministic theology; they project their static ideology upon God and end up with a fatalism that is hardly different from that found in the Muslim belief in Allah. The Christian view of God is one that recognises that 'as the heavens are higher than the earth, so are His ways higher than our ways and His thoughts than our thoughts' (Isa. 55:9). Isaiah raised the question, 'To whom will ye liken God, or what likeness will ye compare unto him?' (Isa. 40:18). And thus the Apostle Paul, when dealing with this question of the destiny of Israel could only say, 'How unsearchable are his judgments, and his ways past finding out! For who hath known the mind of the Lord, or who hath been his counsellor?' (Rom. 11:33f).

Most of us are not happy with this . We are not content to let God be God. We want to tie Him down to a creed which we can rationally understand. And then we tend to deduce from some well-proven axiom another axiom which we also think must be true. This is the way our minds naturally work and we think it is so easy to understand the secret will of God. If we can understand one thing about Him, we often deduce another view which we think also to be true.

For example, take again Romans 8:28. 'And we know that all things work together for good to them that love God, to them who are the called according to his purpose.' Because all things work together for good there is the immediate temptation to say, 'Well, what happened is the way it was *supposed* to be.' Thus if evil turns to good we want to justify the evil. But this is wrong. The fact that God can turn things around and set our path in such a way that we are able to see His hand, does not mean that what wrong we did then was right. The very fact that God can take our sin and bring good from that sin does not mean the sin was not sin. And I say we have no right to excuse ourselves. We are not given a mandate from Scripture to do it. Our problem is that we see clearly one doctrine and assume that the same fits with the other.

Now, for example, when it comes to the doctrine of election, there should be no difficulty about this. The New Testament clearly shows us that God has an elect, an elect which He chose from the foundation of the world. The elect were chosen not with respect to conditions, nor with respect to our works. It is an election which is unchangeable; it is fixed, it is final; and it is from eternity to eternity. It is at this point that I concur with the Westminster Confession. The number of the elect is so definite that such number cannot be 'increased nor diminished.' And when Spurgeon prayed that prayer, which I love to quote: 'O Lord, bring in all thine elect, and then elect some more', he was using poetic licence!

But who is to say that the doctrine of the providence of God is to be understood precisely in the same way that we understand the doctrine of election? But you may say, 'If election is determined, unconditional and unchangeable, so must the doctrine of providence be.' 'If God knows the future', you will say, 'that means He determined it.' And so, if a glass of water falls from an upper storey on Buckingham Gate 872 years from now, you may want to say it was foreordained.

But that is sheer human reasoning. You may have deduced that simply because you may understand *one* phase of God's truth. Perhaps you are like the predestinarian who fell down the stairs and then, wiping his eyebrow, said, 'I am glad that's over.'

When we begin to bring one facet of the knowledge of God into another because they seem similar, and deduce from the doctrine of election a doctrine of providence that is static and predetermined, we err. Are you like that? That is sheer human reasoning and is an unbiblical deduction. You thus simply suggest you do not want to believe that God's ways are *past* finding out. We should avoid foolish questions such as, 'Was I foreordained to be in this place with this particular person at this time?' Because as soon as you begin thinking like that you inevitably make God the author of sin, which I don't think you want to do. I have counselled by the hours with people in the vestry who have used this view of the providence of God as a cloak for their own sin. They said, 'I fell into it, but, after all, God ordained it from the foundation of the world.' That was enough for them. This is human reasoning and it is a trap that, if you fall into it, makes you vulnerable to the manipulations of the enemy of your soul. And God help us to see it.

We are wise, then, to adopt the position of the king of Nineveh who said 'Who can tell?' God seeks those who ask the question, 'Who can tell if He will change His mind?' He doesn't seek those who know it all. It does not surprise me that in the course of church history God has used a variety of people: John Wesley, the Salvation Army, the Pente-costals. I could go on and on. Many strict Calvinists are confounded that God would use men like that. But He is not seeking those who know it all. He looks for those who raise the question, 'Who can tell?' He uses those who begin to explore the possibility that God *will* do something.

But we are also told that 'God saw their works, that they turned from their evil way and God repented of the evil that He had said He would do unto them; and He did it not.' Thus I said there are two grave theological questions raised in this section. The first: Does God change His mind? The second: Does God reward works? Although this question is closely related to the first question, the answer to which we cannot always be so sure of, we can move closer to an answer to this question. And we can feel certain, in the light of New Testament theology, of the answer to the question, Does God reward works? Because we do have the New Testament which gives us an advanced theological maturity not found in the Old Testament. While the New Testament sheds more light on the question, Does God reward works?, it delays giving us the answer to the problem of evil and the question of God's secret will, as whether or not He changes His mind. We will have to wait until we get to heaven to know the answer to the first question. But the New Testament does speak directly to this issue of reward for works and it enables us more clearly to understand the Old Testament. We can even grasp the grace of God in a way the characters of the Old Testament themselves did not do.

And so I say, we can come closer to the answer to this question. And another reason I give is this. The New Testament more explicitly shows God's work in redemption as being by grace alone. Paul could not have said it more clearly. 'For by grace are ye saved through faith; and that not of yourselves: it is the gift of God: not of works, lest any man should boast' (Eph. 2:8–9). Because we have the unmistakable word in the New Testament that God is a God of grace we can re-live the experiences of the Old Testament and also appreciate them more fully. Yet the New Testament proclaims the providence of God as a *mystery* so that we can never understand fully how the mind of God works.

Very well then, we continue the story of Jonah's experience in Nineveh. Having been given a second chance after his miraculous preservation, he delivers the message: 'Yet forty days and Nineveh shall be overthrown.' The people believed and proclaimed a fast; the word even reached the king. The king might have adopted a humanistic position. He might have said, 'It's absurd.' He might have said, 'Let us eat, drink and be merry for tomorrow we die.' But, instead, that head of state proclaimed a fast and then raised the question: 'Who can tell if God will change His mind?' And God saw their works and repented of the evil that He said He would do.

We look now at this question of whether God rewards works. God 'saw' their works. The same God, mind you, who saw their wickedness. Now we are told, He 'saw their works.' He saw their works and this was because He chose to do so. He chose to see their works in the same way that He chose to see their wickedness.

Thus God discovered the wickedness of Nineveh. Now He saw their works. Do works produce faith? Or does faith produce works? We must see here a doctrine which I have implied earlier –the doctrine of accommodation: how God speaks to men. God has a way of speaking to us very simply. God reaches men *where they are*. That is the doctrine of accommodation. It is not necessary that God makes us understand fully *everything* He is doing at the time. For example, many times on our pilgrimage we feel we are doing something in our own strength; only in our maturity do we see it was God all along who enabled us to do it. Many people, when they become Christians, see their conversion as an act which they brought about (alas some never grow up to see that it was *God's* act). In any case, this is the way our pilgrimage often is. And in the Old Testament God accommodated men so that they understood themselves in a way that the New Testament gives more light on. David could say: 'I have walked in mine own integrity; therefore judge me' (Psa. 26:1). And he would say, 'Judge me according to my righteousness' (Psa. 7:8). And yet, the New Testament comes along and shows us that it is a God of grace at the bottom of it all, working in man. Therefore with the New Testament advancement in theological maturity, we know the God of the Old Testament also to be a God of grace.

Thus here we have this incident that God 'saw their works'. Now, we might put it like this. The Apostle Paul as well as the writer to the Hebrews urged men to come to the place where they could receive the meat of the Gospel. The writer to the Hebrews said, 'I have had to feed you with milk. You ought to be much further along than that but I cannot deal with you this way, so I must just give you milk' (Heb. 5:12f). And consequently we must understand many verses in Hebrews as dealing with men who were weak. This is why he could say in Hebrews 6:10: 'God is not unrighteous to forget your labour of love and the work that you have done.' But do not forget that the New Testament clearly says that we are saved by grace. Not only that, not only are we saved by grace, but the Apostle Paul put it like this: 'Whosoever shall call upon the name of the Lord shall be saved' (Rom. 10:13). And many people put a full stop there and never go beyond. But he goes on. 'How then shall they call on Him in whom they have not believed?' He does not stop there. 'And how shall they believed in Him of whom they have not heard?' He does not stop there. 'How shall they hear without a preacher? And how shall they preach except they be sent . . . But *they have not all obeyed* the Gospel. For Isaiah said, Lord, who hath believed our report? So then, faith cometh by hearing and hearing by the word of God' (Rom. 10:14–17). This is Paul helping us more fully to understand *how* God works in men. God uses preaching, preaching to produce faith, and faith to produce repentance. That is the order, and if we don't understand this order it will lead us to all manner of theological confusion.

Well then, does Paul's theology correlate with the Book of Jonah? The answer is, absolutely Yes. Jonah went to Nineveh. The first thing is, he preached. The preaching produced faith. 'Forty days and Nineveh shall be overthrown. So the people of Nineveh *believed* God.' First came the preaching, then the faith, and then the repentance. They 'proclaimed a fast, and put on sackcloth, from the greatest of them even to the least of them.' Therefore when 'God saw their works', it was another way of saying that God *affirmed* the work *He* had done *in* them! This is the way God has always done it. It is the consistent biblical pattern. God created the birds, the fowl, the trees, and said, 'It is good.' God created man and proclaimed His creation 'Good'. God *affirmed His* creation. And so, in the same way, we are 'His workmanship', said Paul, 'created in Christ Jesus unto good works' (Eph. 2:10). And when God saw Nineveh's works *He affirmed what He had effectually produced*. God always does it this way. In the same way He affirms His own Son, His Son who was from the beginning with God and was God. When Jesus came into the world there came that voice out of heaven, 'This is my beloved Son, in whom I am well pleased' (Matt. 3:17). And those in Christ likewise are affirmed by the witness of the Spirit but also by their obedience. So it is, we who are in Christ find God's affirmation again and again. God blesses our obedience, He blesses our self-discipline, He blesses those who pray, He blesses those who study, He blesses those who give. And consequently God affirms *His own work* in us.

Very well then, what God did to the Ninevites was to respect the fruit of their repentance. But we may ask: What are the fruits to which God paid His respect? You may well wonder what it is that *you* can do that God will bless. In what sense may you have an understanding that God will bless you, even reward your obedience? Look at what happened here. Since we are told God saw their works, that they turned from their evil way and God repented of the evil that He said He would do, we would do well to see what they did. This gives us a hint as to the kind of work God affirms, that God blesses.

The first thing they did was to fast. They believed God and proclaimed a fast. Why fast? We fast, or should fast, because the Bible teaches it. There is one of the most rewarding studies in store for you. Explore throughout Scripture and note how the people of God have been blessed by fasting. Now there is no virtue in fasting for its own sake, unless you are overweight! And some of us might do that! But fasting is a biblical teaching. The Psalmist once said, 'My knees are weak through fasting' (Psa. 109:24). Fasting was also a practice of Jesus; it was a practice of Paul and other Apostles. And so fasting is a practice God sanctions. He affirms it. That is why we should fast.

When should we fast? I would say, first of all, when the burden is so great that you do not want to eat. When the burden is so great that food is undesirable that may be God's hint to you to fast and to wait before Him. Another good time to fast is when there is a stupendous task forthcoming, a major decision to be made, and you do not want to make a mistake. It is a timely moment to fast. This was the practice in the New Testament. We are told in the book of Acts: 'As they ministered to the Lord, and fasted, the Holy Ghost said, Separate me Barnabas and Saul for the work whereunto I have called them' (Acts 13:2). So if you are wanting to know when to fast, I would say, when you are facing a major decision and you want to be sure that the right one is made in the power of the Spirit, try fasting. And I would offer a third basis for fasting, and that is, when God hides His face. Is God hiding His face from you? Maybe it has been lasting for days, or for weeks, or for months? Try fasting. Here is how Jesus put it. We are told that the disciples of John and the Pharisees used to fast, and some came to Jesus and said, 'Why do the disciples of John and the Pharisees fast but the disciples fast not?' Jesus said unto them, 'Can the children of the bride-chamber mourn while the bridegroom is with them?' As long as they have the bridegroom *with* them, they need not fast, but 'the days will come when the bridegroom shall be taken away from them, and then shall they fast' (Matt. 9:14–15). I challenge you, you who are experiencing the hiding of God's face. Try fasting. It can be a rewarding experience.

There is yet more to be said about this matter of fasting – how to do it. Jesus spent more time in the Sermon on the Mount telling us how *not* to do it. You don't want to fast in such a way that everybody can tell that is what you have been doing. As surely as you do that, you have forfeited straight away the good that would have come. Many of us like to wear our piety on our sleeves and if we do anything extraordinary such as giving, or praying, or witnessing, or fasting, we have to tell it. I never will forget a lady in the States who came to me and said that she had been fasting all week. And I listened. She should have quit while she was ahead, but she went on to say, 'The reward is in not telling it.' 'But you have just told me,' I said. 'Well', she said, 'I am not going to tell anybody else.' Jesus said, 'Be not like the Pharisees, the hypocrites, of a sad countenance: for they disfigure their faces, that they may *appear* unto men to fast. Verily I say unto you, they *have* their reward' (Matt. 6:16). That's it. If you call attention, the attention is the reward you get. 'When thou fastest, anoint thine head and wash thy face; that thou appear not unto men to fast, but unto thy Father which is in secret: and thy Father, which seeth in secret, shall reward thee openly' (Matt. 6:17f).

However, the Ninevites had proclaimed a public fast and it was a time of humiliation. It was a different situation. There was no chance for any self-righteousness. They knew they were going to be destroyed in forty days, and it was indeed a time of humiliation. But I mention this to you for it could be that this is an area unexplored in your own life. That is the first mention of the work that God blessed.

The second work that God blessed was humiliation. Now it is a sensitive matter to talk about humility. I always think of the apocryphal book entitled *Humility – and How I Attained It*. Humiliation is the recognition that our ways have offended God. Humiliation is the recognition that we have no bargaining power with God. Humiliation is the recognition there is nothing we can do in ourselves. It brings home Jesus' words, 'Without me ye can do nothing' (John 15:5). 'It is the Spirit that quickeneth; the flesh profiteth nothing' (John 6:63). This is not mere intellectual assent. It is the conviction of helplessness driven home – and God has a way of doing that. God has a way of bringing us to humiliation; we see such not merely intellectually but by conviction of the heart. And this was the experience of the Ninevites.

The third work I mention, which God blessed, was prayer. The king decreed that they put on sackcloth and that they 'pray mightily' to God. I suspect that this subject of prayer, perhaps the most familiar yet the least understood subject in the Bible, is one we ought seriously to reconsider. I find prayer something that everybody understands and nobody understands. There are three levels of prayer. First, communion, which all of us as Christians enjoy. It is daily fellowship with God, assurance, blessing, the sense of His presence – communion. The second level I would call supplication. This is when we bring to God our needs and perfunctorily the needs of our friends, our loved ones, the church, the pastor. Most of us never get beyond this level.

But there is a third level of prayer. I think this has almost perished from the earth – *intercession*. I read a tract years ago entitled 'Where are the intercessors?' Intercessory prayer. Do you know what that is? We are too busy to do that. We are too preoccupied to do that. We have our own problems, our own schedule to meet. To intercede, to stand in the gap between God and desperation we do not do. Who *will* do it? Yet I think we can learn from history that when God is about to do a great work He usually precedes it by producing a spirit of intercessory prayer. It is the highest form of prayer. Most of us know little about it. I never will forget a lecture I heard by a very popular theologian who was strong on communion and strong on holding hands with others in a circle and praying for one another. But when someone asked him about intercessory prayer he said that his theology had little place for that. He was embarrassed by the question. Intercessory prayer is carried out when we plead on behalf of others that God will miraculously intervene. We can stand in a circle and hold hands, and I am not putting that down; it has its place but this is usually only more communion itself and a feeling of sharing. Intercessory prayer is asking for God alone to do something that transcends nature; it is beyond ourselves. It is pleading for that which, when it happens, can be explained only by saying that it was wholly of God. This is why I have stressed the point that, if the Holy Spirit were taken from the church today, the work would go on as though nothing had happened. For what *we* do can be understood in human, psychological terms. But intercessory prayer is geared to produce the transcendent power of God, an event which cannot be humanly explained. Do you know what I am talking about? When there is an absence of intercessory prayer in the land, it is a bad sign. And when there is the presence of intercessory prayer in the land, it is a good sign. You may ask whether I have seen intercessory prayer lately. I answer: I have not. Most praying I have witnessed has been perfunctory, superficial and mechanical. If God is about to do something great, He usually precedes the event by bringing upon His people a spirit of intercessory prayer, and I confess I have not seen it, at least for many years.

The final thing I mention, a work which God blesses, which He rewards, which, mind you, He affirms because it was His effectual working, is a general turning away from wickedness. Most of us want to have it both ways, holding on to God and to the world, simultaneously. But Jonah's message made sense to the Ninevites. When he said, 'Forty days and Nineveh shall be overthrown', they knew why. They did not have to look for a reason. Embedded upon their consciences was the light of nature. And so the people fasted; the king of Nineveh gave it his official sanction. They prayed. They prayed 'mightily'. They were humiliated. And the final thing in the king's decree: 'Let everyone turn from his evil way' – *his* evil way. It was personal sin they turned from. It is one thing to pray about the sin of others, but quite another to say, 'Are *my* hands clean? Is *my* heart pure?' Have you been one of those who, when I preach, say, 'I wish so and so were here to hear that'? You do not need it? Is that it? Let everyone turn from *his* sin and from the violence that is in his hands. What you do that affects another – lying, stealing, gossiping – destroying another man's reputation; hate, adultery – a sin, when you commit it, will affect the life of another for ever, not to mention your own.

'Who can tell?' 'What if God will repent?'

Mind you, there was no guarantee. Let none of us be so foolish as to think that if we do certain things, then there is the guarantee what God is going to do. Beware of that. That was the great error of Charles G. Finney in his lectures on revival. He said there are certain things we can do which will guarantee the Holy Spirit to come in power. Now it is true that Charles G. Finney was mightily used at one time in his life. (In the last several years of his life, incidentally, he scarcely was used at all.) There is a story that when Charles Finney visited a factory in New York, before he left the factory every single soul in that factory was converted. There was an unusual power there. You may ask: Did that really happen? Yes; *once*.

There is no guarantee that doing these things like fasting and turning from sin will bind God, as it were. You cannot do that. And so let us not forget that the attitude of the king was, 'Who can tell?' The spirit of intercession is one where we *plead* with God, not manipulating, not handcuffing Him. After we have done what the Spirit has enabled us to do we are back with the king of Nineveh: 'Who can tell?' And the result was: God saw their works and passed by.

19 The Jonah Complex

Jonah 4:1-3

A FEW YEARS ago an American psychiatrist wrote a clever book, a best-seller, which was apparently an attempt to wed two psychological theories, one the 'client-centred' school and the other the Freudian school. It was an effort to existentialise Freud and the new idea became known as transactional analysis. The thesis is that there are three possible stances for one to assume psychologically. The first is that of 'I am not OK. You are OK.' This is the way the child looks at a parent. The second position is 'I am OK. You are not OK', and that is the way the parent looks at the child. And then there is the third position, the healthiest: 'I am OK. You are OK.' This reflects the good self-image simultaneously with the same respect for others. It was a very popular book and there is much to be said for it.

We should also notice that the two possibilities: (1) 'I am not OK. You are OK' and (2) 'I am OK. You are not OK' indicate complexes. The first, an inferiority complex – 'I am not OK. You are OK.' The other, the superiority complex – 'I am OK. You are not OK.' Only the third state is one without a noticeable complex. It describes one who has a healthy self-image and who respects others.

Most of us are in the first state, 'I am not OK but you are OK.' Most of us have feelings of inferiority and we tend to think that others do not have the problems we have. We tend to look at others as being a bit better than ourselves. I am sure it is true that most Christians tend to take this position, especially when they compare themselves with others. Most of us, when we become acquainted with our own infirmities and maladies, assume that other Christians are not plagued with the same problems. We tend to project

223

a mature state of grace, one of much more spirituality, upon others, especially older Christians and those who have been Christians longer than we have.

A typical projection of many a Christian might be like this: 'If I could only experience unmistakably the power of the Lord in my life, that would surely solve my problem.' We tend to have the idea that *other* people have seen the glory of the Lord in a way we have not and therefore *they* are free of the problems *we* have. Therefore we fantasise, if only we could see the glory of the Lord in an unmistakable way, then we too would be 'set'. We therefore would never have doubts again, we would never have problems resisting temptation or with losing our temper; we would have certain victory over all spiritual maladies. If only we could have that clear, undoubted glimpse of the glory of the Lord!

We come now to examine the most astonishing part of the Book of Jonah. We witness the unthinkable, the unbelievable, the irrational. We see sin at its worst. We examine one who had been miraculously preserved in the belly of the fish, one who had all you and I could ever dream of insofar as having an intimate, undoubted experience with God is concerned. Jonah had that. Jonah had such a marvellous revelation of God's mercy and grace to him that, humanly speaking, we might expect he would never have a serious problem again. For, after once seeing God in this extraordinary way in his own life, that 'should' set him up for life. Not only did he *have* this miraculous preservation, he even *saw God work* in a most extraordinary way. He went to Nineveh, preaching a message. It was a message that, humanly speaking, might easily be rejected; but that message was believed. And not only that; the people repented and God honoured their repentance: God affirmed the work He had done in them by passing over them and not destroying them. I say, Jonah saw God work in this unusual way in his own life, and now in the Nineveh revival.

Then came the unexpected for Jonah. God saw their works, that they turned from their evil way and 'God repented the evil that He said He would do unto them; and He did it not.'

Sheer common sense would dictate that anybody would be happy about that. All should rejoice. It is something that should thrill all: to see God move in such an extraordinary way, and show wonderful mercy to men and women.

But here comes the unthinkable. It displeased Jonah. 'It displeased Jonah exceedingly, and he was very angry.' Now, how can we explain that? Jonah's reaction was completely irrational and it shows just how profound sin is in the human heart. Jonah could not rejoice; he was displeased, he was angry.

We now come to examine 'the Jonah complex'. Can you not see already what the Jonah complex is? We witness the example of one who became unbalanced in his judgment and his behaviour, even after seeing God work in this extraordinary way.

This story ought to be of comfort to all of us. We can see that God can use such a frail person as this. If you identified with the Jonah who ran from Nineveh to Tarshish; and with the Jonah who was swallowed by the fish, I must ask you, can you identify also with the Jonah in chapters 3 and 4? Most of us know what it is to have 'the Jonah complex'. Do you? This account can be of comfort to us; we may see that God can use men that are still frail. It shows also how one may still have problems, maladies, infirmities, weaknesses – even after seeing God work. Never think, then, just because you experience God's blessing that you are 'set'. For many times after God blesses us in the most wonderful way it is followed by severe depression and self-pity. There is also a pattern in church history of this. We need to think realistically along these lines lest we have a wrong or romantic view of what it would be like if God were to bless us in an extraordinary way.

This points to the weakness of those who preach what they call the 'victorious life', the 'deeper life', the 'higher life'. There are all kinds of names for it. The idea is projected that there is a place where one can get so that one no longer has serious spiritual problems anymore. This is non-sense. If it were possible for anybody to arrive at that kind of a state of grace, Jonah would have been there. Nobody was operated on more than Jonah. Nobody saw the Lord work in himself or others more than Jonah. No one became more obedient than Jonah. But God has a way of reminding the most godly, the most holy, that we are *still* frail children of dust. And so, I thank God for this story. I can identify with it. We must remember this, that when we see the Lord work mightily in us, we will still be sinners.

The same is true in fantasising and romanticising with regard to revival. We tend to think if revival comes it will solve all of our problems. Let me tell you, revival solves some problems and creates others. The church at Corinth was born in revival. Let us not forget that.

But I must say, having presented the case that Jonah is a type of how the Christian may still behave carnally after seeing the glory of the Lord, that Jonah was *without excuse* in this state. While we can get comfort from it, it does not give us the ground to make excuse when we are in the same situation. Jonah, I say, was without excuse and I am going to show you why.

What is a complex? A complex is a word used in psychology to denote unbalanced thinking. It is an obsession. It is a preoccupation with an idea that is grounded in projection, not reality. We may speak of one who has a chip on his shoulder; that is a complex. Or if you are ever feeling sorry for yourself, feeling persecuted, feeling that nobody understands you – that is a complex. A complex is the result of repression. Repression is a defence mechanism we use unconsciously to avoid pain. All of us at times repress. What we do is, when we face a situation that is too painful we brush it aside. We push the reality down into our unconscious and what emerges is an idea that we nurture. We fondle an idea that is less painful than that reality we push down into the unconscious. Now the human body works this way. For example, when the human body has extreme pain, the mind goes unconscious. The body works this way; extreme pain brings about unconsciousness. And so we work this way also with our minds : we have a way of avoiding pain by pushing the reality into our unconscious self and accepting an idea instead that is less painful, grounded not in reality but in a projection.

Very well then, Jonah had a complex. We will also see

the reality he pushed aside. Jonah's complex may be described also like this. He took the work of God too personally. He was right in a sense to take God's work personally; he accepted the mandate; he received orders; he assumed them. After all, it was that to which he was called. But Jonah took the work *too* personally and began to take himself too seriously. He became so involved in the work that he forgot that it was *God's* work. Jonah became so involved that he thought the outcome was up to him. He himself became the object of extraordinary dealings, both in the fish and in the Nineveh revival. But he began now to think that he had some kind of a monopoly on the glory of God. In fact, Jonah was so obsessed with his own reputation as a prophet that he wanted personal vindication of his prophecy more than he wanted to see Nineveh spared. This is the height and depth of sin but that is precisely what Jonah experienced. He wanted to be vindicated. He had laid himself on the line. He had a message; he preached it – 'Yet forty days and Nineveh shall be overthrown'. The people believed him. They proclaimed a fast. The king gave it his official sanction. God passed over Nineveh after all. But now there was an embarrassed prophet who had preached a sermon – 'In forty days Nineveh shall be overthrown'. Full stop.

What Jonah wanted was to go to the edge of the city and watch Nineveh burn. And perhaps one or two would come along and say, 'Well, you were right.' And Jonah could say, 'Yes, I told you so.' Jonah aspired to be able to say, 'I'm OK. You're not OK.' He feared the opposite. It did not surprise Jonah that Nineveh *believed*. It surprised Jonah that *God did what He did*.

But yet it did *not* surprise him. And this is where we come into the complex. This is how we see that Jonah was without excuse. For he *knew* some things that *were* too painful for him. He brushed these aside. He repressed what he knew.

Jonah took the work of God too personally and a church can do this, you know. We as a church want to see ourselves blessed, don't we? We had better be careful about this. We must be willing to let God be God and manifest

His glory wherever He wants to do it! If God wants to bless men in some other place, can you rejoice in it? We want to be the centre. Jonah wanted to be the centre. And churches can get so involved in their own work that they think they are the only church, chapel, or congregation that matters. One of my favourite stories is that of two churches in a southern state, where there was a Methodist and a Baptist church across the street from each other. They were real rivals. They had argued with each other for years and years, Baptists claiming 'once saved, always saved'. The Methodists replied: 'You can lose your salvation after you get it.' The two churches were competitive and were at each other's throats. It was that kind of situation. Both of these churches would run what they called 'Revivals'. Now I don't guess you know what that is over here. We in America use that term rather unguardedly, I am afraid, but what we have in America, in the south especially, is what we call 'Revival Meetings'. When I was a boy we used to have about three a year – in the autumn, in the winter and in the spring; and they would run from about Tuesday through two Sundays. Twelve-day wonders, they were! I cut my teeth on revivals in that sense. In any case, they had revivals, these Methodists and Baptists did. And it happened that the Methodist church and the Baptist church had revivals going on at the same time. After both meetings were over, one Baptist was heard to say: 'Well, we didn't have much of a revival but, thank God, the Methodists didn't either!'

That is the Jonah complex. If God is not going to bless me, I don't want Him to bless you. Jonah needed reinitiating into the principles of the glory of God. Jonah's mistake also was that he took God's owning his personal life as a sign he could do whatever he wanted. Be careful about this. This is in all of us. Perhaps you have had some undoubted witness that God was with you and you took that to be a sign that whatever you do is right. The fact that God has protected you, the fact that God has promoted you, the fact that God has supplied your need, the fact that God came to your rescue, the fact that He witnessed to you in an undoubted way does *not* mean that you have a *carte blanche* to live as you please and that everything you do from thereon is right. Jonah took God's owning of his personal life, going through that ordeal of being preserved miraculously in the belly of the fish, to mean he could do anything because God was with him. And not only that, he took God's owning of his ministry in Nineveh as the sign that he must be right in all that he did. After all, when you can preach with success like that, it is easy to think for a moment you are doing something right. It is easy to do that.

Now let us be clear about one thing. Jonah *did* have a God-owned ministry and I want to say further that there can be nothing more wonderful than that. I cannot imagine anything greater in this world than to have a God-owned ministry.

What are the signs of a God-owned ministry? Well, they are all here in the book of Jonah. The first is the right message. Now if you do *not* have the right message God cannot own your ministry. The right message is a prerequisite to a God-owned ministry. And Jonah had the message – 'Yet forty days and Nineveh shall be overthrown'. Now, the message may alter slightly from one generation to another and we who are so rigidly orthodox tend to forget this. Many of us are still playing a one-stringed fiddle. We harp on a particular issue that may have been keen 300 years ago, but is not now. We spend our time answering questions nobody is asking. This is why I keep quoting Jonathan Edwards: the task of every generation is to discover in which direction the Sovereign Redeemer is moving, then move in that direction. To have the right message is to be on the cutting edge, to be on the firing line. In Athanasius' day it was the issue of the Person of Christ. And God won that battle. We may have to defend it from time to time, but that was the issue then and to get up now and keep reciting the Nicene Creed and think that that means a God-owned ministry is folly. The same is true with regard to the Reformation, even the glorious doctrine of justification by faith. We do need to understand it and grasp it more fully, but just because we are *sound* on that does not mean that we have a God-owned ministry. We can repeat the Creeds and be perfectly sound. To be given a God-owned ministry means to be on the firing line. Are we afraid of this? Furthermore, the chances are that the message will only be *one thing*. Jonah had *one message* and that was all he preached – 'Yet forty days and Nineveh shall be overthrown'.

That was the message. We need to discover the message for our day, and do you know how it comes? To find the message that God will use to the present generation will likely cost us much pain and tribulation. When I said earlier that it is my hope that the church today is in the belly of the fish, it is because I hope that when we are ejected we will come forth with *the message* and we will be on the cutting edge and God again will speak. But what we must do now is to travail before God, even like those in the Book of Revelation chapter 6. They cried out, 'How long, O Lord, holy and true ... wilt thou not avenge the blood of them that dwell on the earth?' (Rev. 6:10). Intercessory prayer will likely precede the knowledge of what God is going to say to our generation. May God help us to see it. The first sign of a God-owned ministry is the right message.

The second sign is that you have a hearing. Now, we Evangelicals tend to become so modest about numbers and crowds, especially when we are not having them. And we always want to say, 'Well, numbers aren't everything, you know.' Yet we don't mind saying the opposite when the opposite is true. The fact is, we are living in a day when God is *not* owning our ministries, when the masses do *not* even know that we are here. Churches today are half full, one third full, some closing, while the world outside does not care. But a God-owned ministry will be blessed with a hearing.

The third thing about a God-owned ministry is that it is not only blessed with a hearing; it is blessed with *hearing ears*. Jonah not only had the hearing but the people believed God.

And, finally, a God-owned ministry is blessed with undoubted confirmation. Jonah's ministry was God-owned. God saw their works, they turned from their evil ways. He repented of the evil that He said He would do unto them; and He did it not. And so we must be clear about this. God gave Jonah a ministry which He Himself owned.

But behind a God-owned ministry is a very ordinary man. Jonah was displeased; he was angry; he complained; he was not willing to lose face. 'It is better for me to die than to live'. He could not bear the thought of people coming to him and saying, 'You said this, but that didn't happen.' Jonah's pride was hurt; he was devastated; he could not bear this thought. He loved his own vindication more than the glory of the Lord. Elijah experienced a similar thing. Do you remember how Elijah complained? 'I have been very jealous for the Lord God of hosts: for the children of Israel have forsaken thy covenant, thrown down thine altars, and slain thy prophets with the sword; and I, even I only, am left; they seek my life, to take it away' (1 Kings 19:10). The Elijah complex. But behind a God-owned ministry is an ordinary man.

But I say, while this can give us comfort to know, as James put it, God uses men of 'like passions as we are' (James 5:17), Jonah was without excuse. He ought to have rejoiced in the glory of the Lord. He assumed that his own preservation was the end in itself, for God indeed protected and delivered him. He completely forgot that he was God's *instrument*. He was thinking of himself, neglecting the fact he was a *tool* to reach the *Ninevites*! He wanted to be the hero and say – 'I told you so'.

We come to see then that the same Jonah who needed a lesson the first time – having learned some lessons in the belly of the fish, still had *more* to learn, even lessons more painful than being swallowed by a fish! His first lesson was to prepare him, prepare him for the mission God had for him to do. Moreover, the first time, Jonah's sin was that of active disobedience. His second lesson was geared to remind him that he was but an earthen vessel. For this time, he was guilty of sinning by being passively disobedient. That was Jonah's problem. We sometimes think that we have not sinned simply because we have not overtly transgressed God's commandments. And we tend to forget that the *quality* of sin, the potential that resides in the heart is capable of the most heinous and obnoxious sins in the sight of God, and can be more repulsive to Him than some of these outward sins that we get preoccupied with.

Jonah, then, had a second lesson to learn. God was not finished with him. God has a way of doing this. God has a way, after blessing us so that we think we are set, of bringing us back to *zero* all over again and reminding us that 'we have this treasure in earthen vessels' (II Cor. 4:7). Do you know what it is to be blessed in extraordinary ways and then suddenly you are at rock-bottom? Just yesterday Elijah was rejoicing in seeing the glory of the Lord. But today he is depressed – the Elijah complex.

And so we too have lessons to learn. Perhaps like Jonah we need a further disclosure of our own depravity. Or perhaps we need to see that God may use one man to do one thing in a particular way and *not repeat it*. Don't forget. God needs no precedent to do what He wants to do, nor does He have to do anything twice. There have been times in the great Revivals of the past when particular ones were chosen to do certain things, when the time of great blessing was there; but then the Revival subsides and those same people are left utterly devastated because they are not being used that way again. Perhaps you are one of those? You may have been used in a particular way in the past and you say, 'Why isn't God using me that way now?' Maybe that was *all* you were supposed to do then and God has a new path for you now. Your mistake is living in the past. The way God used you then was wonderful and it is over. He has something else for you to do now. Get out of that complex, feeling sorry for yourself because you are not used in that way now. Forget the past; you have a new thing to do. God wants to show you something new. This is the way God works with individuals. He also works that way with churches.

I have already made reference to that expression 'earthen vessel'. When I read Jonah chapter 3 and then 2 Corinthians chapter 4 I cannot help seeing the contrast between Jonah, a man who loved his own vindication more than the glory of the Lord, and Paul, who loved the glory of the Lord more than his own vindication. Now, I don't know what it took to bring Paul to that place, I don't know how many fish swallowed up Paul. I don't know how many lessons he had to learn in Arabia. But I know one thing, this man Paul saw himself as a servant, as a slave. So he could say, 'We preach not ourselves, but Christ Jesus the Lord' (II Cor. 4:6). He also learned not to take things personally. He could say to the Ephesians, 'We wrestle not against flesh and blood but against principalities and powers' (Eph. 6:12). So that if flesh and blood were to say something derogatory to Paul, Paul did not take it personally. He knew that the *devil* was behind that. He knew who his enemy really was. And in the same way, when he was used among the Corinthians, he could say, 'I have planted, Apollos watered; God gave the increase. For neither is he that planteth any thing, neither he that watereth; but God that giveth the increase' (I Cor. 3:6-7). Paul saw himself as a slave and his humanity as a treasure; he saw it as something he could cherish and enjoy because, he said, 'We have this treasure in earthen vessels, that the excellency of the power may be of *God* and not of us.' He saw his humanity as a ground for rejoicing in God's glory.

But the most extraordinary thing of all about Paul, when you compare him with Jonah in this way, is that Paul showed how he completely avoided the complex syndrome. Look at it. 'We are troubled on every side, yet not distressed; we are perplexed, but not in despair; persecuted, but not forsaken; cast down, but not destroyed' (2 Cor. 4:8-9). This was an extraordinary thing about Paul. He appeared quite free of a complex. Persecuted, not forsaken; cast down, not destroyed.

But Jonah could not avoid showing that he was selfish and carnal. Now I said earlier that the complex was his own fault. And I said that a complex is the result of repression, brushing the reality aside and nurturing a fantasy that is less painful than that reality. Did Jonah do this? What was it that Jonah repressed? What reality was too painful for Jonah? What was it that he pushed aside? Well, he tells us himself. Jonah indicts himself by his own testimony, for he said: 'I fled unto Tarshish: for I *knew* that thou art a gracious God, and merciful, slow to anger, and of great kindness and repentest thee of the evil.' Jonah knew this but that was too painful for him.

This was Jonah's problem. He repressed the truth that he *knew* about God. He repressed his own theological understanding. There was not anything wrong with his theology. He was angry because he did not put his own theology into practice. Mark you, there was nothing wrong with Jonah's theology; it's as sound as it can be. But, he was not living according to it. And how many of us are indicted by the very theology we claim to believe. We claim to believe the sovereignty of God, yet we doubt. We claim to be owned by Jesus Christ, but we run our own lives. Jonah should have known because he had known. 'I *knew* that thou art gracious.' He pushed that aside and chose, instead, to get angry. He repressed the truth he knew about God.

Finally, there is one more comparison between Jonah and Paul that I think is in order. While we may say Jonah's theology was sound, it was sound only in theory. Theoretically, Jonah was sound. Paul's theology was alive, he lived by it. It was fresh, vigorous. How do we know this? Well, simply this. Jonah said, 'I knew'. Paul said, 'I know'. Jonah said, 'I *knew* that thou art a gracious God'. Paul said, 'I *know* whom I have believed, and am *persuaded* that he is able to keep that which I have committed unto him against that day' (II Tim. 1:12). 'I knew' – theory, and living in the past. 'I know' – persuasion, and living in the present. Paul could say: 'We *know* that all things work together for good to them that love God . . . Who is he that condemneth? It is Christ that died . . . I am *persuaded*, that neither death, nor life, nor angels, nor principalities, nor powers, nor things present, nor things to come . . . shall be able to separate us from the love of God which is in Christ Jesus our Lord' (Romans 8:28–39). It is one thing to say 'I knew'. It is far different to say, 'I know', because it is real, it is present. May God give us the grace to rejoice in the fact we *have* this treasure in earthen vessels. We can rejoice in this.

Our complexes indict us. We are without excuse. Our complexes suggest we know things in theory only. We need to learn from one who says, 'I know'. Do you have the

Jonah complex? Are you persecuted? Paul said, 'I am persecuted but not forsaken.' And that is the difference. We leave ourselves without excuse when we boast of what we believe in theory only. For if it is only theory that motivates us, we are sure to be in the complex syndrome and the world outside will never be affected by us. For when they see us like that they see no life, they see no vigour, they see no cause for rejoicing.

But, thank God, we serve One who is alive! We serve Christ who is at God's right hand! And if God be for us, who can be against us? 'I know.'

20 Jonah's 'Body of Divinity'

Jonah 4 : 1-4

WE HAVE COME to see that the Book of Jonah is really divided into two parts. Part one, chapters 1 and 2. Part two, chapters 3 and 4. A key word to the second part is the word 'second'. Jonah was given a second chance. The Lord came to him a 'second time' saying, 'Arise, go to Nineveh that great city and preach'. We know the story well by now. The initial command was, 'Arise, go to Nineveh'. Jonah, instead, rose up to flee from the presence of the Lord and determined to go to Tarshish. Then we see that long beautiful process of God's transcending grace. God sent the storm; God brought about Jonah's confession by which his real identity was disclosed. Then came the only solution to calming the storm : Jonah had to be thrown overboard. For a while Jonah had his lodgings not on that ship but in the sea – in a fish, three days and three nights. At last, he was ejected from the fish; he was forgiven, he was given renewed hope, was even given a second chance. Thus the word 'second' is a key to this second part of the Book of Jonah.

We might spend some time profitably looking at 'Jonah's second prayer'. You remember the first prayer; it begins in chapter 2. 'Then Jonah prayed unto the Lord his God out of the fish's belly'. But now, in chapter 4, we find him praying again – in Nineveh. But note the contrast between the two prayers. The first prayer was in the belly of the fish; the second in Nineveh. The first prayer was in humility; the second prayer in carnal pride. In the first prayer Jonah was found crying; in the second prayer he was found angry. In the first prayer, he was empty of himself; in the second prayer he was full of himself. In the first prayer, he was found justifying God and accusing himself; but in the second

236

prayer he was accusing God and justifying himself. He said: 'Therefore I fled.' Mark you, Jonah was desperate in both prayers. In the first prayer he was praying to live; in the second, he was praying to die: 'Take from me my life, for it is better for me to die than to live.'

We might also take a look at what could be 'Jonah's second sin'. The first sin was 'active disobedience'. The second: 'passive disobedience'. The first sin was voluntary and deliberate; the second, involuntary and unwitting. The first sin was overt; the second inward.

Part two of Jonah, then, is really Jonah's 'second lesson'. The first lesson he learned came about in the belly of the fish. When it came to the second lesson, it too was very painful, perhaps more so. It is one thing to learn a lesson as a consequence of going through physical pain; but psychological, emotional pain can at times be even more painful. Thus during the first lesson, Jonah was partly motivated by the fear of losing his life; but in the second there was the fear of losing face. He was humiliated both times but in different ways. After all, physical pain, I say, is not necessarily the worst kind of pain, nor is the fear of death always the worst kind of fear; for Jonah was praying to die. These are clues to this second part of the Book of Jonah.

However, I want to concentrate on Jonah's knowledge of God. I want us to focus our attention upon this verse in which he discloses his own theological grasp of God. We find here Jonah's 'Body of Divinity', his 'Systematic Theology'. 'For I knew that thou art a gracious God, and merciful, slow to anger, and of great kindness, and repentest thee of the evil'. Jonah the theologian lays out his abstractions before the God of heaven.

Now, the astonishing thing is this. After having experienced God's forgiveness, Jonah reverts to his original disobedience and justifies it. Imagine this. Here is a man who simultaneously discloses his theology and his carnality at the same time. The 'Jonah complex' and the 'Body of Divinity' emerge together, at once. The astonishing thing, I say, is that this man who has experienced forgiveness now raises the sin of which he was forgiven and justifies it. Here is one who once said: 'I am sorry, I want forgiveness' but turns around and says, 'Well, I still think I was justified in what I did.' Double talk. Have you ever done that? It is much like a husband who will apologise to his wife and say, 'I see now I shouldn't have done that; I am sorry. Will you forgive me?' And she says, 'Yes, I forgive you.' And then they continue talking and all of a sudden he says, 'But that is why I did it!' 'Ah, you said you were sorry.' 'Well, but the more I think about it, I see I was right.' 'Well, you wanted me to forgive you; now you don't mean it.' This is what happens. This shows how deceitful our hearts are, how determined we are to justify ourselves. Sometimes, when we ask for forgiveness, we only *think* we mean it. For if we get the slightest ray of hope along the way that we might have been right we will go back every time and justify ourselves.

And so, here is what happened. Jonah is forgiven, He is given a second chance. He preaches. Nineveh repents. A great awakening follows. God passes over them. Now Jonah comes to *God* and says, 'I told you so.' 'This is why I fled in the first place.' 'Therefore I fled, for I knew you could do that.' 'I knew that thou art a gracious God, and merciful, slow to anger.' Thus we have here the disclosure of his theology and the exposure of his carnality in the same breath.

We must ask the question: Is there a connection between the two? If a man's carnality emerges with the disclosure of his theology you immediately want to ask, Is there a connection? We must look very carefully now at Jonah's knowledge of God – his theology, his doctrine.

We can say, first of all, that it was a sound knowledge of God. Does this surprise you? This may indeed come as a surprise to some of us. Surely, we would say, a carnal man like this is to be found out and understood in terms of a defective theology. 'This explains that man; his theology is rotten.' The immediate conclusion then that we might draw is that Jonah's carnality goes back to his theology. But I am prepared to say today, there was nothing wrong with his theology. It was sound, impeccable, immaculate, sound. 'Surely not', you might be saying.

When did he learn his theology? Well, some might say

that he had learned this theology in the belly of the fish.
After all, going through that would make him more theologically exact. But this was theology he had learned long
ago. This is not theology that he learned in the belly of the
fish. We are dealing with a man whose theology goes back
beyond his disobedience. You may be wanting to say all the
more, 'Well, that shows there was something wrong with his
theology.'

I want us to see that there is nothing wrong with this
theology; it is as sound as it can possibly be. Look at it.
Jonah's knowledge of God meant that God is a God of
grace. Now, there is a scandal in this. The most offensive
thing about God to the natural man is that He is a God of
grace, that God would give a man what he does not deserve.
Jonah says: 'I knew this.' He is a gracious God. He is a
God of mercy. This means that God may give something
that is contrary to justice. God may give you justice. He
doesn't have to if He does not want to; He can give you
mercy. For that is God's prerogative. And whenever God
gives mercy it is sovereign mercy, and it is the Sovereign
who alone has the right to give or withhold mercy. God
said to Moses, 'I will have mercy on whom I will have
mercy.' Paul repeated it in Romans 9:15. Jonah also believed that God is a God of patience – 'slow to anger'. That
means that we are dealing with a God who is not trying to
get even, measure for measure. Perhaps you are the type
that, if somebody offends you, you snap back and you can
lose your temper – just like that! Not God. 'Slow to anger'.
'God', says Jonah, 'is of great kindness.' God delights
in giving you benefits along the way. He supplies your
needs. He goes before you, prepares the way. And He is a
forgiving God. 'I knew that thou repentest thee of the evil.'
This is *vis-à-vis* giving the condemnation that is deserved.
Now, these may be redundant expressions that Jonah is
giving here. Actually, they each have a slightly different
shade of meaning. But here is the point. Jonah has just
witnessed a great awakening. He is full of his subject and
what the great awakening did for Jonah was to vindicate
his theology. But his theology, he thought, also justified his
disobedience. Again, it is not Jonah's theology that is

wrong. We must remember that. It is not Jonah's theology. It is more subtle than that.

What do you think it is? Christian people, there is nothing wrong with Jonah's theology but there was plenty wrong with Jonah. This makes the difference. You see, sometimes there is a defective theology and sometimes the theology needs correction, but not in this case. Jonah had a sound knowledge of God. Jonah's theology was sound, *but his deductions were not*. This is the difference: Jonah had a knowledge of God that was correct and precise and exact but he *deduced* from that knowledge false conclusions.

Moreover, he equated his deductions with the absolute truth. He had the audacity to say 'I told you so' to God. He was virtually saying, 'I didn't do wrong after all.' Now what Jonah was doing is this. He was saying that if God is gracious, merciful, slow to anger, kind and forgiving, that implies this – One, two, three, four, five. The affirmations were right, the conclusions were wrong.

You see, Jonah immediately concluded that this knowledge of God meant something else. Jonah thought that since God so easily forgives sin, then evangelism is unnecessary. Jonah actually thought that if God can freely forgive then he himself was not even needed. God could have forgiven Nineveh in the first place, apart from preaching. And so, it was his *deduction* that led to his sinning, not the infallible revelation of God's mercy and grace.

Now what we have before us here are the 'two scandals' of Christian doctrine. We might say, the two scandals of Reformed theology. They are: the charges of passivity and Antinomianism. The moment the natural mind sees God's grace, the natural mind concludes Antinomianism is inevitable. That is the way the natural mind works: free grace means licence. Or take the doctrine of God's Sovereignty, of His free and sovereign election. The natural mind concludes there is no need to preach: man is not needed. So, what we have here is a knowledge of God which is right but conclusions that often follow which are wrong.

Jonah assumed his natural conclusions were equal to the

truth. I have stated repeatedly in this series that Jonah had
assurance all along. He did. He said, 'I knew that thou art
a forgiving God.' But he took that assurance to mean that
his obedience to God's command was an optional thing.
And this is where Jonah got into trouble. And then, after
being forgiven himself and seeing God freely forgive the
Ninevites and pass over their malady, Jonah *went right
back* to his original position. 'Well, this is exactly what I
thought. You *are* forgiving. You did *not* need me. You
are a forgiving God. Why didn't you just forgive them
anyway? Why did I have to go and tell them?'

Now, let's be clear about this. Jonah concluded that a
forgiving God would wink at his own disobedience and he
concluded that such a God did not need a human instrument. He could say to God, 'You can surely forgive men
apart from works; you can just as easily deliver men without my preaching to them.'

Thus embodied in Jonah's two objections we find the
two scandals of Christian theology implicit here: the doctrine of justification by faith alone and the doctrine of
God's free electing grace. It is interesting that the Apostle
Paul had to deal with these two truths throughout the
Epistle to the Romans. After having dealt with the doctrine
of justification by faith, he knew someone would say, 'Shall
we continue in sin that grace may abound?' (Rom. 6:1).
So after having written chapters 3 to 5 in the Epistle
to the Romans, Paul had also to throw in chapters 6 and
7. And then in the eighth chapter he introduced God's
predestination, elaborated upon in chapter 9. But he knew,
in preaching that, someone was going to say, 'Well, why
preach?' So in chapter 10 he had to show: 'Faith comes by
hearing and hearing by the word of God'. 'How can they
believe if they have not heard? How can they believe if
they have not had a preacher? And how can they preach
unless they be sent?' There it is: preaching and faith
work together. But what often happens is, when we first
hear the doctrine of justification we conclude a certain thing
that is natural. That was Jonah's error. He concluded and
equated his conclusion with the very truth that he saw. And
so, it did not bother him at all to flee. He also concluded

that he was not needed. 'Why should I be an instrument of God?' And so he is saying here to God, 'You have done this. You have forgiven the Ninevites. You could have done it in the first place without me.'

The natural man always reasons this way. We must remember that Christianity is not a philosophy that can be reasoned. Christianity is a revelation. It is not anti-rational, it is not irrational; it is supra-rational; it is above reason. But the natural man, when he sees certain things concludes certain things. As Alexander Pope put it, 'All looks yellow to the jaundiced eye.' Men can naturally see only one thing.

Alas, Jonah's conclusion was precisely what a natural man concludes. He did not realise that the conclusions that he drew from seeing who God is were *his own* conclusions. This is a great lesson to us as we seek to understand God's Word. After seeing a great truth, when we turn around and use natural reason to grasp it, we are violating the very principle, the very epistemological principle that Christianity is founded upon. This was the great error in the Middle Ages, with the scholastics such as Thomas Aquinas. He had a natural theology; it was also the tendency of Protestant scholasticism in the seventeenth century. We must watch it ourselves today.

Jonah's sin, then, was to apply natural reason to revealed knowledge. Hence Jonah's sin can be traced to unbelief. He used worldly wisdom to explain God's word. He was afraid simply to believe God's word, and the consequence was that this natural reasoning of Jonah became an *arrested theological development*. This was *his* conclusion. He jumped to the conclusion: 'God is forgiving, therefore it does not matter how I live.' And he believed that.

It is amazing how a person can come to a conclusion early on and never change. I wonder how many of us examine our own conclusions – things that we have assumed to be true which we have concluded long ago. Many people believe a certain thing because they have read one book. But they have not had a new idea since. Or perhaps they heard one sermon or they heard one preacher. Many times we do this sort of thing, we never think twice. Christianity ought to teach a person how to think. The easy way out is to come to a natural conclusion and then just ride it for all it is worth.

If we are right, however, we can afford to criticise ourselves. If we are right, we can take criticism. The problem with most of us is that we have an arrested theological development. We go back to the way we always thought and don't want to be shaken. Jonah even said, 'When I was yet in my country'. This is the way we all like to talk. 'Well, back in the hills of Kentucky here is the way we did it.' Or, 'I am from Yorkshire'; or, 'I am from Scotland and we do it this way'. 'When I was yet in my country'. When we go against our familiar surroundings we get very uncomfortable.

But we need to learn to question. When we were spoonfed certain truths we may have come to conclusions that are but natural conclusions, the way the natural man thinks. There was nothing wrong with what Jonah saw in God. Jonah's knowledge of God was sound but the conclusions he derived, which he equated *with* that knowledge, were not and they led him to his problem.

You see, what also happened was, it not only led to his disobedience but it led to his psychological problems as well. There is a great case to be made that when we come to false conclusions, theologically, and begin to live disobediently, that we can also have all kinds of psychological problems as well.

What were Jonah's psychological problems? He said: 'I am not needed'. It led him to self-pity. He concluded it was better for him to die than to live. Jonah's false conclusions led him to believe he was no longer needed and so he prayed to die. Have you ever prayed to die? I have. I never will forget a few weeks after my mother died I actually prayed that God would take me. I did not want to live. Many Christians pray to die. I knew a Christian man that prayed to die every night for the last twenty years of his life. He died in his eighties. The Christian Gospel should give a man dignity and with that a feeling of being needed. We need to come back to this point: Jonah forgot it, that God needs us. Now if I were to preach God does not need you, I would be preaching the truth because God

243

doesn't. But I can also preach He does need you because He does. You see, most of us want to use natural reasoning and say, 'Well, God doesn't need us'. Full stop. He doesn't need us. That is a natural conclusion. We must see the antinomy – two parallel principles that are naturally irreconcilable but both true. God does *not* need us. He *does* need us. But Jonah did not want to accept that. His conclusion was, 'If God can forgive as He did with the Ninevites, I am not needed'.

Do you know something? God needs you. Maybe you feel worthless. Maybe you feel so dull. Maybe you feel so unnecessary. God needs you. Maybe you feel that you are so untalented; you think you have no gifts that God can use. 'Surely', you say, 'I am not needed'. Are you feeling not needed because you are getting older? God needs you. It is God's prerogative to take life, and He is not finished with you yet. Maybe you are ill and you feel you are in the way. But you are needed, you are needed. Jonah felt unnecessary; he came to that conclusion and the conclusion produced self-pity.

But not only did he have that problem, Jonah's natural reasoning led to his anger. This could have been avoided had he seen the whole truth of God's Word and let God be God and not try to put God in a strait-jacket or tie Him up in a box, to manipulate Him, to corner Him. Had Jonah done that then he could have been in a position not to take himself so seriously. But instead, he was angry and he directed his anger to God. In a sense, every time you get angry you are getting angry at God. That is because you have falsely concluded something about God and you are mad at Him. It is so easy for us to do.

However, the true object of Jonah's anger was not really God but his own unwarranted conclusions about God. He wanted to blame God. He was angry, he was blaming God. But the truth is, it was his own unwarranted conclusion that led him to this. It is much like Martha who said to Jesus, 'Lord, if thou hadst been here, my brother had not died' (John 11:21). And maybe you have done the same thing, you lost your temper and then you said to God, 'Why did you let that happen? If you hadn't let this happen I would not have lost my temper.' Or, you may have fallen into sin and you say everything happened in such a way, it was all so convenient; and so you blame God. That is your conclusion. And so when you begin to think like this you may blame God but the fact is, it is because you have not understood God. The problem is not with God; it is with you. You see, anybody can complain about his malady and ask, 'Why am I in this mess?' But it is the mature Christian who will respond and try to redeem things. And so Jonah lost his temper because he took himself too seriously. We lose our tempers because we won't let *God* vindicate us. We are determined to vindicate ourselves.

Jonah did a foolish thing by quarrelling with God and trying to justify himself. Do you know, the more you quarrel with God, the more you expose yourself? Jonah's very quarrel told on himself. You are better off not to quarrel with God and blame Him, but rather to see yourself as you are. But we love to justify ourselves. Let me illustrate what I mean. Miami Beach, Florida, is that luxurious city full of hotels, one after another. On Collins Avenue there is one hotel after another for miles. It is a beautiful sight. One evening I was driving in front of the magnificent Fontainebleau Hotel. I was driving about 35 miles per hour, admiring the view. I was coming to a traffic light; the light was green but before I knew it, it had turned red. I was going at about 35 miles per hour so I went on through. I looked in my rear-view mirror and saw a blue light. It was going off and on, off and on. So I pulled over, got out and went back to the policeman. He was looking at me, smiling. I knew what I had done. He knew I knew. I looked at him and said, 'I hope you won't give me a ticket.' He said, 'Why?' 'Well', I said, 'I would appreciate it if you didn't.' 'Well', he said, 'I have given out 19 tickets today, and I am wanting to give away 20 so I can go home.' I said, 'I will appreciate it if you don't give me a ticket.' He said, 'Give me one reason why I shouldn't.' I said, 'I will say this. I live in Fort Lauderdale and when the light turns yellow there it stays yellow for 3 or 4 seconds and you can go on through but here the light turned red so fast and I was going 35 miles per hour . . .' He said: 'The speed limit is 25.' The more I talked, the more I was condemning myself.

This is what Jonah did. He told on himself.

But you may think, 'How blasphemous Jonah was, talking like this to God.' You may say, 'Surely God would rebuke him. Surely, for Jonah was praying yet angry at the same time.' Did *you* ever pray when you were angry? Don't we normally say that when we come into God's presence, we come humbly and meekly? There was none of that here at all. Jonah was mad. As we used to say in Kentucky, 'mad as fire'.

I mentioned Jonah's two prayers. I referred to the first prayer in humility, and this prayer in pride; the first prayer when crying, and this time he is angry. The first prayer he was emptied of himself; the second, he is full of himself. The first prayer, justifying God and accusing himself but now he is accusing God and justifying himself. In the first prayer he was praying to live; now he is praying to die. But there is one more comparison to be seen in the two prayers and that is, the two prayers are just alike in that they achieved the same result. In the first prayer, Jonah said, 'I cried by reason of mine affliction *and He heard me.*' Now, angry Jonah prays. *And God heard him.* Does that surprise you? God heard him. God was so gentle. You will say, 'Surely not, for God only hears us when we are humble.' But, have you forgotten? Even your tears need to be repented of. You see, God still listened to Jonah because God *is* slow to anger. The same result: God heard him. The reason is that we have One at the right hand of the Father who has already pacified God's justice and His anger. And God deals with us in tenderness. And so, how gentle He was to Jonah.

God simply replied: 'Doest thou well to be angry?' The answer, of course, is No. We do ourselves no good, we are never better off when we take matters into our own hands. Jesus said, 'How can ye believe which receive honour one of another and seek not the honour that comes from God only?' (John 5:44). Thus we have here: Jonah's second chance, his second prayer, his second sin, his second lesson.

But we also have his second forgiveness. The same God who forgave him for fleeing is still with him. 'Doest thou well to be angry?' God deals with us in the same way. We do not deserve to have Him talk back to us. We have sinned. We have been irreverent. We have done those things that could cause us and should cause us to blush. 'Doest thou well to be angry?' 'There is forgiveness with thee that thou mayest be feared' (Psa. 130:4).

21 Jonah's Gourd

Jonah 4 : 4–8

WE LOOK NOW at Jonah's famous 'gourd'. We know little more about Jonah's gourd – that is, what it actually was, than Jonah's fish. It was probably a castor-bean plant, a fast-growing perennial which may reach the height of 10 feet; it looked something like a palm tree with large leaves.

In any case, the same God who prepared the fish prepared the gourd. In the end it does not matter whether there is a plant in Palestine today that would make the story more credible any more than having to know that there is a sufficiently large fish that still swims in the Mediterranean to make Jonah's nightmare more credible. God 'prepared' both; He does not need a precedent for what He is pleased to do, neither does He have to do anything twice. We know the Bible is true owing to the inner testimony of the Holy Spirit; he who does not have that witness will not believe the book of Jonah even if science proves it a thousand times.

I look at Jonah's gourd in much the same way we can look at things that take place when there is a great outpouring of the Spirit. Now, when God comes in great power unusual things happen. For example, I love to hear people talk about the Welsh Revival. There are a few still living that can relate stories they were told, some actually were witnesses. If you were to hear them you might say, 'Unbelievable'. But God does things in an unusual way when He is unveiling Himself for a special reason. Thus we need not dwell any longer on the explanation. There is no natural explanation for Jonah's gourd. We do greatly err when we look for a natural explanation for this sort of thing.

Now then, what is the situation? Well, Jonah is angry because God did not vindicate His prophecy. Jonah lost face and he is pouting. And then Jonah comes up with this. He claims that he really disobeyed God's initial command because God *is* merciful, gracious, and slow to anger. Jonah felt that God could have forgiven Nineveh without him and thus, God's forgiving the Ninevites over and above Jonah's head, as it were, came to Jonah as the very vindication for his disobedience that he was looking for. Jonah is found saying 'I told you so' to God Himself. The problem then was not with Jonah's knowledge of God, for it was an impeccable knowledge of the most high God; the problem was with Jonah and with his logical deductions, his natural reason, his conclusions from that knowledge. He concluded Antinomianism and irresponsibility and it was these deductions that led to his anger and to his self-pity. The truth is, God did need Jonah and the truth is that Jonah was not justified for his anger.

We have a splendid opportunity to examine ourselves now in a rather painless way. We can watch Jonah who endured much pain. We have an opportunity really to see ourselves. It is like being in an operating theatre, to look from above and see a patient being operated on. And so, in this case, God is the surgeon. Jonah, in whom we see ourselves, is the patient and we can vicariously feel Jonah suffer. We can behold God, the master surgeon, operating on Jonah with His two-edged sword. Or I could put it another way; we can watch God, the master psychologist, deal with His client. If you are studying medicine and you hope to go into psychiatry or psychology, you will do well to look at this lesson, for any psychiatrist or psychologist would do well to observe how God treated Jonah. It is very interesting. We can also see here the way a minister should deal with somebody in the vestry or how a parent may learn how to deal with his child. For here is the way God dealt with childish, pouting Jonah. It is an extraordinary thing to see.

The first thing to be noted is God's patience. You have heard of the patience of Job. Have you heard of the patience of God? Paul refers to the God of patience (Rom. 15:5), and John refers to the Kingdom and 'patience' of Jesus

Christ (Rev. 1:9). When we think of the various attributes of God we often overlook this one; it is patience in its perfection. We know that God is holy and He gave us His law. We know that He is just, that He must punish sin. But consider this attribute of God: His patience. He is 'slow to anger, plenteous in mercy'.

There are three ways of counselling people. One approach, when you see somebody who is overcome with hostility and anger, is to say: 'You are right to be angry; you do well'. That is the existential approach. Sometimes it is called indirect counselling, or non-directive therapy. A person may or may not see any guilt in what he has done and the therapist says, 'Get it out of your system; you *are* right to be angry'. Thus the person goes on his way and feels justified. That is one approach. Another approach is to say, 'You are *wrong* to be angry'. That is the legalistic approach, moralising, making the person feel guilty. Now there are some, you know, who thrive on that. Some people want to be told they are wrong. Some people just enjoy feeling more guilty. When they come into the vestry they just want to be given more moralising.

There is a third way: 'Doest thou well to be angry?' (Jonah 4:4). In fact, a free translation from the Hebrew is: 'You are very angry, aren't you?' Perhaps the best way a parent can react when the child is angry is: 'You're angry, aren't you?' Because this shows you understand. You are not condoning, you are not condemning; you understand. See the masterly way God dealt with Jonah: 'You are angry, aren't you?' But this is God's patience. James described the wisdom of God as being 'first pure, then peaceable, gentle, and easy to be intreated, full of mercy and good fruits, without partiality, and without hypocrisy' (James 3:17). That is the way God dealt with Jonah. I am amazed that God continues to go to extraordinary pains with this man Jonah. Why did not God give up on Jonah a long time ago?

God had every reason, justly, to drop Jonah. He could have done it when Jonah first fled. But God sent the wind. He could have done it when Jonah went to the sides of the ship to escape the storm. But God had a way of overruling the mariners' gambling and they went right to Jonah. And then when Jonah was thrown overboard, that could have been the end of Jonah. But God prepared the fish. Jonah was even given a second chance. Surely by now he is mature, surely he has learned his lesson. A man who has been three days and three nights in the belly of a fish and has repented and is so glad that God still loved him and cares – surely such a man would never sin again! There is that in all of us that makes us think when we learn a lesson we have learned them all. Or, if we overcome one malady we have overcome them all. But sin is so deep and subtle and the extent of our depravity is infinite; and the same man whom God stayed with all this time now has the audacity to get angry with God and say, 'I told you so'. God could have finished him off. Jonah thought he knew everything. Oh, the patience of God! Most of us would have thrown Jonah out of the church a long time ago. Could a man who has true faith act like Jonah? Where is his repentance?

This cuts across our popular, pietistic thinking that God only communes with the very godly. But if God only communed with the perfect, He would never commune with anyone. Does He commune with you? Is it because you are very godly? Where is Jonah's repentance? Can a man who has true faith act like this? This is another illustration of the very fundamental point that true repentance does not precede faith in the *ordo salutis*. If repentance had to come first then we must say Jonah is not even a man of God. There are those who are so anxious to say, 'There must be repentance, there must be repentance!'

But repentance *follows* faith. But, I must tell you, sometimes it is slow in coming. Some people worry about new converts when they don't see a quick change in them. You know, what worries me is *old* converts who still have all kinds of maladies. Sometimes these old saints cannot see their *own* maladies. But consider how patient God has been with you. 'You who are spiritual, when you see a brother overtaken in a fault, consider such an one in the spirit of meekness, because you too may be tempted' (Gal. 6:1).

Oh, how I identify with Jonah, not only the Jonah who

ran but the Jonah who is angry. There is that Jonah in all of us. God help us to see it. And so the fact is, God was patient with him. You too have done things for which God could have justly finished you off. God could have done it. But He didn't. And how many times have you quarrelled with Him? But He listened. You knew He understood, that He accepted you. There is Mary and Martha, one after the other coming to Jesus, blaming Him for their brother Lazarus' death. 'Lord, if thou hadst been here, my brother had not died' (John 11:21, 32). 'You could have been here, but you were not.' They were angry. What did Jesus do? He wept (John 11:35). They wept; He wept. Is there somebody like this here today – nobody will weep with you? They do not understand you, even Christian people do not understand you, even church members do not understand you, and you cannot talk to them because they are going to moralise? They are going to say, 'Shame on you'. And so you just suffer within. Is there anybody here like that? Listen:

> Standing somewhere in the shadows you'll find Jesus;
> He's the only One who cares and understands;
> Standing somewhere in the shadows you'll find Jesus;
> And you'll know Him by the nail-prints in His hands.

'Doest thou well to be angry?' Well then, God was patient.

But that is not all. Look at Jonah's recalcitrance. Here is a man who did not even reply to God. Jonah did not even answer. We are just told that he went out of the city, sat on the east side of the city and made a booth. This was a trellis. He sat under it in the shadow 'that he might see what was going to happen to the city'. Isn't this extraordinary? God had already passed over Nineveh! It was a great awakening. But Jonah would not give up. He was convinced somehow he was right. He could have been dining with the king of Nineveh right now. Jonah was a hero. He could have been in a cool chamber dining with the king but instead he built this little trellis. He preferred sitting out in the sun and watching for 'vindication day'. And so God says: 'Do you well to be angry?' Jonah says to himself: 'I am going out to the edge of the city to see what happens.'

The fact that God understood Jonah's feelings so perfectly may have been an indication to Jonah that God sanctioned his ways. You see, sometimes God gives us a special assurance, even when we are in the wrong, but that does not mean He is sanctioning our ways. It is the mature Christian who realises this. But Jonah may have thought otherwise. Now, it is an easy mistake to make, simply because you feel God with you, simply because you have the witness of the Spirit, you assume God is sanctioning your attitude in everything you do. Two people can have opposite opinions and both have assurance. You will say, 'One cannot be right'. But no, God accepts us *that He might teach us repentance* and God comes to us not to sanction us but to accept us. I used to sing as a boy:

It's just like Jesus to roll the clouds away,
It's just like Jesus to turn the night to day.

But the fact that He does that does not mean that we are justified in all that we do. God help us to see it. May He make us mature enough.

But Jonah could not think like that. Here was Jonah still waiting for vindication. He refused to abandon his conclusions regarding the knowledge of God. It happens to us, doesn't it? We get a certain theological idea in our minds; we like it and we will not give it up: a theological fixation, being in a theological strait-jacket. I have had people come to me and ask about a particular matter or doctrine and they will say, 'I see it, I see it'. And do you know something? Two months later they are back the way they were. We will not give up easily, for we love that obsession which makes us feel more comfortable.

Jonah was back to his original conclusion. Here was his reasoning, here was his rationale: 'God can show mercy and forgiveness, He can do it without me therefore I am not needed. But, if I am needed it must mean that God cannot show mercy without me, therefore my prophecy was right. I said, "Forty days and Nineveh shall be overthrown." God needed me, He imparted to me the message. That means my prophecy is right.' You see, for Jonah it was either black or white. 'God can forgive, therefore I am not needed.' Or, 'If I am needed then my forecast is correct.' So many of us look at things that way; it is either black or white. 'If this is true, then *that* has got to be true.' 'If *that* is true, then *this* is true.' And there we are. That is Jonah.

And so Jonah, still in the spirit of self-justification, opted for this side: 'I am needed. Therefore, my prophecy will be vindicated. God would not have sent the fish in vain,' he says to himself. And so he is out on the edge of the city preferring to stick with his logical deductions rather than listen to the voice of God. There he is, under the trellis watching for the day when Nineveh will go up in flames. We may ask again: why does God stay with a man like that? Here is a man so recalcitrant, so obdurate, so opinionated. Why would God stay with Jonah? But Jesus said to the church of the Laodiceans: 'As many as I love, I rebuke and chasten' (Rev. 3:19).

And so, God said, 'Very well, Jonah, you are going to go out to the edge of the city; you are not going to listen to me. I see you have built yourself a booth there; it is helping you a bit, isn't it? I can do much better than that.'

And God prepared a gourd. Jonah woke up one morning and saw this beautiful palm-like plant. Jonah said, 'Well, this is more like it! I knew God was with me!' Jonah took the gourd to be the final sign God *was* with him indeed.

We are told that Jonah was 'exceeding glad of the gourd'. The gourd protected him, the gourd comforted him. Mark you, God intended the gourd to bring comfort to Jonah. That is precisely why God did it. Now perhaps you would not have dealt with Jonah that way? You would have rebuked him? You would have moralised, sermonised, legalised? But God made him a gourd. It was far better than the booth and Jonah was quite happy about it.

But the gourd was *not* intended to be the ultimate proof that God was with him. The gourd was a *temporary measure* to encourage Jonah. For Jonah had yet another lesson to learn.

And so do we. What is the lesson? The gourd is analogous to experimental knowledge in the Christian life. You will recall from an earlier sermon that experimental knowledge is mainly for the world to see. See chapter 6, pages 64–76. Experimental knowledge is primarily given that the world may see there is something different about us. And you may recall that the mariners were converted when they saw this experimental knowledge. They saw that there was something authentic about Jonah. They could see that what was going on was beyond nature. It was despite Jonah, mind you. And so the main thing to remember about experimental knowledge – what God does through us, is not primarily for ourselves to see that *we* might get comforted but for the *world* to see. For our own comfort is not to be derived primarily from experimental knowledge.

However, sometimes God allows us to reflect upon what God has done in us as a *temporary means* of comfort. It is a *subsidiary* ground of assurance. And it is to the weaker Christian. We see it in the Epistle to the Hebrews. We know these Hebrew Christians were weak Christians, for the writer said to them, 'I ought to be giving you meat; I can't, so I give you milk' (Heb. 5:12f). So he is treating them like weak Christians throughout the epistle. He could say to them in Heb. 10:32f: 'Call to remembrance (that is, reflect upon experimental knowledge) those days after ye were illuminated, ye endured a great fight of afflictions; partly, whilst ye were made a gazing stock both by reproaches and afflictions; and partly, whilst ye became companions of them that were so used.' And he goes on to show them certain things that happened. So he says, 'Look at this and this could give you some comfort.'

Sometimes God does let us reflect on ourselves in this way and derive comfort. It is the mature Christian who realises it is not the ultimate ground of comfort; it is subsidiary and it is a temporary measure God gives in our *waiting* for the real ground to be seen and to be stood upon.

And so Jonah needed comfort. He did not deserve it but he needed it. And God prepared the gourd. I once asked you: What is your fish? I ask you now: What is your gourd? God prepared a fish to preserve Jonah. God prepared a gourd to comfort Jonah. What is your gourd? Maybe it is an extraordinary answer to prayer. Have you seen this happen lately? Maybe you felt very weak as a Christian and you wondered whether God had forsaken you, whether you did not matter any more. Thus what you needed was a gourd to spring up and God gave you an extraordinary answer to prayer and, like Jonah, you were exceedingly comforted and glad. Maybe you have been given special grace with some temptation or trial and heretofore you were not able to handle a particular situation, but suddenly God has given you special grace and you are amazed. That is your gourd which God has prepared for you. Maybe you are in a period when the fruits of the Spirit seem to flow endlessly out of your life and you are very happy. Your Christian life is at a peak and you are enjoying this. Maybe there has been some special providence in your life and you needed it and God accommodated you by working something out in an extraordinary way. That is your gourd.

Perhaps God has given you an unusually clear mind in a particular situation, and you can say, 'God is surely with me'.

But remember, God does not intend such experimental knowledge to be the *permanent* ground of assurance. You see, I begin to rejoice a little bit too much in the 'fruit' and, if I am not careful, that will become idolatrous. Or, I will begin to get proud. I will say, 'I have at long last found out how to handle this situation. I have conquered it.' Or perhaps you have a particular infirmity, or a particular weakness and then you go through a period when God gives you special grace, and you say, 'I have mastered it'. You feel so good. And you might see other people with *their* problems and you say, 'Look, let me tell you, I *used* to have that problem but I don't any more'.

Do you know what happens? God sends a worm and the gourd withers. And you wake up and you say, 'What happened? I had a clear mind, I could feel God's presence. But He has left me'. God does not intend that experimental knowledge be the permanent ground of your assurance. Because you will get too proud every time.

256

Our assurance is to be the Word of God, the Truth of God, His Son the Lord Christ. The ground of our assurance is Christ! Take for example the principle of guidance. Providences confirm. But they are not the final ground. If you go entirely by providences, the experimental way, to know God is leading your life and make that the ultimate ground, then you will have many reasons to go against principle. Look at the three Hebrew children, when nothing 'providential' was happening yet. They were about to be thrown into the fiery furnace. 'Providentially' they could justify themselves and say, 'We see God must want us to bow to the golden image'. But they said to the king, 'We are not careful to answer thee in this matter. Our God is able to deliver us from the burning fiery furnace. *But if not* we will not bow down!' (Dan 3:16ff).

The ultimate ground of assurance is the principle of God's Word. Thus the foundation of Christianity is not scientific verification; it is the Word of God. We must remember that if science happens now and then to verify something we like, we should not get too much comfort from it any more than we should get too much comfort when suddenly God helps us through a matter and we say: 'Well, God must be with us'. Mark you, the gourd is prepared by God for your comfort but it is a temporary measure to take you through a situation.

Furthermore, there is a danger if we derive comfort from experimental knowledge for *too long a period*. Here is what happens. The very nature of experimental knowledge is to demand that we reflect upon what God has *done* rather than *God*. The very nature of experimental knowledge makes you see the effect, not the cause, and so you concentrate on the effect and you are getting your comfort from the effect – what God is *doing*, what He has *done*, *what* He is *working* through you. But then, when that goes away, you are down! The fact is, the ultimate ground of comfort should have been *God* not the *gourd*. I worry about people who love godliness more than God. There is danger therefore when we derive comfort from experimental knowledge for too long. Jonah was exceeding glad of the gourd, we get exceeding glad of what God has done through us in answer to prayer, victory over temptation, when we prosper.

You can see the danger too when a church begins to do this. Here is what often happens. The church stops; rather than looking to Christ it begins to reflect with pride upon what God has done in the past. And every time we will become like the church of the Laodiceans and say: 'Look at us; we are rich, we are increased with goods, we have need of nothing' (Rev. 3:17). It will happen. We get proud when we begin to reflect. God wants us to look at Him. But He does prepare gourds. Yet it should remind us of the transitory nature of the fruits of repentance and other gifts God has given us. Jonah should have known that these things are transitory. The Apostle Paul was later to say, 'Whether there be prophecies, they shall fail' (I Cor. 13:8).

Well then, God has a way of intervening because He knew just how long to let Jonah get comfort from the gourd; He knew how long Jonah should have it. You see, the same God who knows how long we can take discouragement also knows how long we can take encouragement. In Jonah's case, one day was enough. 'God prepared a worm when the morning rose the next day, and it smote the gourd that it withered.' Jonah's gourd came when he needed it.

Now let us talk about Jonah's worm. Jonah's worm came when he needed it. You will remember the words of Ecclesiastes, 'There is a season and a time to every purpose under heaven, a time to be born, a time to die, a time to plant, a time to pluck up that which is planted, a time to weep, and a time to laugh, a time to mourn and a time to dance ... He has made everything beautiful in his time' (Eccl. 3:1–4, 11). I ask you, you who have been deriving your joy from the gourd, what do you do when the gourd withers away; you that have been encouraged by these things? What do you do when you do not have them? What happens when God is not answering prayer? What happens to a church, if people are not being converted? What happens if God hides His face? What happens when the gourd is gone? This is why our primary ground of assurance should never be experimental knowledge. Some of the old hymn writers knew this. Thank God for the one who said:

> When darkness seems to hide His face,
> I rest on His unchanging grace;
> When all around my soul gives way,
> *He then is all* my hope and stay.
> On Christ the solid rock I stand,
> All other ground is sinking sand.

I must trust Christ even if He hides His face from me. I must live by a principle whether God blesses me or not. I must preach the Gospel whether there are any converts or not and I must stand for the Bible if science does not vindicate it. What do you do when the worm comes and withers away the gourd?

Jonah needed the worm that he might look to God rather than the gourd. So it is, the danger of reflection for too long. We begin to feel complacent and happy with ourselves. The only thing to do is to go back to Christ. He is to be the ground of our assurance.

So, I ask you, What is your worm today? Is God hiding His face? Have you been humiliated lately before friends at work, before family? Have you found out you did not have victory over that particular temptation, after all? Thank God for the gourd. But thank Him also for the worm to bring us to the place where we see our nakedness and flee to Him.

22 Jonah's Final Lesson

Jonah 4:8-11

Now THAT WE are at the end of the Book of Jonah we may
well want to ask a question, Why did Jonah himself tell
this story? Indeed, the conclusion of the book itself demands
that we raise this very question. What is the real purpose of
the Book of Jonah? I think we could already say we know,
in a sense, and we could give several answers. We could say
that the purpose of the Book of Jonah is to demonstrate the
folly of running from God. We could say that the Book of
Jonah dramatises how futile and unproductive disobedience
always turns out to be. Or we could say that the Book of
Jonah is one that shows how God is ruler over nature, that
He is the Creator of the universe and the preserver of all
nature. Or we could say that the Book of Jonah is written
to show us the singular mercy of God to His own, how He
deals with them so tenderly. Or we may be tempted to say
the real person involved in this story is the one who has
been chastened of the Lord, so that we can see how God
chastens those whom He loves. These are no doubt reasons
for the Book of Jonah.

But these are subservient reasons for the Book of Jonah.
For we have not yet come to the ultimate thesis and Jonah
waits to the very end to show this to us. The reason perhaps
the Book of Jonah itself exists is because it is in a sense
unique in the Old Testament canon of Scripture. You may
be interested to know that the Book of Jonah was controversial in Israel's history and, humanly speaking, we may
wonder how it even got into the canon. But it did get in
the canon, as did the Book of Job, another controversial
book. We see in the Book of Jonah a definite contribution
to the sacred history of Israel. For, after all, other books

show the folly of disobedience; other books show that God is Creator; other books show that God is tender toward His own and show that God chastens whom He loves.

The real contribution of the Book of Jonah, which is saved to the very end, is that the very revelation of God to Israel (that He *is* slow to anger, that He *is* gracious, that He *is* merciful) shows that mercy and grace are universal and not limited to Israel only. This idea of limitation had been the assumption. But the very knowledge of God that Israel claimed to espouse proved that grace is by nature universally offered. And so, this is an indictment of Israel's insularity and introspectiveness because it shows that they had not taken seriously what they themselves claimed to believe about God. For Jonah said, 'I *knew* that thou art a gracious God and merciful, slow to anger, and of great kindness, and repentest thee of the evil.' How do you think Jonah knew that? This was not Jonah's contribution, nor was it David's, although the psalmist refers to it in Psalm 103:8. This knowledge of God goes back to Exodus 34:6. It is inherent in the very law of Moses, given to the children of Israel. But they had taken that to mean that God loves only Israel, that they are peculiar to the degree that nobody else can be the object of God's mercy. And so Jonah must learn that the very fact God *is* merciful assumes universality; it is therefore an indictment of Israel's insularity for thinking that they are the only ones to whom mercy is offered. Hence we come to this final verse, when God says, 'Should I not spare Nineveh, that great city, wherein are more than a hundred and twenty thousand souls that cannot discern between their right hand and their left; and also much cattle?'

This, then, is the ultimate thesis of the book. It is also a reminder to us what a Christian book this is. Now this could be truly said of any Old Testament book. But in a special way the Book of Jonah is a Christian book because it shows that Israel's very concept of God prefigures God's giving grace to the Gentiles. It foreshadows what would come more explicitly later, that God would openly turn to the Gentiles. And so we today should not be surprised, nor should it have been a surprise to Israel, that God would turn

261

to Nineveh. Nor should it surprise anybody that God would turn to the Gentiles. This is seen in other books in the Old Testament. The Prophet Isaiah said, 'I am sought of them that asked not for me; I am found of them that sought me not: behold a nation that was not called by my name shall behold me' (Isa. 65:1). And this, of course, was seen by other prophets as well. But it is the Book of Jonah that dramatically exhibits this. Thus all of us today have more reasons than we have perhaps recognised for being thankful for the Book of Jonah, and especially for the *God* of the Book of Jonah. For most of us are among those who make up that 'wild olive tree' that has been 'grafted in' to the natural olive tree (cf. Rom. 11:17). The point to remember is that Israel's very knowledge of God assumes and prefigures grace not just to Israel but to all men, and Jonah's experience is to dramatise this point.

We must also say that it is the very knowledge of God that was disclosed by Moses which not only prefigures grace to the Gentiles but points to Jesus Christ as Messiah. This simply means that the Jews today are without excuse; they are utterly, absolutely without excuse, for all that is in the Old Testament is mirrored again in the New Testament. This is seen so clearly by the Apostle Paul and he labours to show this. Of course, the Jews are blind; but the fact is, the Old Testament in its entirety should be a source of great joy for us all. Do not ever accept the idea that there is discontinuity between the Old Testament and the New Testament; it is one great continuous covenant, God showing free grace throughout. Therefore the ultimate purpose of the Book of Jonah is to show that the very knowledge of God given to Israel shows the universality of grace. Yet the Book of Jonah does make us encounter other profound truths along the way and we have seen, perhaps most of all, that we are all Jonahs. We can read this book and see ourselves in almost every episode.

What is the situation? Jonah is angry because God did not destroy Nineveh. Jonah is angry because his prophecy was not vindicated. Although he had every reason to believe that God would pass over Nineveh and not destroy it, Jonah continued to delude himself by thinking that somehow Nineveh would still be destroyed. So he goes outside the city and waits for the catastrophe – and also for congratulations from everybody. While he is waiting there he decides to build himself a little booth, a trellis, so he can have protection from the sun. Then God does one better than that; God prepares the gourd, this castor-bean plant, that shadows his head from grief and pain. And Jonah was 'exceeding glad of the gourd'. But this joy was short-lived. The next day the Lord prepared a worm; it 'smote the gourd' and it withered.

There is more to be seen concerning how a patient God handled an irrational, angry Jonah. We may see how a patient God brought Jonah to *see for himself* this ultimate truth of universal grace. Now how is this done? Well, God begins by adding insult to injury, you might say. For after taking away the gourd we are told that, when the sun arose, God prepared a vehement east wind; the sun beat upon the head of Jonah 'so that he fainted and wished in himself to die'. He said, 'It is better for me to die than to live.'

God had already sent the worm to destroy the gourd. Jonah therefore did not even have 'props' to his faith. Jonah's gourd had brought him out of the doldrums, from severe depression. The gourd became a ground of comfort; the gourd was Jonah's basis for saying that God was with him after all. We saw that the gourd is analogous to experimental knowledge in the Christian life. We also saw that it is dangerous for experimental knowledge to be the ground of our assurance for too long a time. God knows how long to let us derive comfort from the gourd. God sends the gourd and we rejoice. But the same God, eventually, sends the worm and the gourd is gone. Have you had it happen? Bud Robinson was a Nazarene preacher back in the 1920s and 1930s. My parents used to tell me about him. He was a colourful, eccentric, unlearned but brilliant preacher. They called him 'Uncle Buddy'. He tells the story that after preaching once somebody came up to him and said, 'Uncle Buddy, that is the greatest sermon I have ever heard'. And Uncle Buddy bowed his head and said, 'Lord, don't let me get puffed up'. But a minute later somebody else came and said to him, 'That is the worst preaching I have ever heard in my life'. And Uncle Buddy bowed his head and said, 'Lord, don't let me get puffed down'. The gourd, the worm. God knows how long to let the gourd give us comfort. What will you do when the gourd disappears? What are you going to do when all around your soul gives way? What if you don't have that victory? If you don't have that answer to prayer? If you don't have people to cheer you up? If God hides His face and you are left to yourself? If somebody makes that nasty comment or relates something ominous that somebody has said about you? What do you do then? What do you do when the gourd is gone? There comes a time when the things that gave us temporary comfort become nothing, and we have no choice but to lean on God Himself. God wants to teach us to delight in Him alone. And so Isaiah put it like this: 'Thou wilt keep him in perfect peace whose mind is stayed on Thee' (Isa. 26:3). The Apostle Paul could say: 'For to me to live is Christ' (Philip. 1:21). 'I know *whom* I have believed' (II Tim. 1:12). God was teaching Jonah to rejoice in God only, not in things that please Jonah; not in the gourd but in God, not in godliness but God. But oh, how painful the lesson can be.

And so, God added insult to injury; He not only took away the gourd but now sent an affliction. Then came the east wind and 'the sun beat upon the head of Jonah so that he fainted'. We find moreover that the old malady had not gone away. He prays the prayer he had prayed earlier. 'It is better for me to die than to live.' May I remind you again of the differences between an affliction and oppression? God may afflict; the devil oppresses. See Chapter 9, page 102. Paul said, 'God sent to me a thorn in the flesh lest I be exalted above measure' (II Cor. 12:7). God sent an affliction to Jonah to show Jonah who he is in himself – lest he be exalted above measure. The affliction in Jonah's case brought to the surface the real Jonah; and what do we see here? We see these extreme changes of mood – from anger to ecstasy to anger. The gourd comes, and Jonah is happy. Then comes the worm, and he is down again.

What are the causes of his extreme changes of mind? The answer is that Jonah's mood was dependent upon the changing circumstances and conditions of life rather than the unchanging God who controls conditions and circumstances. And so, when there is the gourd, he is happy. When the gourd is gone, he is unhappy. And then comes the affliction, and he is dejected. Christian people, when we have these extreme changes of mind, when we vacillate like this, we betray that our ground of comfort is also in conditions external to us rather than God Himself. We thus show the world we are little, if any, different from the man outside the church who too gets his joy from things external. Verse 8 is a grim reminder that Jonah's malady did not go away when the gourd appeared. And this is why I warn against experimental knowledge as the ground of our assurance. If it becomes 'too permanent' it is dangerous. Because we think ourselves sufficient. But God knew just how long Jonah could take the gourd. The gourd disappears and, sure enough, the malady is still there. Sometimes we are tempted to think that, because we are doing so well – when the gourd appears and we are feeling good, even ecstatic, that we have 'arrived'. 'Ah, I have got victory.' And that lasts as long as the gourd is around. But once the gourd withers we find the old malady is still there.

Jonah found this out, and his vacillation was due to these changing conditions. You may be a happy Christian because you have every reason to be happy, for everything is given to you on a silver platter. Why shouldn't you be happy? You have comforts; you have income. What will you do when the gourd is gone? Would you be like Job who said, 'The Lord gave, and the Lord taketh away: blessed be the name of the Lord' (Job 1:21)? Could you be like the Apostle Paul who actually could say, 'I take pleasure in infirmities, in reproaches, in necessities, in persecutions; for when I am weak, then am I strong' (II Cor. 12:10)? How could Paul say that? It is because his ground of comfort was *God*. What is yours?

But Jonah is found complaining of the same malady. He once prayed to die. Now the same prayer comes back. But notice how God so patiently deals with Jonah. God pinpointed the immediate source of Jonah's anger. 'You are very angry about the *gourd*, aren't you?' You see, God could have said, 'You are angry about the wind'. God could have said, 'You are angry about the sun beating your head, the extreme temperature'. Many times when we deal with problems we only deal with symptoms and think we have uncovered the problem.

But God the great surgeon of the universe knows how to locate and to operate on the very malady itself. And He said to Jonah, 'You are angry about the gourd, aren't you?' And Jonah says, 'You're right, that is it. I am angry, I am mortally angry, I want to die.' And God says, 'You are angry because I gave you a prop to your faith and I took it away, that is why you are angry. I gave you relief, now it is gone. You have enjoyed my mercy, my patience and these things I have done for you, but they are not there any more and you are angry.' And He continues: 'You had nothing to do with the gourd, did you? You did not produce it, you certainly did not deserve it, you did not work for it. I did the whole thing, right?'

And now Jonah is ready for the final lesson. God says, 'I was good to you and you did not deserve it; why shouldn't I be good to *others* who don't deserve it?' In fact, God puts the point in terms of a question that Jonah could not answer. And the book abruptly ends. 'Should I not spare Nineveh, that great city, wherein are more than sixscore thousand persons that cannot discern between their right hand and their left hand; and also much cattle?' The book ends, abruptly but perfectly.

How could Jonah answer that? Some of the great verses in Scripture are put like that, put in terms of a question that cannot be answered. 'For what shall it profit a man, if he shall gain the whole world and lose his own soul?' (Mark 8:36). How do you answer that? 'How shall we escape if we neglect so great salvation?' (Heb. 2:3). You cannot answer that one. This is the way Scripture often puts profound truths. Thus, comes this question. It is a way of saying, 'Jonah, I saved you and you did not deserve it; why shouldn't I save somebody else who doesn't deserve it?' And the book ends.

This book, I say in closing, even as I said when we began, is one of the most relevant books at the present time. There are some finer points in this lesson that we would do well to look at. The first is, that not only the root of salvation but also morality and ecology is in God alone. 'Salvation is of the Lord.' Jonah had concluded that. Morality too is from God. 'Should I not spare Nineveh that great city wherein are more than a hundred and twenty thousand souls that *cannot discern their* right hand from their left hand?' Morality ultimately finds its source in God. There are those who talk about the inherent goodness of man, that man is basically good. This is nonsense. 'The poison of asps is under his lips. Man's throat is an open sepulchre' (Rom. 3:13). And when man is left to himself he will always seek the lowest level, and another generation will be lower, and in yet another generation, lower still. This is what Paul described in Romans 1. 'When these would not retain God in their knowledge' – they wanted another god – they ended up with a god of 'creeping things, fourfooted beasts' (Rom. 1:23). Because nature left alone will always go to a lower level. Morality is not to be found in man; it is in God. We who want to see Parliament or Congress do this or that may want to see them do it but as long as they derive their wisdom from nature they will continue to make laws that accommodate man as he gets lower and lower and lower. Thus new laws nowadays accommodate man in a lower state.

Morality is not in man; it is in God. Jonah too had to learn this. 'Should I not spare Nineveh?' 'These people who are so desperate, they cannot discern right from wrong.' 'And also spare much cattle.' This points to ecology. Ecology and God's favour are inseparable. Furthermore, God is interested in the cities. We are living in a time when people are fleeing to the suburbs, or are going to the country. We can take comfort, that God is interested in the cities. 'Ought I not to spare Nineveh, that great city?' We ought to claim this as a promise. If God is interested in the city of a hundred and twenty thousand, how much more ten million? We can see also that God is interested in numbers. Look at God's strategy on the Day of Pentecost. Why do you suppose the Holy Spirit came on that day? Because there were many people there.

God is interested in numbers, in the cities, and in

ecology. There is much talk about clean air, clean water, the population explosion, the fear of liquidation of our natural resources. We are to learn from the Book of Jonah that God regards ecology as a serious issue. But we don't improve things merely by dealing with the things themselves. We must go back to our Creator. For God is saying here, had He not had mercy on Nineveh not only would 120,000 souls have been annihilated but also the cattle, everything. By having mercy upon Nineveh, ecology is spared. All you have to do is to read church history and see that, wherever God has been on the scene with an outpouring of His Spirit, it changes the whole atmosphere; morality, ecology, everything qualitatively is advanced. It has always been that way. Oh, the folly of thinking that we need merely deal with the things themselves. It cannot be done that way. We must go back to God. He will reverse the whole trend, in morality, in ecology and in these things that ought indeed to concern us.

In conclusion, we may ask a question. Why did God even bother to tell Jonah these things? In other words, why did God even bother to *teach* Jonah this? After all, Jonah accomplished the mission; he was used of God, so why didn't God answer his prayer? 'Take my life from me, I am no use.' God could have done this. God did, after all, accomplish His purpose in Nineveh. Why return to Jonah himself and give him all this attention? Why bother to explain to Jonah? God did not have to tell him these things. Jonah deserved nothing. God had used Jonah; He could have said, 'OK, you are finished'.

But in coming back to Jonah God treated him with the highest dignity. Jonah did not deserve it but that is the way God treated him. God came back, nursed Jonah's wounds, and let Jonah even see for himself the way in which God was dealing with him. I ask you, Is God still teaching you things? Is God still showing you things? Are you learning? You may say, 'I don't know much. I am of no use'. But maybe you can also say, 'I don't know what I want to know, I don't know what I ought to know, I don't know what I hope to know. But I do know more than I used to know, and God *is* still showing me things'.

God dignifies us by showing us Himself. And as long as God is showing you things, He is treating you with the highest dignity.

But now the final question: Did Jonah learn his lesson? This recalcitrant, proud man – did he learn? I answer: He did. He wrote the book, didn't he? He became self-effacing after all. He laid himself bare. And, in telling the story, he let God have the last word.

Believing God
Studies on Faith in Hebrews 11

R.T. Kendall

It was Martyn Lloyd-Jones who lent Kendall the expression 'Believing God' as a definition of faith. And focusing on the mighty stalwarts of faith catalogued in Hebrews 11, Kendall is at pains to remind us that the writer of the Epistle was more concerned about the nature of faith itself than about these people of faith.

ISBN 0-85364-652-x

PATERNOSTER PRESS

CARLISLE, UNITED KINGDOM

EUROPEAN THEOLOGICAL MEDIA

For a book service that offers you up-to-date information on new publications and discounts of up to 50% on a wide range of academic titles, ask for the free Nota Bene quarterly catalogue from:

European Theological Media, PO Box 777, Carlisle, Cumbria CA3 0QS, UK.